sponsored by

# the good Membership guide

## for the voluntary sector

a relationship marketing toolkit for growing your support

by Stephen Iliffe

Published by NCVO Publications
(incorporating Bedford Square Press), imprint of the
National Council for Voluntary Organisations
Regent's Wharf, 8 All Saints Street, London N1 9RL

First published 2004



Typeset by JVT Design
Printed and bound by Latimer Trend and Co. Ltd.

British Library Cataloguing in Publication Data
A catalogue record for this book is available from the British Library

ISBN: 07199 1619 4

## Author's acknowledgements

At NCVO, thank you to Ben Kernighan for commissioning the book, to Julia Childerhouse and Diane Lightfoot for their ongoing support, and to Emma Moore and Josephine Finn for seeing the project through.

For their help with fact-checking, case studies, advice or suggestions, thanks are due to:

Tesse Akpeki, NCVO
Nick Barratt, The Ramblers' Association
Bryan Bland, RSPB
Tom Brembridge, Macular Disease Society
Tim Butler, The National Trust
Sarah Denner Brown, SDB Talking Direct
Peter Dyer, NCVO
Bill Gunns, SRIC
Stephen Last, Soil Association
Tony Lewis, The Caravan Club
Kevin Mills, Diabetes UK
Julia Pounds, Fisk Brett
Adrian Ritchie, The Ramblers' Association
James Rogers, RNIB
Melanie Sallis, Associa
Philip Shipway, Woodland Trust
Winifred Tumim
Chris Underwood, RNID

The book also draws on 15 years' experience in the voluntary sector. My appreciation to Austin Reeves, Maggie Woolley, John Healey, Stuart Etherington and Joe Saxton for their personal support at crucial points of my career.

For their love, patience and support during the 18 months of preparing this book, my grateful thanks to Emma, Ben and Sophie, to Pat and Derek Iliffe, and to Winifred Tumim.

In memory of Véronique Serafinowicz whose outstanding proofreading skills graced many voluntary sector publications.

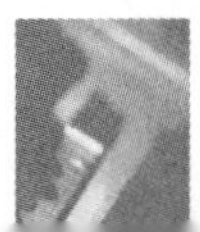

# Contents



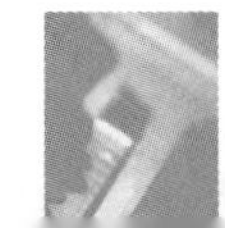

# The Good Membership Guide

The need for this guide indicates that many voluntary organisations are finding it increasingly difficult to recruit and retain members. Social factors such as a greater sense of individualism, economic trends such as increased borrowing and therefore debt, and wide spread political apathy all play a part in decreasing the attraction of an individual investing time and/or money back into the community. In light of this sort of resistance, today's voluntary organisations must take a considered approach that appeals to the charitable side of human nature that is precariously balanced against the pursuit of personal wealth.

There are many lessons charitable organisations can learn from commercial companies in terms of using modern business techniques to their advantage. We are surrounded by clever media campaigns aimed at capturing the imagination – as well as the finances – so activities designed to attract new members and constantly enthuse existing ones need to be equally as appealing to the general public. Once convinced, a member's ongoing affiliation relies on effective administration, regular communications and high levels of responsiveness comparable to the customer care facilities we expect from service providers such as banks and mobile phone vendors (even if they do often fail to live up to expectations!).

Associa is pleased to be able to sponsor a publication that is attempting to provide organisations with the tools necessary to be successful in the modern marketplace. This guide will explore the ways to: present an attractive proposition to potential members; continually communicate with members to maintain interest and avoid the dreaded apathy; and also utilise modern technology to dramatically enhance results.

Illustrated by real examples and with standardised action points to get things moving, we are confident that this book will become an invaluable resource to voluntary groups wanting to attain, regain or retain healthy membership numbers.

# Introduction

Type the keyword 'membership' plus your special interest into the Google internet search engine, whatever your need – from managing diabetes to indulging a love for line dancing – the chances are you'll soon find an organisation that serves it. From the cradle to the grave, there is a scheme for every conceivable need. During pregnancy and the early years, the National Childbirth Trust offers practical and emotional support. For young people, the Scouts and the Guides bestow fun and adventure. At work, professional associations and trade unions represent millions. In the third age, recent arrivals such as the Association of Retired People are making the grey lobby a force to be reckoned with. For death-related causes, you can be a member of, for example, the Stillbirth and Neonatal Death Society or the Voluntary Euthanasia Society.

So why is a guide to membership needed? Despite the huge number of membership organisations in the UK, a stark contrast can be made between academic and research support for people who fundraise and those who run membership schemes. The voluntary sector collates annual statistics and trends in public giving. Fundraising managers and staff join support bodies such as the Institute of Fundraising (formerly ICFM), attend fundraising conventions or undertake professional development courses in fundraising. There is a wide range of best-selling books, journals and email groups to keep fundraisers up to date with best practice. By comparison, people involved with membership schemes have few such resources.

Why this should be so is a matter for debate. Fundraising is vital and immediate. It makes money and it funds vital research, development, campaigns and services. It also attracts a cohort of highly skilled professionals, well versed in the art of networking and information sharing.

In contrast, membership is a more multifaceted activity; it generally exists to serve a softer (though no less essential) set of goals. Your scheme may have any number of reasons to exist: to underpin governance and democracy, to build support for the cause, as an information distribution channel, to provide services, to generate income and so on. Perhaps it is this diverse set of goals (and skills required) that explains why, in the UK, membership tends to fall between several stools when it comes to developing national support structures and publications.

In 2002, NCVO took a lead with the establishment of the Membership Forum which meets two to three times yearly. This book evolved as a direct result of the demand from Forum delegates for a guide to membership best practice.

## Relationships and relationship marketing

One of the challenges in writing this guide is the sheer diversity of the third sector's 80,000 membership schemes. Just what is it that all these disparate schemes have common? During my research for this guide, I found that whatever the scheme's objective – whether to change the law or to support a football club – they are all in the same business of managing one-to-one relationships. Taking this as my cue, this guide explores how recent developments in 'relationship marketing' can be applied to grow your own membership support.

Relationship marketing is a term for a new–old concept; not a new discovery so much as a rediscovery of an ethos that, for many membership schemes, has long been the key to success.

**Relationship marketing is a member-focused approach to building relationships between the host organisation and its members**

In essence, relationship marketing is a member-focused approach to building relationships between the host organisation and its members. You might be the secretary of a social club or the marketing manager of a large charity. Your members may be individuals, or organisations, or other membership bodies who have joined an umbrella scheme. Whatever cause you serve, the ultimate goal of relationship marketing is always the same – to build long-term relationships between your host organisation and like-minded people. The glue that binds these relationships is the two-way flow of value – that is, the member gains real value from the relationship which converts into value for the organisation.

This guide provides a relationship marketing toolkit with a chapter devoted to each of the following tools:

- Intrinsic motivations
- Mission and strategy
- Market research
- The marketing mix
- Recruitment
- Loyalty and retention
- Membership databases
- Governance and representation

### Which organisations does this book apply to?

This book is a non-specialist's guide to relationship marketing to be used to unleash the full potential of a membership scheme. The key principles apply to any third-sector organisation or group, including:

- **charities** including all bodies that conform to the registration criteria set by the Charity Commission;
- **voluntary organisations** made up of other bodies with social aims that have not registered as charities, eg sports and social clubs, friends' schemes, pressure groups, owners clubs;
- **not-for-profits** (a broader classification originating from the United States) which covers trade unions, cooperatives, professional associations and other organisations that may make a profit but do not distribute it.

The dividing line between the third, private and public sectors isn't as rigid as it might appear. So while the core of this book relates to the voluntary sector, the key principles of relationship marketing are also relevant to:

- **organisations on the cusp of the third and public sectors** such as museums and art galleries who receive their core funding from the government but also rely on voluntary membership and donations;
- **membership bodies on the cusp of the third and private sectors**, for example, the friendly societies and cooperatives who do not pay dividends to shareholders but operate like commercial companies, loyalty schemes, travel clubs and product user groups.

Given the range of different membership models, it is inevitable that some of the examples or situations this guide covers, or the terms it uses, may be unfamiliar to you. In some cases, you will have to translate the general principles outlined in the book to apply them to your own unique situation. For example, if you are a local group leader it may seem wishful thinking to believe that you can learn from the million-member-strong RSPB, but as this guide will demonstrate, some of the key principles that underpin its success are just as applicable to a local play scheme or an astrologers' club.

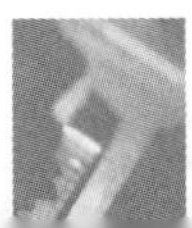

## Who is this guide for?

Anyone involved with third-sector membership schemes, including:

- the trustees who govern membership organisations;
- the management team, who must work with trustees to formulate policy and deliver services;
- the staff and volunteers who require a clear strategy and plans in order to fulfil their day-to-day roles and meet the needs of their members;
- the membership coordinator (professional or otherwise) whose role, even in the smaller organisations, is being transformed from the 'membership secretary' (who merely collects the subscriptions and keeps the records in a card index box), to a multidisciplinary skilled person (or team) who coordinates a wide range of organisational functions – from database marketing to volunteer management.

Whatever your status or setting, I hope that you find many of the ideas in this book thought-provoking and useful.

## Making the most of this book

### Case studies

Case studies are used throughout the book to illustrate ideas and approaches for dealing with real-life situations.

### Exercises

Exercises can be found in most chapters of the book to encourage you to apply key ideas and techniques to your own membership scheme. These can be done either on your own to assist your thinking or together with your work team/manager/trustees. And they work too: the exercises have been used widely by all kinds of organisations for problem solving and generating ideas. So use them!

### Key action points

Successful membership schemes don't come about just by reading books. By setting out key action points at the end of each chapter, this guide encourages you to move straight from theory to practice.

### Other NCVO Good Guides

This book is the seventh to be published as part of the NCVO Good Guide series. The other guides include *The Good Management*

*Guide; The Good Financial Management Guide; The Good Employment Guide; The Good Campaigns Guide; The Good Trustee Guide;* and *The Good Investment Guide.* As many of the themes tackled in those books overlap with the membership issues explored here, at certain points in this book, readers are signposted to these titles for further guidance on the wider skills and competencies that can aid the running of a membership scheme. See www.ncvo-vol.org.uk/publications for more information.

**NCVO Membership Forum**

If you would like to know more about the NCVO Membership Forum you can visit NCVO's website at www.ncvo-vol.org.uk, contact NCVO's HelpDesk on 0800 2 798 798, textphone 0800 01 88 111 or email helpdesk@ncvo-vol.org.uk.

The Forum, which meets two to three times yearly, enables people involved with the running of membership schemes to get together to share information and learn about best practice. If you have any ideas about issues that the Forum should cover, please do not hesitate to contact NCVO. We need your help and suggestions in order to improve.

**Your feedback please!**

Finally, we would appreciate your feedback to help ensure that future editions of *The Good Membership Guide* are as relevant as possible. So please do spare a few minutes to fill in the feedback form at the back of the guide and return it to NCVO, or contact me directly at Stiliffe@aol.com.

**Stephen Iliffe**

# Prologue: a history of membership schemes

**No man is an island, entire unto itself. We are each a piece of the continent. [John Donne, Meditation XVII]**

Membership schemes are not a modern invention – in fact, their roots go back to prehistoric times. *Homo sapiens* is a social animal, primed to seek out membership of a group (family, tribe, village, school, workplace, membership scheme). This deep-rooted instinct has its origins between 100,000 BC and 10,000 BC when humans became the dominant species on earth. A crucial factor in the ongoing 'survival of the fittest' was the acquisition of language and speech to foster cooperation within tribal groups for mutual benefit: to hunt and gather, to share out the food, to seek safety in numbers and care for the young, the elderly and the sick.

### The beginnings of mutual self-help

Early agriculture would have been impossible without mutual cooperation among farmers. They relied on one another to defend land, harvest crops, build barns, and to share equipment. These examples of early informal cooperation were the precursors of modern cooperatives.[1]

With the emergence of the great civilisations of ancient Egypt, Greece and Rome we see the first appearance of membership-type groups outside of the immediate tribal unit. With food and shelter now in plentiful supply, these groups could focus on the higher social needs. In Rome, military governors jealous of their power base would view suspiciously any citizen petitioning to form a self-help group. But such groups did flourish and even had what we would recognise as a scheme. For example, the burial societies founded to ensure that ordinary people of modest means had a decent send-off, were, in practice, cooperatives that charged a monthly subscription and became a focus for social events.[2]

### The early Christian church

By Anglo Saxon times, the Church was using certain features of what we would recognise today as a membership scheme to become the hub of every British settlement. For example, while members of the congregation could rely on their priest for spiritual worship, weddings, baptisms and funerals, the cost of all this – ie the subscription – was the annual tithe, which was equivalent to one-tenth of their agricultural produce or earnings. Failure to pay invariably brought exclusion from the Church and its benefits.

### The medieval guilds

The rapid growth of medieval cities ushered in the medieval guilds. People who made and sold the same products often lived close together (in London, the bakers could be found on Bread Street, the goldsmiths on Goldsmiths Row and so on). In time, this led to the formation of over 157 trades and crafts guilds. With formal charters and democratic structures governing a mix of self-interest and altruism, the guilds were the precursors of the modern trade unions. For example, the White Tawyers Guild of leather dressers enabled members to agree a uniform price to avoid ruinous price-cutting and unfair competition. In 1347, it adopted a statute which also stipulated that members support each other in hard times:

> *The members of the trade are to provide a candle to be kept burning before the shrine of Our Lady in the Church of All Hallows near London Wall. Contributions toward the cost shall be put in a box. From this charity box seven pence a week is to be provided for any member of the trade of good repute who shall fall into poverty and for any widow of a member.*

### The emergence of modern membership schemes

It is no coincidence that the modern third-sector membership scheme has its roots in the aftermath of the first Industrial Revolution. Until the mid-18th century, most people still lived in agrarian communities that had no need of such schemes. Each village had a deep-rooted ecosystem of social, cultural, fiscal, altruistic and other benefits, a caring and sharing network that looked after its members; the young, sick, disabled, elderly and widowed. If a child was orphaned, the extended family cared for it while she or he contributed to the shared pool of labour. From tavern to church, the locals found fulfilment through gossip, folk song, dance, religious and pagan festivals and other shared rituals.

Much of this rich and mutually supportive social fabric was torn by the transformation of Britain from a rural society to one whose wealth was driven by industrial production. That sparked the mass migration of workers to hastily built new towns and cities (Manchester and Leeds had been mere villages 70 years earlier). The resulting alienation caused a desperate need for new forms of social engagement and representation. Such was the government's fear and loathing of the new self-help groups – in particular the emergent trade unions – that it passed the notorious *Combination Acts* of 1799/1800. Fearing the spread of ideas that inspired the French Revolution, the acts banned every kind of unofficial 'combination' (a membership-type body) or meeting leading to one.[3] Yet the groups persisted because they met a vital human need.

The first general trade union, the Grand National Consolidated Trades Union (GNCTU) and its members thrived on the kind of multiple benefit 'packages' that drive membership schemes today.

## Grand National Consolidated Trades Union (GNCTU)

During the 1830s, the GNCTU came under enormous pressure to desist from its activities. Yet it and its constituent member unions survived by evolving a sophisticated mix of mutual benefits:

**Social**

Local branches offered a place to meet and drink, an attempt to replicate the old social bonds of the agrarian communities.

⇧⇩

**Cultural**

Branches held marches, dances and folk events to invoke a sense of belonging and loyalty among members and their families and friends.

⇧⇩

**Informational**

Workers were informed of their rights and responsibilities during a time of rapid and fluctuating legal and political change.

⇧⇩

**Fiscal**

⇧⇩

Some early unions had mutual investment schemes (a precursor to the later emergence of the friendly societies).

⇧⇩

**Access to services**

⇧⇩

Paying their dues gave union members privileged access to services such as individual casework.

⇧⇩

**Representational**

By joining, individuals gained the strength in numbers to bargain often hostile employers on pay and conditions.

⇧⇩

**Altruistic**

To gain wider public support, many unions had the discretion to disburse funds to related causes or worthy individuals.

⇧⇩

**Central resource**

The GNCTU acted as a conduit between the smaller unions and as a central repository of information and knowledge.

So powerful were the bonds that the GNCTU formed with displaced workers that government attempts were made to destroy it and its member unions. Most infamously the arrest of six people from the village of Tolpuddle in Dorset for forming an association under the name of the Friendly Society of Agricultural Labourers. These six men (known as the Tolpuddle Martyrs) were found guilty at a show trial of 'administering illegal oaths' and transported to Australia. The episode retains a hallowed place in the lore of the GNCTU's modern equivalent, the Trades Union Congress (TUC), whose 69 unions represent 7 million members today.

But it wasn't only self-interest and mutual protection that inspired the emergent third sector. Parallel to the early trade unions, the non-conformist churches were among the first to set up a membership scheme for what would today be recognised as a strategic and altruistic purpose.

## The Anti-Slavery Society (ASS)

The ASS is a striking early example of how a single issue campaign can unite members from very different backgrounds. Its earlier incarnation – as the Quaker-dominated Committee on Slave Trade – had succeeded in abolishing slavery in England in 1777. But it was one thing to prick the public conscience about slavery at home and another thing to abolish it in the colonies. By creating a mechanism for shared governance, debate and policy making, the ASS membership scheme united a broader coalition than was hitherto possible, of Quakers, Baptists, Methodists and other sympathetic people. With this non-denominational base of support, the ASS was able to widen its sphere of influence and to lobby the government to keep its promise to legislate for the colonies.

In the 1830s, it did so, and yet still the slave trade flourished by other means. However, by now an underlying national structure of social, networking and representational activities had given the ASS the longevity to keep the issues in the public mind and on the long-term parliamentary agenda. By 1860, the ASS had:

- a coalition drawn from different social, religious and political groups
- a constitution
- 100 local societies
- 850 direct members
- elections to a central governing committee
- a regular journal – *The British Emancipator*

With this sophisticated mix of activities, the ASS understood the intrinsic motivations of its members to do the right thing and act out their religiously inspired altruism; to feel a sense of self-esteem; to enjoy social friendship through local societies and gain public recognition from their peers; to have the chance to exercise influence via the Society's governing structure, journal and campaigning work.

Now known as Anti-Slavery International, their vital work continues to this day.

From the early 19th century to the present day, membership schemes have evolved adapting to different conditions, innovating a wide variety of forms to serve almost every conceivable individual or organisational need:

- **Professional associations**
  1823 – The now 120,000-strong British Medical Association was the first of the modern professional associations to bring together people with similar qualifications, career goals and interests. Members of similar bodies join to gain privileged access to services; to gain formal recognition of their skills and knowledge; or to gain protection against external threats.

- **Cooperatives**
  1843 – The Rochdale Equitable Pioneers Society became the birthplace of the cooperative movement – set up to create democratically owned entities where the members (workers, consumers, farmers and producers) could balance each other's social and economic interests.

- **Trade unions**
  1851 – The Amalgamated Society of Engineers (ASE) became the first of the new model trade unions that were highly centralised, levied high membership dues and were able to employ full-time officials and provide material benefits as well as representational advocacy.

- **Friendly and mutual societies**
  1854 – The Cheltenham Mutual Society empowers ordinary people to pool their money for financial self-protection. To ensure that people of all social classes gain access to affordable fiscal products – such as insurance and life assurance – the societies are owned and governed by the members.

- **Charity institutes and associations**
  1866 – In this year, RNIB unites local groups for blind people across the UK. Since the Middle Ages, charities had been secretive and isolated with little shared understanding of the root causes of poverty. Many similar national bodies emerged to unite and coordinate the disparate local self-help groups of disadvantaged people.

- **Sports clubs and associations**
  1868 – Increased social mobility through the new rail and transport networks allowed people to travel further to pursue sport and leisure activities. The Football Association came into being when a meeting of the leading clubs decided to cooperate and frame a unified set of official rules under which everyone could play.

- **Owners' clubs**
  1907 – The Caravan Club is an early example of what we now call an owners' club – gathering together people who own a particular product whether generic (eg motorcycle clubs) or branded (the Morris Minor Owners Club).

- **Social clubs**
  1915 – The Women's Institute reflects the emergent trend for women to mobilise. Operating at both national and local level, similar bodies bring together social clubs with shared interests into an overarching federated (or similar structure) of branches with a central resource of knowledge and expertise on which to draw.

- **Pressure groups**
  1926 – Like many other pressure groups founded out of a fear of losing something valued, the Campaign to Protect Rural England (CPRE) began by lobbying to stop the erosion of green spaces by indiscriminate development. Members join local pressure groups too, such as residents' associations, founded to influence local economic, social or legal decisions.

- **Friends' schemes**
  1968 – The British Museum Friends joins a now well-established tradition of people banding together to support a library, hospital, archive, museum, art gallery and so on. The scheme, which exists either independently of the host organisation or is managed by it, provides members with an opportunity to show their support (financially or by volunteering) often while benefiting from discounts or invitations to special occasions.

- **Fan clubs**
  1973 – The founding of the Doctor Who Appreciation Society (DWAS) reflects the modern trend for fan clubs (or supporters' groups) of causes ranging from rugby clubs to pop groups.

Every decade of the 20th century saw the birth of third-sector membership schemes which still exist today. Here are some of the more well-known ones (with their 2003 UK membership size):

1903 National Art Collections Fund (100,000)
1903 Workers' Educational Association (16,500)
1908 Scout Association (476,000)
1909 Girlguiding UK (600,000)
1918 National Council for One Parent Families (3,000)
1919 National Council for Voluntary Organisations (3,200)
1920 Royal British Legion (500,000)
1930 Youth Hostels Association (310,000)

1934 Diabetes UK (180,000)
1935 The Ramblers' Association (131,000)
1935 Voluntary Euthanasia Society (35,000)
1946 Soil Association (15,000)
1947 MENCAP (15,000)
1957 Consumers' Association (700,000)
1958 Tate Gallery Members (50,000)
1961 Amnesty International (195,000)
1961 Pre-school Learning Alliance (16,000)
1963 National Children's Bureau (4,500)
1964 National Childbirth Trust (53,000)
1966 National Women's Register (8,000)
1970 Gingerbread (4,100)
1971 Friends of the Earth (104,000)
1972 The Woodland Trust (124,000)
1973 National Association of Toy and Leisure Libraries (852)
1977 Greenpeace (230,000)
1979 Business in the Community (700)
1979 Alzheimer's Society (25,000)
1980 National Day Nurseries Association (2,500)
1983 English Heritage (460,000)
1983 Alcohol Concern (2,000)
1987 Amicus MSF (730,000)
1988 Action for ME (9,500)
1988 Association of Retired Persons (65,000)
1990 National Asthma Campaign (15,000)
1992 The Wildlife Trusts (440,000)
2000 Eden Project Friends (10,000)

As a glance at this list suggests, the only slowdown of new membership bodies occurs in the 1940s and 1950s. As a result of the Labour government's post-war ambitions to create a cradle to grave welfare society, many third-sector functions were subsumed into government departments, state hospitals and social services. Then the 1960s saw a dramatic second wave of new schemes. The impetus for this came from:

- the growth of the third sector itself, as the state contracted out more services;
- the increasing self-awareness and mobilisation of women, minority ethnic groups and disabled people;
- the continued growth of the professional sectors;
- smaller niche organisations addressing needs not tackled by existing or larger monolithic organisations;

- the constant identification of new needs not previously recognised;
- the popularity of single-issue campaigning;
- increased economic prosperity making paid-for membership affordable to all.

In more recent times, observation suggests that the number of schemes has continued to grow, at least in part due to:

- the spread of computer databases making it easier to collate, store and strategically analyse membership data;
- the emergence of desktop publishing and cheaper print which have made membership magazines and newsletters more affordable;
- the internet, which offers new forms of connectivity and collaboration.

**Membership in the 21st century**

As anyone over the age of 70 will tell you, the UK today has a very different social landscape compared to 50 years ago. The well-ordered pre- and post-war municipal society – family, school, church, council, large industries, the welfare state – has fractured and reassembled into new shapes.

Society today is more complex. It is like a jigsaw puzzle of interlocking (and sometimes ill-fitting) private, public and third-sector organisations, alliances and groups. The UK's 80,000 plus third-sector membership bodies[4] represent just some of the individual pieces in that complex puzzle. According to the most recent World Values Study[5], the trend is international. The table overleaf shows the international membership levels of voluntary organisations and participation within those organisations.

| Country | % of the population who are members of a voluntary organisation | % of members who volunteer |
|---|---|---|
| Sweden | 85 | 46 |
| Netherlands | 85 | 42 |
| Denmark | 81 | 32 |
| Norway | 81 | 45 |
| USA | 72 | 64 |
| Germany | 67 | 45 |
| Canada | 65 | 67 |
| Belgium | 57 | 49 |
| Great Britain | 53 | 41 |
| Ireland | 49 | 54 |
| France | 39 | 60 |
| Italy | 35 | 68 |

**Membership plays a vital role in maintaining the fabric of a civic society.**

Today, membership plays a vital role in maintaining the fabric of a civic society. A groundbreaking piece of social research by Andries van den Broek and Paul Dekker[6] examined widespread fears in the Western world that three aspects of modernism were eroding civic values:

- *rationalism*, which erodes traditional, religiously inspired values and moral obligations;
- *individualism*, which champions autonomy, self-expression and personal freedom;
- *the calculative citizen*, where individual self-interest predominates, inhibiting social concern in general and volunteering in particular.

Contrary to these fears, van den Broek and Dekker's analysis of the World Values Survey data stressed how voluntary membership schemes led to the enhancement in American and European democracies of *social capital* (which equates to "networks, norms and social trust that facilitate cooperation for mutual benefit") and *public discourse* ("the ability of a society to express collective values, to be aware of social problems, and to develop political goals").

**From ancient Rome to the internet**

Today, online members of the Consumers' Association's internet scheme, Whichnet?, can download comparative reports on different funeral plans or visit the bulletin boards to exchange ideas and socialise. Two thousand years may separate the social hubbub of imperial Rome's burial societies from the collaborative intimacy of today's internet schemes, but the needs that people fulfil when joining them don't change (much).

*Homo sapiens* has an innate capacity to cooperate in groups for the purpose of securing mutual benefits. For much of our history, we have lived in small family and tribal groups. Group life produced many benefits and people still instinctively seek it out. The more things change, the more they stay the same – membership, it seems, is here to stay.

---

1 www.cooplife.com.
2 Hudson, M (2002) *Managing without Profit*, Directory of Social Change
3 The History of the TUC. www.tuc.org.uk
4 Extrapolated from Charity Commission data, 2004
5 World Values Study data, as distributed in Inglehart, R (1990)
6 Van den Broek, A and Dekker, P (1998) *Voluntary Organisations –The Civil Society Perspective*, CAF

# 1 An introduction to relationship marketing

Membership schemes existed in ancient Greece (the debating societies) and still flourish in the internet age (Globelink). They take myriad forms – from a charity (MS Society) to a pressure group (Billericay Residents' Association) and a fan club (the Blackburn Rovers Supporters Club). Some gain influence through mass strength in numbers (the National Trust), others with a small but influential membership (the Green Alliance). Some are hosted by organisations primarily funded by donations, contracts or government (RNIB), others by those who eschew any funding except members' fees and sales (Consumers' Association). There are left-wing bodies (the Rail, Maritime and Transport Union) and right-wing (the Freedom Association). Some are international (the World Wildlife Fund (WWF) and others are local (the Aberystwyth Hard of Hearing Club).

But what do all these disparate schemes have in common? Regardless of their objective, all are in the same business of managing one-to-one relationships. This chapter explores how recent developments in relationship marketing can be applied to grow membership support. It covers:

- How members get value
- How organisations get value
- Achieving win–win situations of mutual benefit
- What relationship marketing can do for you
- The six stages of the membership journey
- A relationship marketing toolkit

Whatever kind of scheme you operate, it is a channel for managing relationships between your cause and like-minded people. The two-way flow of *value* binds these relationships, ie the real value gained by the member from the relationship converts into value for the organisation.

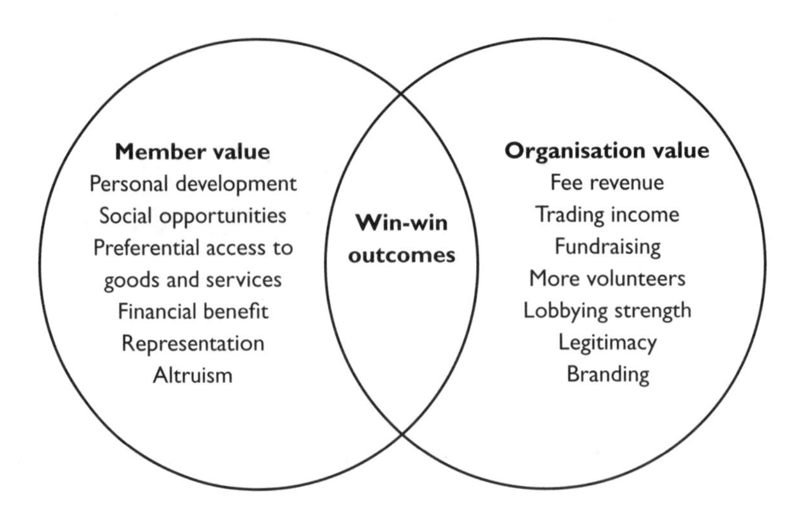


## How members get value

Relationship marketing is a *member-based* approach to the business of growing membership support. This means starting from where your prospects or your members are now. What kind of value are they seeking from your scheme? Your members will most likely look for a combination of the following benefits.

**Personal development**
From medical self-help to career development to learning a new hobby – membership can offer a focus for personal development.

**Social opportunities**
A scheme can bring together like-minded people seeking to meet and mix with each other, to gain self-esteem, status, a sense of belonging or to form relationships.

**Preferential access to goods and services**
Another key motivation is preferential access to a members' only benefit that would otherwise be unobtainable – a magazine, a telephone helpline, a chance to book tickets to the opera before the show opens to the public.

**Financial benefits**
A scheme may offer discounts or the opportunity to purchase goods and services more cheaply than from other sources.

**Representation**
Whether pursuing an ideology or belief, or acting out of self-interest, people know that they have a far greater chance of

influencing social, legal or political change by joining a group rather than by acting on their own.

### Altruism

Helping others – whether through donating, volunteering or campaigning – can be a source of well-being or pride, giving people a feeling of being needed, or of public recognition for their contribution to a cause.

### Umbrella bodies

The above values can also benefit organisations or membership groups who elect to join an umbrella body that offers services, networking and representation to enable member bodies to enhance the value they offer to their own members.

## How organisations get value from members

If relationship marketing starts from where the members are, it explicitly acknowledges that the organisation will seek a return on its investment in the scheme by getting value from its members.

### Revenue from membership fees

Membership fees can generate a regular source of revenue for an organisation. Assuming that the costs of running the scheme are fully recovered, they can make a net financial contribution towards the host organisation's work in other areas, such as research and campaigns. If the running costs of a membership scheme are not fully recovered from the members' fees, the scheme may still prove its worth by delivering one or more of the following benefits.

### A warmer audience for trading activities

The warmth felt by members towards the organisation's cause can be turned into an effective source of trading income. When buying your products or merchandise – from gift catalogues, bookshops, visitor sites etc – members are inspired by knowing that any profit will be ploughed back into the cause (it doesn't go to shareholders).

### Boosting fundraising income

From the ubiquitous raffle to the legacy pack, a committed membership base also makes a warm audience for fundraising promotions.

**More volunteers**

As a means of affordable staff, volunteers can dramatically enhance any organisation's outreach or impact. Not all volunteers will be members and not all volunteers may wish to join, but compared with people who make only one-off or infrequent contact with your organisation, members will generally be a more fertile source of volunteer support.

**Greater lobbying strength**

There is no argument: any organisation that can command a vocal and active pool of advocates will have more lobbying clout. Members make great advocates: they are already well informed about the cause and can be quickly mobilised into a rapid response force.

**Stronger governance and representation**

Member input into governance is both a source of valuable user feedback (if well managed) and potential conflict (when poorly handled). Nonetheless, third-sector bodies invariably gain enhanced legitimacy when they are able to show that their governance takes account of the constituency it serves.

**Improved branding**

Membership affords legitimacy to the organisation by virtue of demonstrating to the general public that it both serves and responds to a constituency. This engenders healthy respect from government, the media and corporate sponsors, all of whom are more likely to pay attention to, or do business with, the cause.

The following exercise offers a quick way to evaluate whether your membership scheme facilitates a balanced two-way flow of value between the organisation and its members.

## Exercise: Does your scheme facilitate two-way value?

Estimate the value that your membership scheme offers both to the members and to your organisation. 1 = excellent value, 3 = satisfactory value, and 5 = poor value. You can circulate this exercise to your trustees, colleagues and members and compare the results.

### Member value

| | | | | | |
|---|---|---|---|---|---|
| We offer our members scope for personal development | 1 | 2 | 3 | 4 | 5 |
| We offer social and networking opportunities | 1 | 2 | 3 | 4 | 5 |
| We offer privileged access to goods and services | 1 | 2 | 3 | 4 | 5 |
| We offer financial benefit | 1 | 2 | 3 | 4 | 5 |
| We offer representation | 1 | 2 | 3 | 4 | 5 |
| We offer altruistic opportunities to help others and gain satisfaction from doing so | 1 | 2 | 3 | 4 | 5 |
| We offer ... (describe and rate any other values you deliver to your members) | 1 | 2 | 3 | 4 | 5 |

### Organisation value

| | | | | | |
|---|---|---|---|---|---|
| Our membership fees generate revenue income | 1 | 2 | 3 | 4 | 5 |
| Our members generate profitable trading income | 1 | 2 | 3 | 4 | 5 |
| Our members donate to the cause | 1 | 2 | 3 | 4 | 5 |
| Our members are a source of volunteer support | 1 | 2 | 3 | 4 | 5 |

| | |
|---|---|
| Our members give us greater lobbying strength | 1 2 3 4 5 |
| Our members afford us legitimate governance and representation to outside bodies | 1 2 3 4 5 |
| Our members enhance our brand | 1 2 3 4 5 |
| Our members ... (describe and rate any other values to your organisation) | 1 2 3 4 5 |

Few membership schemes will facilitate all of the above types of value, but the respective aggregate scores for organisation value and member value should be roughly equal. The greater the disparity of the two scores, the greater the risk that one party will not value the scheme as much as the other.

Is your two-way flow of value more or less equal in both directions? Where could it be improved?

## Achieving win–win situations

The ethos of relationship marketing holds that few schemes survive for long if one party – the organisation or the members – does not value it as much as the other.

If a theatre friends' scheme, specifically set up for fundraising purposes, loses money, and theatre trustees and staff see no other value in it – for example, as a source of volunteers to staff the box office – then investment in the scheme will most likely fail, even if its members appreciate the ticket discounts.

LOW organisation value +
HIGH membership value

= *lack of organisational investment and commitment*

The reverse is also true if the same friends' scheme has fundraising value for the theatre's management but the members do not perceive any tangible value (such as privileged access to premières) or any intangible value (a feeling of gratitude from the theatre management) then the scheme will suffer from a lack of public support.

HIGH organisation value +
LOW membership value

= *lack of membership recruitment and retention*

With a genuine commitment to relationship marketing, the friends' scheme will achieve a two-way flow of value to secure win–win outcomes of mutual benefit. With members feeling satisfied and cared for, the theatre management will gain friends for life – a group of loyal supporters and advocates in both good times and bad. Enthusiasts who will volunteer, fundraise and introduce new members even when the going gets tough.

Relationship marketing understands that one plus one equals three:

HIGH organisation value +
HIGH membership value

= *a third presence*

It's like the Chinese fable of the moon shining its light on a man drinking wine. Each night, the man's shadow acquires a life of its own and becomes a third presence in the story. It guides the man through a series of trials and tribulations to achieve wisdom. This happens as long as the man makes a little time each night to drink wine by the moonlight. On nights when the man is preoccupied and fails to keep his moonlit appointment, he loses his way.

Likewise, if we (the organisation) always pay attention to our shadow (the membership) we too can achieve better win–win outcomes.

The management guru Rosabeth Moss Kanter uses the term *synergy* to define how disparate work teams can harmonise so that the host organisation punches above its natural weight.[1] In this context, synergy equates to the *combined knowledge, resource and energy of the organisation plus the membership.* When both act in concert, the whole is greater than the sum of its parts.

Susan Kay-Williams of Girlguiding UK has a clear view of how synergy can enhance a charity's work.[2] She recalls her time with the British Lung Foundation and visiting a local Breathe Easy club for people with lung disease:

> *One particular lady lived in a small village. When I arrived she proudly said that she had told all her family (four generations), her neighbours, her doctor and the local newsagent that I was coming to see her. By the time I got there, most of the village knew I was coming. Talking about the visit gave the lady the opportunity to talk to all these people about the charity and what it did for her. She was a more effective advocate for the British Lung Foundation than any amount of advertising and direct mail.*

Now take the impact this single member had on her local village and magnify it to a local, regional or national scale. You'll create a buzz that will spread to dozens, hundreds or thousands of people with a similar desire to be advocates for the cause. Our first case study explores the transforming power of organisation–member synergy.

## Royal National Institute for Deaf People (RNID)

When I joined RNID in the early 1990s it had just adopted the voluntary sector's new contract culture – taking on services from the public and business sectors and tailoring them to the specific needs of deaf and hard of hearing people. In the process, the charity doubled its multi-million pound turnover and was reaching out to more beneficiaries than at any time in its 90-year history. At the same time, attitudes to charity were undergoing a sea change. In a delayed reaction to the 1970s civil rights movements, deaf people were no longer content to be passive beneficiaries. They wanted an active relationship with those organisations that claimed to speak on their behalf. With just 300 members, RNID's membership scheme had fallen behind the times.

The scheme was revamped in 1997 and within six years our support had grown from 300 to 34,000. The key to this dramatic turn-around was the launch of a new magazine, *One in Seven*, as a relationship marketing channel to empower members to be more than just passive service users and to become supporters and advocates too.

*One in Seven* inserted a number of membership surveys to enable the readers to tell us about their day-to-day experiences – from hearing aids to television subtitles. In the following issues, the magazine fed back to members on the survey results and explained how their experiences fed into our campaigning policy statements.

With each bi-monthly issue of *One in Seven*, we raised the commitment levels of our members until they became our supporters; that is to say, people who had moved from the one-off transaction of becoming a member to also being a donor to the cause, a purchaser of some of our other goods and products (knowing that any profit would be ploughed back into the cause) or a volunteer in our national and regional offices.

This new-found synergy reached its peak when more than two-thirds of the members were nurtured to an even higher level of commitment to become advocates – people who move beyond regular transactions with the organisation to advocate the organisation and its cause to other people. This followed a mass lobby of the four UK parliaments and assemblies to introduce free digital hearing aids on the NHS. RNID staff had researched an impressive case for change but found that still more public pressure was needed to force the government's hand. So *One in Seven* gave the members the facts and figures. They wrote letters to the press. Tens of thousands of their postcards and letters filled MPs' postbags. Eventually the pressure persuaded the government to commit over £100m to upgrade the NHS audiology service.

It was a classic win–win outcome. Members had the prospect of a modernised NHS hearing aid service. For RNID, upgrading our members to supporters and advocates dramatically boosted our renewal rates. Thousands signed up as advocates in our newly created 'campaign network' to boost our lobbying strength for future campaigns. Each year, over half a million outpatients use the NHS Audiology Service, so the campaign's impact went far beyond the 34,000 RNID members involved.

**From transactions to relationships**

Of course, not all members want an active relationship with their organisation. And members are not the only people who bring value; there are customers, donors and volunteers. Yet contact with these latter groups is transactional – a one-off exchange of custom or support, vital all the same but without any deeper commitment. The churn rate of transactional contact is very high. These people appear and disappear, their longer term potential to the cause oddly unfulfilled. A key aim of relationship marketing is to turn transactions into *relationships*.

**A key aim of relationship marketing is to turn transactions into relationships.**

A charity coordinator once told me that the hardest part of her job was to nudge her contacts into supporting the cause. Why? Because so much of her time was taken up with one-off enquirers who rang the helpline, the one-off purchasers of their publications and merchandise, the one-off donors who did not respond to future appeals. Here today, gone tomorrow.

**Why relationships matter**

Setting up a membership scheme is just the start. The ultimate goal is to develop more lasting relationships, yet this is the aspect that often gets less attention than any other. Cue an all-too-familiar scenario: the more existing members who lapse, the more time and money is spent recruiting new people to replace them. For example, if 25 per cent of members lapse in one year, then the entire membership base must be replaced within four years. At an NCVO Membership Forum, Nick Beeby, formerly of English Heritage, told the audience that membership is like a bath: you can turn on the taps and fill it up (recruitment) but if there is no bath plug (retention) your members drain out as quickly as they arrive (lapse). His point was crucial; treating your members in a transactional fashion and overlooking the need to build long-term relationships is akin to forgetting to put in the bath plug.

Too many schemes do all they can to recruit members and too little to retain them. Members who might have been friends for life leave at the end of the first year. The net wastage to the UK's third sector is huge – financially and timewise. For more enlightened bodies, relationship marketing offers the best safeguard against such wastage.

## What relationship marketing can do for you

Like most marketing ideas, relationship marketing originated in the private sector but can be applied with equal success elsewhere. It is a new–old concept, coined by Theodore Levitt[3] who made a distinction between:

- **transactional marketing** which focuses on the initial sale
- **relationship marketing** which reaches beyond the sale to deliver customer satisfaction throughout the lifetime of the product or service

Much of today's transactional marketing practice originates from the USA in the 1950s. In an era of unprecedented growth and prosperity, the onus was on the push for a quick sale in a manufacturing-led industry of fast-moving goods such as cars, vacuum cleaners and baked beans. Brand loyalties were strong and people took the hard-sell techniques in their stride so long as they delivered instant gratification. By the 1970s, many brands faced declining profits. Levitt linked this to an obsession with closing the sale at the expense of delivering lifelong customer satisfaction. He noted that:

- customers were less likely to make repeat purchases from the same company once they had experienced poor service;
- it cost four times as much to recruit new customers than to retain existing ones;
- loss of profitability was often directly linked to customer retention failure.

While it is easy to be distracted by Levitt's goal to maximise company profit, his thinking applies to non-profit bodies too. Whatever type of scheme you have, the ability to sustain long-term relationships is crucial because:

**Whatever type of scheme you have, the ability to sustain long-term relationships is crucial.**

- individual (or organisational) members who renew are satisfied members;
- satisfied members are more likely to support you in other ways, from buying merchandise to volunteering to making a donation;
- they are also more likely to become your advocates, actively championing your cause and introducing new members;
- they deliver membership growth which inspires the confidence in your trustees and management to invest further in your scheme.

In the 21st century, the rules of engagement have changed. With a global economy of bewildering choice and competition, customer (and member) loyalties are more fickle. They are easily able to transfer their custom (or membership) if unimpressed with their existing provider – be it supermarket, car dealer, travel firm or social group or charity. With people aware of their power to shop around, even leading brands such as BT and Marks & Spencer have to work much harder to keep traditionally loyal customers. Likewise, the third sector is no longer immune. For example, the Scouts Association must work harder and smarter to keep itself relevant in an age when boys are immersed in a fiercely competitive environment of aggressively marketed children's television, electronic games, fads and fashions. Yet third-sector membership schemes can compete for people's loyalties. With good relationship marketing, they even have certain advantages. They can:

**With people aware of their power to shop around, even leading brands have to work much harder to keep traditionally loyal customers.**

- move people beyond a transaction (purchasing goods and services) to a relationship (joining as a member);
- exploit the interactive nature of membership newsletters or events to nurture a more intimate bond with their members;
- lever greater financial commitment from members (their subscriptions and donations reward the cause, not shareholders);
- legitimately appeal for further support and advocacy because the win–win outcomes that flow from this benefits both organisation and members;
- use the cyclical nature of membership (annual renewals) as the mechanism for building longer term relationships;
- use voluntary governance to empower members to have a stakeholding in the organisation, not merely to be customers of it.

**Pyramids and trapezoids**

Ken Burnett argued that by the 1990s the best third-sector fundraisers were ahead of much of the commercial sector in their use of relationship marketing to create long-term relationships.[4] He cited the development of strategic models such as the donor pyramid.

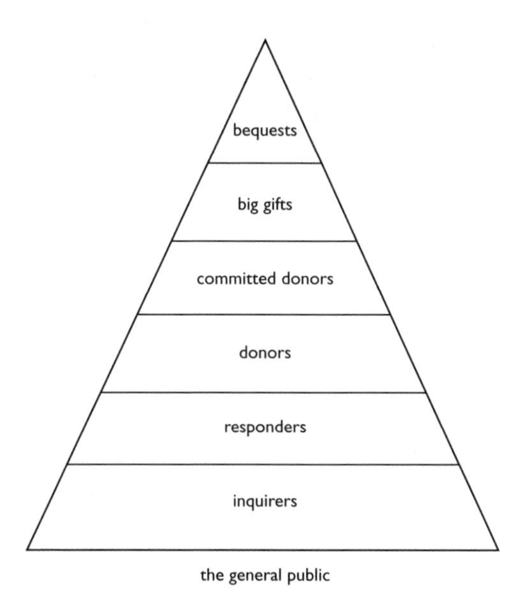


**The donor pyramid**

Like any model, the donor pyramid simplifies what happens in real life but encapsulates an idealised life cycle of a typical donor. It shows how donors often start a relationship with the cause as an inquirer. Then, suitably impressed with the way the charity fights for the cause, he/she makes a donation. The charity's gratitude for this support, and carefully timed follow-up appeal, leads some responders to become a donor, a person who has given more than once.

When a certain pattern of donations becomes obvious, the charity then nurtures some donors to upgrade into committed givers – people who donate on a regular basis, for example by giving monthly through direct debit. Of these, a small number become so inspired by the charity's carefully constructed programme of communications, appeals and thank you letters that they move up to the next level and make a big gift – a larger than average donation. At the apex are the legacy pledgers who leave behind the ultimate gift, a bequest.

Of course, not all donors conform to this model – the majority may donate once and never contribute again. Some may leave a bequest without any prior contact with the charity. But the principle is clear: the greater the care in nurturing relationships at all levels, the greater the commitment to upgrading relationships to the next level of the donor pyramid, the more long-term income for the cause.

### The membership trapezoid

If fundraising success is pyramid shaped, then what does membership success look like? While the process of engaging with donors and members has certain similarities there are differences too.

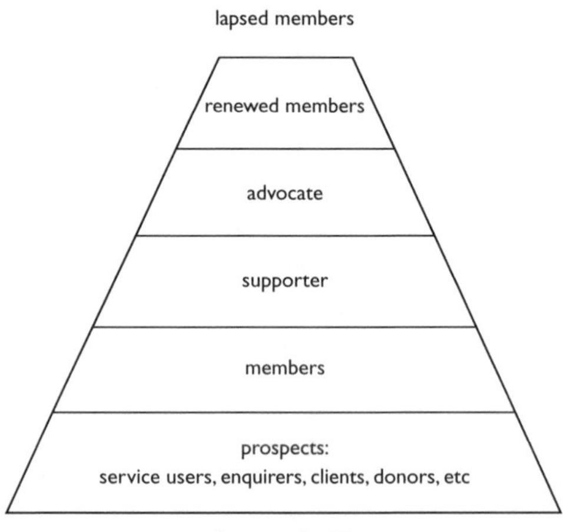


A pyramid isn't quite the right shape. The cyclical process of membership renewals means that compared with a typical donor base, fewer people lapse from one year to the next. The trapezoid is wider as membership numbers don't taper off quite as dramatically as they do for a typical donor base.

### The six stages of the membership journey

The trapezoid resembles a path receding to the horizon, as if inviting the members to travel down it, as indeed they can. The journey has six stages:

- **Prospects** – your users, enquirers, donors, etc, who have not yet joined but who are most likely 'warm' to your cause.
- **Members** – those prospects who have consolidated their transactional contact with your organisation by joining it.
- **Supporters** – members who give further transactional support by purchasing your goods and services (knowing that income supports the cause) by volunteering, making a donation, etc.
- **Advocates** – members who go one step further and actively promote your cause to others, eg by supporting a campaign or recruiting new members.
- **Renewed** – satisfied members, supporters, advocates who make the commitment to renew for another year.

- **Lapsed** – those who have left your scheme but who may be reactivated at some point in the future.

We will further explore these six stages in the succeeding chapters and look at how relationship marketing can nurture long-term relationships.

## The role of databases

Relationship marketing has grown in tandem with the emergence of affordable computer databases as eloquently explained by one of the NCVO Membership Forum's most inspirational speakers to date, Sarah Denner Brown of SDB Talking Direct:

> *Think back 50 years before supermarkets to the days of the old corner shops. Think about what those corner shopkeepers knew about their customers. They knew literally everyone who walked in. They would know who they were, who they lived with, what they bought, how much they spent, whether these people were creditworthy and if they would deliver on the slate or not. These humble shopkeepers had lots of information in their heads and they used it in dialogue with their customers and ensured that the shop had the right goods in stock, that it could tailor a personal service to the customers, or tell them about new products that might be of interest. Today, that is essentially what we are trying to do with our membership schemes. We are trying to personalise our service to as many people as we can and to retain their loyalty. The concept is nothing new. Where things have changed very much is with technology. We are trying to follow the same principle as the shopkeepers all those years ago, but now we are trying to talk individually with hundreds, or thousands, or tens of thousands of members, sending personal messages to even millions in some cases. And the technology, of course, is the marketing database.*

**Databases are more than a necessary evil: they can segment your membership into different groups and allow you to tailor your relationships.**

Databases are more than a necessary evil: they can segment your membership into different groups and allow you to tailor your relationships – if not quite on a truly individual basis in the way the old shopkeepers did, at least at a level of offering your members a choice and reflecting their preferences. With rapidly declining IT costs, the database is now an accessible resource for even the smallest groups. Whether used in-house or via an external membership bureau, they are not just a tool for automating your membership administration but also for personalising your services. While many members will match a certain

profile for age, gender, personal interests etc, there are many that don't. A scheme may include young and old, men and women, left-of-centre and conservative types. In your personal life you wouldn't communicate with them all in exactly the same way. You need 'different strokes for different folks'. Databases can segment by an individual's type or duration of membership; their choice of benefits; their desired level of support; or by any relevant criteria. If you collect and store this data (with their permission) you can personalise your relationship with them and convert them into supporters and advocates. Members of Diabetes UK who have the condition will have either the type A or type B condition. Diabetes UK segments accordingly and the result is a similar but tailored product for each group.

Such attention to detail can make the difference between some remaining on the long-term journey and leaving after one year.

## A relationship marketing toolkit

Before we take action to implement the principles of relationship marketing, it helps to have a practical toolkit. What might such a toolkit look like?

Now it actually doesn't matter whether you have 34, 340, 3400, 34,000 or 340,000 members – the relationship marketing toolkit is effective for third-sector bodies of any size. Whether

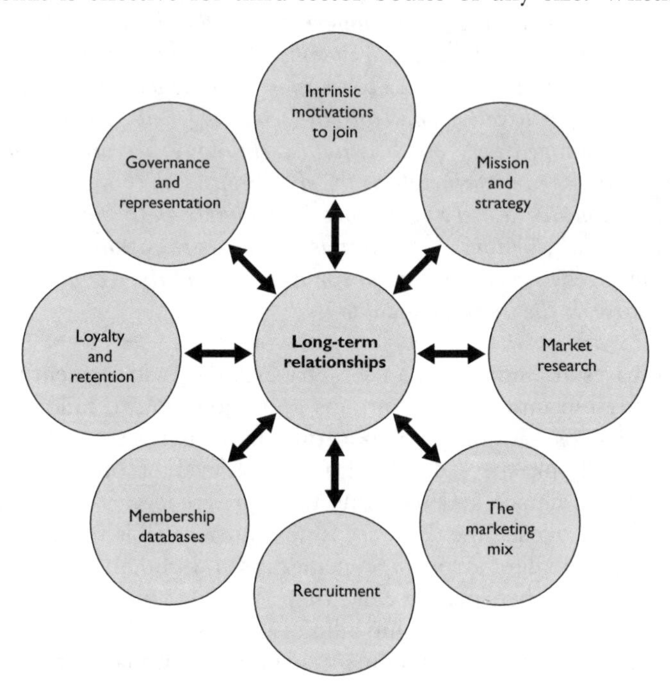

your scheme is local, regional, national or international, the same tools can help to grow your support.

All kinds of membership bodies can gain from an understanding of the *intrinsic motivations* (physiological, social, ego, etc) that people have for joining membership schemes. These must be matched to your *mission and strategy* to facilitate a two-way flow of value and secure win–win situations of mutual benefit to both the organisation and the members.

Whether you command a large or small budget, you can utilise *market research* either informally (talking to your members) or formally (mass questionnaire surveys). For developing effective membership packages, there is the *marketing mix* (philosophy, product, price, place, promotion, people, process, physical evidence) which can be adapted to almost any membership scheme's own situation.

We'll explore how to build *loyalty and retention* by using the membership trapezoid model (see page 34) to upgrade your members' commitment to your cause and build long-term relationships. Even small groups can now access affordable *membership databases* to tailor a personal service to each and every member. Last but not least, no scheme can afford to overlook the vital importance of good *governance and representation*.

### What does failure look like?

Ultimately, *long-term relationships* are at the heart of this map. Our first exercise asks you to read the case study of a charitable (and dysfunctional) cricket club and think about how the toolkit might have helped to turn their situation around. It may help you to take notes as you read and think.

## Exercise: Anytown Cricket Club (ACC)

The ACC began out of a 1950s campaign to transform council-owned wasteland to sporting use. An ex-professional cricketer was brought in to coach inner city youths in the fine arts of a game that had previously been assumed to be the preserve of the suburban middle classes.

The club's first steering committee was elected from the original group of parents. Then business sponsors were invited to join the committee, along with the ex-professional cricketer. He was resolute in his determination to widen access to youngsters who could not otherwise afford the kit and equipment to play.

By the mid-1960s, the club ran 12 teams and membership had risen to 640 people. The ex-pro became a paid director and the club obtained charitable status to boost its fundraising efforts. Over three decades, the director worked beyond the call of duty to fund a well-equipped pavilion and train a network of volunteer coaches to work in the local schools. He was single minded and would deflect any criticism of his autocratic management style by merely pointing to his success.

In the late 1990s, the membership affairs of the club fell into disrepute. A property company had approached the now cash-strapped council with a proposal to build a commercial leisure centre on the sports fields. From having sole tenancy of the site, the ACC was confronted with a Hobson's choice: agree to cooperate with the removal of the pavilion to make space for the new centre and convert two of the four cricket pitches into the centre's car park or risk the whole site being sold off to the developers.

The ACC could not stump up millions of pounds to buy the land. To secure the club's future there was no option but to cooperate with the council and developers.

The director faced this immediate threat to the club's existence by forming an unelected subcommittee. The members were given a cursory account of progress in a quarterly newsletter displayed on the club noticeboard. All through the season, the director rebuffed calls for more openness. He said the business was "commercial in confidence" but that negotiations were in his safe hands. When some members lobbied their elected chairman he was more sympathetic but said the director was "doing his best".

After that hearsay and gossip spread quickly. Members heard from each other about the rumoured changes to their club and ground. At the AGM, some members proposed a motion of no confidence in the director and demanded a say in the decision-making process. After the AGM, three members – part of the volunteer coaching team – wrote to the director:

Dear Director

We are writing to express our concern at the current secrecy over the future of the ACC ground. Morale has never been so low among the coaches and we feel certain things need to change if we are to avoid a mass resignation of members.

It isn't enough to keep the two adult pitches for use by the first and second teams, while converting the two youth team pitches into a car park. Without our traditional emphasis on youth, there would be no reason for our charitable status, or for sponsors to continue funding us.

In the ACC's recent 'newsletter', you announced new developments in a one-way fashion that gave members no opportunity to voice their concerns. Our loyal members are threatening to lapse their subscriptions. They are angry at the perceived sell-out to big business. Some members are planning to write to the local newspapers. Surely this will alienate our sponsors? We would like to discuss the option of holding a members' forum to allow them to air their views and suggest alternative plans for the club. Failing that, we feel that coaching at the club will no longer be an option for us.

Yours sincerely

The coaches

In the presence of the chairman, the director met with the three coaches. He was taken by surprise and lost no time in letting his anger show. He was furious at claims of a "sell-out" and what he saw as a lack of respect towards him. After all, he had built up the club from scratch – why should he not have the club's best interest at heart?

The director was dismissive of threatened mass resignation. "Membership is just a way of paying subscriptions," he said. "We can't afford to be romantic about involving them – they'll just make trouble. The threatened resignations don't matter, we'll soon replace them. Just ask around and we'll find some more kids to join us. We haven't got an up-to-date mailing list since the hon. secretary retired last year and took his card index box with him, so some of these people might not be members at all. There is no time to lose. We must move on."

The chairman was cowed by the director's anger. He did not intervene or summarise the discussion other than to say he was not aware that members had any right to a forum. He agreed to check the constitution when he got home, but the coaches heard nothing more.

**Analysing the case study**

It is not difficult to see the key issues that arise from the ACC director's 'short-termist' attitude to member relationships described in this case study.

The following chapters in this guide describe the relationship marketing competencies that make up our toolkit.

Reflect on how using the toolkit could have helped the ACC manage its situation more effectively:

**Intrinsic motivations to join** (Chapter 2)

*ACC's director fails to understand or harness the intrinsic reasons why people join it in the first place ("It's just a way of paying the subs").*

Understanding why people join membership schemes (social, ego, self-actualisation, etc), would help the director to desist from seeing his members as an obstacle and empower him to utilise their energy and resources.

**Mission and strategy** (Chapter 3)

*The ACC strategy has become detached from the members.*

The essence of all good membership schemes is about achieving win–win outcomes of mutual benefit to both the organisation and the members. Chapter 3 looks at how to harmonise your organisational mission and strategy with the members' needs and wants.

**Market research**
(Chapter 4)

*There is no feedback loop between the ACC staff, trustees and members.*

Chapter 4 looks at market research as a problem-solving tool for finding the right fit between the organisation and the members; for example, why doesn't the ACC director set up a focus group with key trustees and members to evaluate views and ideas for accommodating all the team matches on two pitches rather than four by rotating the fixture list?

**The marketing mix**
(Chapter 5)

*External change is seen only as a threat to the club not as a new marketing opportunity.*

Far from being a threat, the influx of visitors to the new leisure centre at the ground could be seen as a potential source of new recruits. Utilising the marketing mix's seven Ps (philosophy, product, price, place, process, people and physical evidence) would enable the club to exploit change and repackage itself to new audiences.

**Recruitment**
(Chapter 6)

*Overdependence on 'word of mouth' to recruit members.*

Using a mix of recruitment channels is essential for growing your support. Like many 'social' membership schemes, the ACC has overlooked the wider options – from direct mail to websites to member-get-member schemes.

**Loyalty and retention**
(Chapter 7)

*While the ACC has rightly gone into crisis management mode it is overlooking the loyal members whose energies are just as vital to the club's survival.*

By adopting a relationship marketing discipline, the ACC would be able to call on its members as supporters and advocates in both good times and bad. This chapter offers practical tips for boosting loyalty and retention.

**Membership databases**
(Chapter 8)

*The club has no central membership records and so cannot effectively communicate with the members when it needs to. The grapevine has taken over with an inevitably damaging effect.*

With the increasing affordability of IT, the director could now invest in a database to manage the club's records and make it easier to reach all members at all times, to segment them into different groups and so build their commitment and loyalty by personalising the club's service to them.

**Governance and representation**
(Chapter 9)

*Members input into ACC governance (they elect the chair) but have no representation (no one listens to their views).*

It is important for the chair to see that there is a vital need to review the ACC's governing structure and communications. In Chapter 9 we will explore how membership schemes can adapt their structures and feedback loops so the trustees, staff and members all pull in the same direction.

## Action points

- ✓ Handle all your organisation's one-off transactions with great care. Be it from enquirers, service users or donors, these warm contacts offer you your best future prospects for membership.
- ✓ Convert one-off transactions into long-term relationships.
- ✓ The ultimate task of any membership scheme is to create a two-way flow of value between your organisation and your members. Make it yours too.
- ✓ Identify the win–win outcomes of mutual benefit to both parties and build your membership strategy around them.
- ✓ 1+1 = 3 (organisation + the members = a third presence); involve your members and your scheme will add up to more than the sum of its parts.
- ✓ Create a membership journey: nurture your prospects to become members, then supporters and then advocates – use the raised level of commitment to renew your members.
- ✓ Remember that membership is like a bath: you can turn on the taps to fill it (recruitment) but without a bath plug (retention) your members soon drain out again (lapse). So give your loyalty and retention programme as much time, resources and care as your initial recruitment effort.
- ✓ 34, 340, 3,400, 34,000 or 340,000 members: relationship marketing can be practised on any scale. So use the relationship marketing toolkit.
- ✓ Ensure that every communication your organisation sends is geared to making your members feel valued.
- ✓ Invest wisely, as your resources allow, in a membership database. Use it not to automate your services but to personalise them.
- ✓ Always keep long-term relationships in mind even when there are short-term pressures requiring your attention.

1 Moss, R K (1990) *When Giants Learn to Dance*, Routledge
2 Kay-Williams, S (2002) *Marketing for the Voluntary Sector*, Kogan Page
3 Levitt, T (1982) *Innovations in Marketing*, Pan Books
4 Burnett, K (1992) *Relationship Fundraising*, Jossey Bass

# 2 Intrinsic motivations to join

What is the fundamental resource of good membership schemes? It is people.

Yet all too often, schemes pay insufficient heed to prospects' reasons for joining or not joining them. I once asked a judo club leader what he thought attracted people to his club. His response was puzzled: "Well, people join a judo club to do judo, don't they?" Up to a point, they do. But those who take this question for granted in fact overlook a rich complex of human motives (and are invariably also the first to complain about the lack of members). Before we can expect our prospects to relate to our membership scheme we must first be able to relate to their needs and desires.

**Before we can expect our prospects to relate to our membership scheme we must first be able to relate to their needs and desires.**

The first item in the relationship marketing toolkit (see Chapter 1), is to understand the intrinsic (inner) motivations that guide a member's decision on whether or not to join a membership scheme. This chapter asks you to take some time out to explore key insights from psychology, sociology and marketing.

- The five levels of individual need
- The six most common benefits sought by members
- How members give and take
- Demographics and psychographics
- Creating and using pen portraits of your target audience

## The five levels of individual need

One well-known behavioural model suggests that there are five levels of individual need:

- physiological needs – food, drink, shelter
- safety needs – protection against danger, threat, deprivation
- social needs – belonging, acceptance, friendship
- 'ego' needs – self-esteem, reputation, status
- 'self-actualisation' – realising own potential for continual self-development

Ivan Maslow categorised these as a hierarchy of needs:

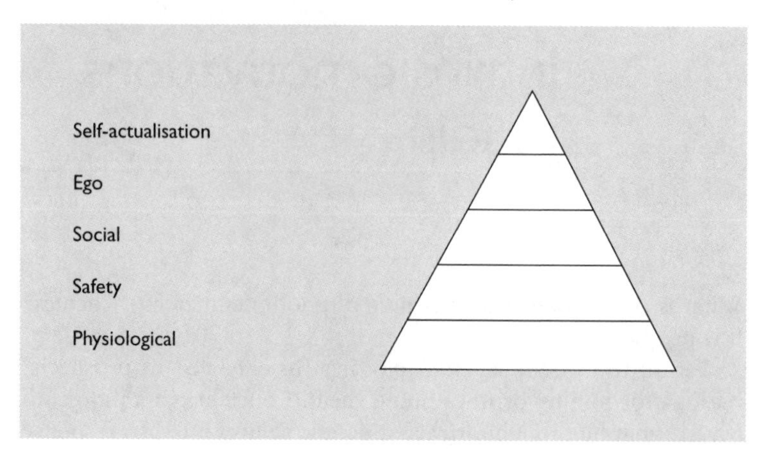


According to Maslow, the reason these needs make a hierarchy is because the lower-level needs have to be satisfied first. It is only after these are satisfied that the individual can pay attention to his higher needs'. In other words, someone who is hungry and cold will naturally be preoccupied with obtaining food and warmth and have no time to think about their higher order needs. But when that same person is properly fed and warm, they move onto the task of being safe. Only then will they seek to fulfil their personal self-development (for example, seeking the satisfaction of taking up a hobby).

Let's return to the question which opened this chapter: Why do people join a judo club? Using Maslow's model, the judo club leader could elaborate answers like these: People may join a judo club for *physiological reasons* ("To get fitter and healthier"); for *safety* reasons ("To protect myself in the event of an assault"); for *social* reasons ("My friends go there, so I thought I'd go along too"); for *ego* reasons ("I'm strong and fit and this my scene!"); or for *self-actualisation* ("To develop my mind, body and spirit").

Like any theoretical model, Maslow's simplifies what happens in real life. An alternative approach from Alderfer (1972) offers a non-hierarchical model of *existence needs*, *relatedness needs* and *growth needs*[2]. Alderfer stresses that different levels may operate at the same time and there is not an automatic progression from one level to the next.

Try the exercise below to explore how a good membership scheme can consciously touch on these intrinsic needs at all levels.

## Exercise: Maslow's hierarchy of needs

Think about an organisation you belong to (or one that you joined in the past).
Use the template below to work through some of your intrinsic motivations for joining. Your motivation may have been conscious or subconscious. Rate them on a scale of 1 to 5 (with 1 being very important and 5 not relevant).
For example, my perception is that my decision to join the Soil Association was triggered by the following motives:

| Needs and wants | Examples | Rating |
|---|---|---|
| Physiological | I'm confused by conflicting media reports. I want guidance on healthy eating to avoid the illnesses linked with industrially processed food. | 1 |
| Safety | I feel that uncritical acceptance of genetically modified food products will lead to an unsafe world for my children to grow up in. | 2 |
| Social | I need that feeling of belonging to a wider movement. | 2 |
| Ego | I want my friends to see this is the kind of person I am: you won't find me eating rubbish! | 4 |
| Self-actualisation | Joining the Soil Association makes me a more politically active citizen and I can help the wider campaign for sustainable organic farming. | 1 |

The relative importance of the psychological triggers that compel people to join will vary from one membership scheme to the next and from one individual to another.

But the best schemes are adept at offering benefit packages that push several different buttons at once.

Use the pro-forma sheet below to do the exercise. If you belong to more than one organisation, why not complete several sheets and compare the results? You can add as many examples as you can think of alongside each level of need and want.

| Needs and wants | Examples | Rating |
|---|---|---|
| Physiological | | |
| Safety | | |
| Social | | |
| Ego | | |
| Self-actualisation | | |

**What invokes the desire to join a membership scheme is the opportunity to access certain benefits that cannot be found elsewhere.**

There are many ways that we can fulfil our individual desires and joining a membership scheme is just one of them – others might include job satisfaction, seeing friends, having a meal, visiting a show, joining an evening class, and so on. What invokes the desire to join a membership scheme is the opportunity to access certain benefits that cannot be found elsewhere (or at least not without significantly greater expense, time or effort).

## The six most common membership benefits sought

**1. Personal development**

From playing a sport to pursuing spiritual beliefs, from career development to learning a new hobby – whatever it is that any individual really wants to do, the chances are there is a scheme to help him or her fulfil it. Being a member can be a form of escapism (joining the Dad's Army Appreciation Society, for example) or the fulfilment of a deeper urge (for example, someone who really wanted to work with animals but who ended up tax collecting may join the WWF to fulfil an inner urge to engage).

**2. Social and networking opportunities**

Membership schemes are ideal for offering people the chance to meet others with similar interests. For those of a certain creed, ideology, culture, hobby, medical condition, disability, profession or niche interest, membership offers a focus to meet like-minded people. Members gain a sense of belonging, of status and acceptance, a chance to make new friendships, the comfort of knowing that they are not alone.

### London Irish Network

The London Irish Network (LIN) was founded in 1989 by a group of Irish people based in London to provide a focus for people from an Irish background or anyone with an interest in Irish culture. In a city as busy as London it can be difficult to find the time and opportunity to meet new people. Independent of party political or religious affiliations, LIN offers a safe and neutral space and is run 'for the members by the members'. It defines itself as a 'multi-activities' social club and the benefits include a printed monthly programme of over 20 events sent to the members' home, online programme updates plus a members' only area on the website. Events range from singing get-togethers to theatre visits, walking events to watching TV broadcasts of traditional Irish events such as hurling. LIN offers a chance to make new friends, try out new activities and develop new hobbies or skills. It recognises that non-members, such as those who are new to London, may initially feel unsure if the network is suitable. So LIN allows guests to attend up to three events before being asked to pay a membership fee.

As thousands of similar schemes attest, social networking in the flesh has long been part and parcel of business or professional life. It may lead to useful new contacts or deals being struck. In the internet age, virtual social networks are becoming commonplace and some schemes no longer find it *de rigueur* to hire a conference room and provide drinks and canapés.

### British Learning Association

The British Learning Association (BLA) is a registered charity that offers a focus for people with an interest in open learning and innovative technology in education. Despite the steep membership fees – ranging from £145 (individuals) to £475 (corporate) – BLA offers value for money. The package includes online access to all members' contact details via region or sector; a keyword search can quickly locate someone with a very specific shared interest. Online forums enable members to scan discussions at a glance and click through to a thread on a specific topic. Time = money. Joining BLA's online community is highly time efficient. It gives members the chance to swap information, know-how, opinions, ideas and vital contacts quicker than it takes to grab your coat and hail a taxi cab.

Such members' only schemes may be open (anyone may join and there is no entry criteria), or closed (ie joining is by word of mouth, by invitation only or by strict entry criteria relating to skills, experiences or qualifications). Membership may bestow access to an egalitarian social circle (such as the Women's Institute), to an elite (such as MENSA the high IQ society), or offer the chance to exercise influence on decision makers and opinion formers in a political, economic or legal field (eg the Institute of Directors).

**3. Privileged access to goods and services**

One of the most common motivations to join is the privilege of obtaining goods and services that are unobtainable to non-members (or at the very least, only available in a less convenient or more expensive form).

## The Caravan Club

With some 850,000 members, the Caravan Club is the largest of its kind in Europe. Membership offers access to over 200 club sites. Only club members can stay at all sites and book in advance (essential for the most popular sites and for peak times of the year). The club also has a network of 2,700 certified locations (CLs) – small sites that will accommodate a maximum of five caravans only. These offer a chance to really get away from it all in rural settings; on farms, by peaceful rivers, even in the grounds of castles. Only members can gain privileged access to the sites directory, club magazine and free legal services.

### 4. Financial benefits

For many people, the key motivation to join will lie with benefits that have a financial value – such as discounts, or preferential rates for regular visitors to a nature reserve or heritage site. Families that have children are often especially price conscious when taking decisions whether or not to join a scheme and will be motivated by the chance to save money. Where a scheme does not directly provide financial savings or benefits, the information and advice given may in itself offer powerful value for money.

## Which?

Which? is a wholly owned subsidiary of the Consumers' Association, a registered charity set up to protect and advise consumers and funded entirely by its members. It is totally independent of government, business and advertising and gets no grants or subsidies from them. Joining Which? delivers value for money through wholly independent advice on purchasing goods and services. According to their leaflets: "Whether you're choosing headphones or health insurance, a microwave or a mortgage, Which? could save you time and money and a great deal more. Saving money's all very well, but peace of mind is vital too. That's what you get with Which?" Members get a quarterly magazine, access to a members' helpline giving up-to-the-minute best buy information.

Schemes that exist mainly to serve other purposes, ie members are not primarily motivated by financial benefits, may nonetheless offer financial privileges or discounts as a reward for the members' loyalty and support for the cause.

## Youth Hostels Association

The Youth Hostels Association (YHA) operates 220 youth hostels throughout England and Wales, plus a network of camping barns. It was founded in 1930 with the altruistic purpose of running hostels to encourage all people, especially young people of limited means, to develop a greater love and care of the countryside. The hostels are open to the general public, so YHA membership adds value to the hostelling experience via special offers and money-off travel opportunities. The outdoor equipment specialists, Millets, offer privileged discounts to YHA members throughout its 247 stores nationwide. The value of these discounts alone can quickly recoup the cost of the original membership fee.

Some membership schemes may offer *indirect* financial value. For example, someone who is admitted to the Chartered Institute of Marketing gains endorsement of their personal skills and qualifications thereby becoming more attractive in the marketplace and enhancing their earning power.

**5. Advocacy and representation**

Whether seeking discrete support on a personal issue or the safety in numbers that comes with belonging to a movement, joining to take advantage of advocacy and representation is another key motivator.

## Royal College of Midwives

There's nothing bashful about the Royal College of Midwives (RCM) publicity: "Almost all practising midwives in the UK are RCM members." The RCM website proclaims its "experienced trade union negotiators with over 600 workplace-based stewards and health and safety representatives". Advocacy services include free counselling and legal support, both in relation to workplace issues and to issues unrelated to employment, including road traffic accidents. Representation takes the form of "having your say about RCM policy and how the RCM is run, by voting or standing in the elections to the RCM's governing council; attending and debating motions at the conference; or by taking a role in special interest groups such as the Ethics Committee". Midwives gain financial benefit too: directly, in the form of personal accident cover and medical malpractice insurance, and indirectly by supplying strength in numbers to RCM's pay bargaining clout.

People may join a representative group for fear of losing something valued (such as the Ramblers' Association which campaigns to retain and improve the right to roam in the countryside) or to regain something that has been lost (like the members of the National Association of Deafened People who seek to recover some of the freedom and ease of movement and socialisation they enjoyed before losing their hearing). Some join to act out an ideology or belief, or to stand up and be counted on a single issue campaign which they feel strongly about.

## The Burma Campaign UK

At the time of writing, Burma is ruled by one of the most brutal military dictatorships in the world, charged by the United Nations with a "crime against humanity" for its systematic abuse of human rights, and condemned internationally for refusing to transfer power to the legally elected government of the country. The Burma Campaign UK is part of the global movement campaigning for human rights and democracy in Burma. It aims to increase economic pressure on the regime by discouraging investment and tourism and it lobbies the UK government and the European Union to increase political pressure. Membership is offered as "one of the most effective ways of supporting the struggle". It provides practical involvement in actions that to date have secured some of the campaign's objectives, including forcing British American Tobacco and a number of tour operators to withdraw from Burma. Members receive a welcome pack and the bi-annual *Metta* magazine with the latest news, campaign actions and information from inside Burma. There are no other material benefits, but (as with an altruistic scheme) members can gain personal satisfaction from contributing to a worthy cause.

**6. Altruism**

Altruism, simply put, means selflessness – or to do something to benefit others. The very act of being a contributor to a cause makes people feel good, needed and valued. Some may join out of concern or belief (as with Greenpeace or the British Humanist Association) or in order to repay a debt (by supporting a friends' scheme for a school, hospital or theatre from which they have benefited in the past). Volunteering is another common form of altruism in membership schemes.

### Friends of Milton Country Park

Like almost all public parks in the UK, Milton Country Park – located on the northern outskirts of Cambridgeshire – is both well loved locally and chronically short of public funds. People who have enjoyed the sanctuary it provides for wildlife and birds, and the walks and picnic spaces, can give something back through the Friends of Milton Country Park. Subscriptions are free as the emphasis is upon building a volunteer force to help the overstretched park rangers with maintaining the park.

As many studies in donor giving have clearly demonstrated, self-interest lies at the core of altruism. The Friends of Milton Country Park are protecting something valuable for themselves, their families and friends. The reward may be modest (a newsletter, the recognition of fellow volunteers and the gratitude of the park management team), but it is nonetheless a reward in kind (if not a financial one). Many schemes have an overt link between altruism and reward.

## Friends of the National Maritime Museum

Founded on Trafalgar Day in 1982, income from the Friends of the National Maritime Museum (FNMM) has funded the restoration of many items – from books to barges – through the Adopt-an-Item scheme. This has enabled the FNMM to buy many exhibits and assist the development of the Neptune Galleries to the tune of £650,000. Its members come from all walks of life and are offered a tiered choice of different levels of support for the museum. Fees range from £22 for concessionary, £30 for adults, £40 for families, £250 for Blue Riband membership which carries additional privileges such as invitations to private views and guest cards. For a subscription of £1,000 or more, a person can become a benefactor which entitles the giver to very special privileges including life membership, free catalogues and transferable guest cards. At £5,000, corporate membership benefits include corporate entertainment events, free use of the lecture theatre, tickets to corporate receptions, invitations to previews, plus 50 complimentary exhibition passes for staff and their families. Corporate members are encouraged to suggest other future privileges and discuss them with the museum. In 2004, the Friends pledged a further £300,000 for a major initiative to create a new permanent display for the museum's Oceans of Discovery exhibition. The museum gains additional financial value from the FNMM's volunteer programme, which increases the museum's staffing capacity by providing additional front-of-house support and tour guides.

Being a Friend of the National Maritime Museum is akin to a 'give and take' process, especially in the higher tier categories. The latent expectation is that in return for their support, friends will be able to access certain privileges and (rightfully) gain a degree of public recognition for their support.

## How members give and take

**Research indicates that most people who give expect to benefit in return.**

Some people hold dear the maxim 'It is better to give than receive', but research indicates that most people who give expect to benefit in return, whether tangible (free tickets) or intangible (a feeling of gratitude from the organisation for their support).

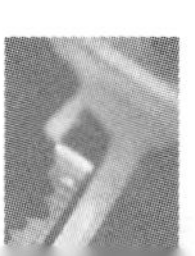

| The organisation gives and the member takes ... | The member gives and the organisation takes ... |
|---|---|
| social opportunities;<br>access to networks;<br>time saving and convenience;<br>privileged access to goods and services;<br>financial benefits;<br>value for money;<br>advocacy support;<br>representation;<br>kudos and self-esteem from altruism to others<br>... and so on. | donations;<br>volunteer time and help;<br>case studies;<br>campaign support;<br>user feedback;<br>market research survey information;<br>legitimacy;<br>word-of-mouth advocacy;<br>introduction of new members;<br>strength in numbers;<br>enhanced brand image<br>... and so on. |

Different schemes (and different tiers) involve different permutations of these win–win outcomes, with different stresses on various aspects of giving and taking. Some start primarily from the giving perspective as we saw in the earlier case study of the corporate Friends of the National Maritime Museum who gain kudos for supporting the cause as well as special privileges. Other schemes begin from the taker's perspective; the average member of the Consumers' Association's Which? is primarily seeking to make an informed choice and get value for money, but also understands that their membership gives legitimacy to the association's wider campaigning work.

**Serving multiple kinds of individual need**

What seems clear from all the above examples is that any one scheme can attract people with different motivations – some more concerned with giving than taking or vice versa.

Read the following case study about two members of the National Trust, and complete the questionnaire below to assess David and Sarah's contrasting motivations.

## Exercise: Is it better to give or receive?

David, 37, is married to Jo and has three school-age children. He drives them out on frequent trips to Trust-owned properties and sites. Their £62.50 family group membership (FGM) represents excellent value for money as he reckons on saving about the same amount again on entrance fees. He thinks the annual handbook is great too; it lists the hundreds of properties and their features, such as availability of car parking, local pubs and restaurants, and the sights en route. The handbook certainly makes life a lot easier when planning day trips.

David does get the magazine (and the appeals) but as a travelling salesman, constantly on the move with little time to read for relaxation, he tends to flick through it and puts it aside. If pressed, David admits to being something of an 'incentive junkie' (a phrase he's learnt from being a salesman). He shops around for the best deal when it comes to weekend outings, and as far as he's concerned, the National Trust is it. He hasn't donated to the Trust's appeals as he reckons it is doing well enough for itself.

His mother, Sarah, is 67 and lives in Kent. She is widowed, suffers from MS and lives alone. She doesn't get out much now and just makes the annual trip to a local Trust site on August bank holidays when David comes south, packs his mother's wheelchair into the boot and drives her over there. Three years earlier, Sarah had paid £540 to become a pensioner life member (PLIF). Ironically the MS kicked in not long after, restricting her mobility (even though she's aware the local Trust sites are largely accessible to wheelchair users).

David thinks he could talk to the Trust and get her life membership changed back to an ordinary one. But Sarah won't hear of it; the yearly trip is still a real pleasure, the thrice-yearly magazines are beautifully illustrated and give her hours of quiet engagement with the cause. The regional newsletter keeps her up to date with local developments. More importantly, she knows her fee is helping a good cause; the Trust cares for the countryside and she feels all the better for helping it out in her own small way. She makes a regular donation as she knows it will be put to good use. Sarah also answered the Trust's appeal to write to MPs about the threat to local wildlife from the government's proposals to concrete over a site in Cliffe, north Kent to build a new airport.

All David will say is that he thinks Sarah is simply careless with her money. But he keeps his counsel as he knows she thinks he's tight with money.

Now fill in the following questionnaire to assess how you see the different relationships that Sarah and David have with the National Trust. What values do you think each place on the Trust's core benefits (1 = very important to the member, 5 = not relevant at all).

**David joins the National Trust to ...**

| | | | | | |
|---|---|---|---|---|---|
| Take advantage of free access to the Trust sites | 1 | 2 | 3 | 4 | 5 |
| Take benefit from free car parking at Trust sites | 1 | 2 | 3 | 4 | 5 |
| Take benefit from the yearbook | 1 | 2 | 3 | 4 | 5 |
| Take benefit from the regional newsletter | 1 | 2 | 3 | 4 | 5 |
| Take benefit from the magazine | 1 | 2 | 3 | 4 | 5 |
| Give active support to the Trust's campaigns | 1 | 2 | 3 | 4 | 5 |
| Give financial support to the Trust's work (via the fee) | 1 | 2 | 3 | 4 | 5 |
| Take pride in supporting the Trust's work | 1 | 2 | 3 | 4 | 5 |

| **Sara joins the National Trust to ...** | | | | | |
|---|---|---|---|---|---|
| Take advantage of free access to the Trust sites | 1 | 2 | 3 | 4 | 5 |
| Take benefit from free car parking at Trust sites | 1 | 2 | 3 | 4 | 5 |
| Take benefit from the yearbook | 1 | 2 | 3 | 4 | 5 |
| Take benefit from the regional newsletter | 1 | 2 | 3 | 4 | 5 |
| Take benefit from the magazine | 1 | 2 | 3 | 4 | 5 |
| Give active support to the Trust's campaigns | 1 | 2 | 3 | 4 | 5 |
| Give financial support to the Trust's work (via the fee) | 1 | 2 | 3 | 4 | 5 |
| Take pride in supporting the Trust's work | 1 | 2 | 3 | 4 | 5 |

How do David and Sarah's results contrast? Who takes more from their National Trust membership? Who gives more?

You may have noted that David is more concerned with taking the benefits, while Sarah takes greater pride in her role as a supporter. But isn't taking pride a form of benefit in kind? Isn't David's keenness to help himself to free access to sites and car parks nonetheless a form of support (his fee helps the Trust, even if he hasn't given this much thought). As we can see from Sarah and David's example, people are predominantly 'givers' or 'takers'. Different people have different motives for seeking different benefits from the same membership scheme. For example, some people may join the local branch of a membership organisation for its social and networking opportunities even if they have little affinity with the organisation's ultimate cause. Some members enjoy getting involved with the governance and running of the branches while others enjoy just being there. Social status is another intrinsic factor that motivates

**Different people have different motives for seeking different benefits from the same membership scheme.**

both 'givers' and 'takers'. Many friends' schemes that support theatre or opera institutions know the difference between people who are mainly interested in rubbing shoulders with the celebrities, and basking in the reflected glory, and those who are more interested in public recognition for their role as supporters of a prestigious cause.

**Offering a choice of membership categories is a powerful technique for recruiting and retaining all the different segments of your target audience.**

The ethos of good membership schemes, like the National Trust, to serve different people with different needs with different benefit packages, and of tailoring different kinds of relationships to maintain their support, is a key principle of relationship marketing (as introduced in Chapter 1). Whether you are a local group or a national organisation, offering a choice of membership categories (or tiers) is a powerful technique for recruiting and retaining all the different segments of your target audience.

The use of the marketing mix to segment your membership benefits for different audiences is explored in further detail in Chapter 5.

## Demographics and psychographics

Two analytical tools that can help us to deepen our general understanding of people's motives to join are demographics and psychographics.

*Demographics* are tangible factors that we can record or measure, such as:

- age
- gender
- marital status
- children/dependants
- geographic address, postcode
- medical condition/disability
- educational attainment
- occupation
- sexual orientation
- racial or cultural type
- political affiliation
- consumer spending patterns

The broad impact of these factors can be demonstrated by taking any subset of the UK population, such as women, and identifying the demographic niches that exist within it. For example: Asian Deaf Women's Association; Black Women in the Arts; British Federation of Women Graduates; Catholic Women's Ordination;

English Collective of Prostitutes; Feminists against Censorship; Grandmother's Federation; Jewish Lesbian's Group; Older Women's Network; Single Mother's Self-Defence; Townswomen's Guild; Wages for Housework; Women in Business; Women's Sport Foundation; Women in Music and so on.

Overlaying demographic factors are the so-called *psychographics*, defined by American sociologist Arnold Mitchell as the collective essence of an individual's attitudes, beliefs, opinions, prejudices, hopes, fears, needs, desires and aspirations that, taken together, govern how he or she behaves and that, as a whole expresses itself in a lifestyle.[3]

Mitchell devised a system called Values and Lifestyle, better known as VALS (a trademark of the SRI Consulting Business Intelligence), for categorising his fellow American citizens by their social values and behaviours. While specific to the USA, and more commonly used in the third sector to analyse groups of prospective donors, it still provides a useful yardstick for thinking about the values of your prospective and actual members.

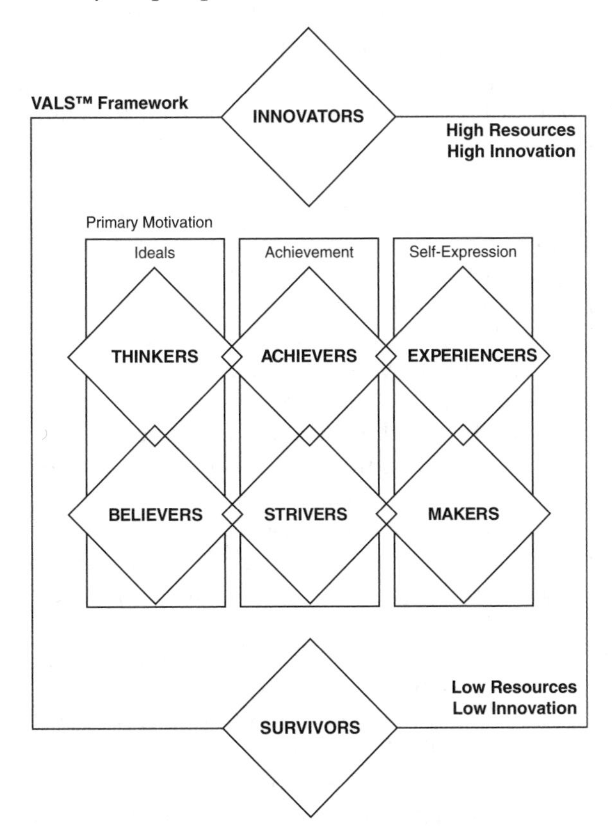

VALS works by emphasising the primary motivations of:

| IDEALS | ACHIEVEMENT | SELF-EXPRESSION |
|---|---|---|

Using these primary motivations, VALS offers eight personality types to create metaphors (such as *thinkers* and *believers* for the different subsets of the general population).

- **Innovators** are successful, active, 'take charge' people with high self-esteem and abundant resources. They are interested in growth and seek to develop, explore, and express themselves in a variety of ways, sometimes guided by principle and sometimes by a desire to make a change.
- **Thinkers** are mature, satisfied, comfortable, reflective people who value order, knowledge and responsibility. Most are well educated and in (or recently retired from) professional occupations. They are well informed about world and national events and are alert to opportunities to broaden their knowledge. Content with their career, family and station in life, their leisure activities tend to centre on the home.
- **Achievers** are successful career and work-oriented people who like to, and generally do, feel in control of their lives. They value consensus, predictability and stability over risk and are deeply committed to work and family. Work provides them with a sense of duty, material rewards and prestige. Their social lives reflect this focus and are structured around family, church and career.
- **Experiencers** are young, vital, enthusiastic, impulsive and rebellious. They seek variety and excitement, savouring the new, the offbeat and the risky. Still in the process of formulating life values and patterns of behaviour, they quickly become enthusiastic about new possibilities but are equally quick to cool. At this stage in their lives, they are politically uncommitted, uninformed and highly ambivalent about what they believe.
- **Believers** are conservative, conventional people with concrete beliefs based on traditional codes: family, church, community, and the nation. Many believers express moral codes that are deeply rooted and literally interpreted. They follow established routines, organised largely around home, family and social or religious organisations to which they belong.

- **Strivers** seek motivation, self-definition and approval from the world around them. They are striving to find a secure place in life. Unsure of themselves and low on economic, social and psychological resources, strivers are concerned about the opinions and approval of others.
- **Makers** are practical people who have constructive skills and value self-sufficiency. They live within a traditional context of family, practical work and physical recreation, and have little interest in what lies outside that context. Makers experience the world by working on it – building a house, raising children or fixing a car – and have enough skill, income and energy to carry out their projects successfully.
- **Survivors** have constricted lives. Chronically poor, with little education or skills, without strong social bonds, and often elderly and concerned about their health, they are frequently resigned and passive. As they are limited by the necessity of meeting the urgent needs of the present moment, they do not show strong self-orientation. Their chief concerns are for security and safety.

## Creating and using pen portraits of your target audience

The more advanced use of VALS is outside of the scope of this book. To date, its use in the third sector has been restricted to the larger and strategically driven charities by professional fundraisers looking to identify affluent and/or socially conscious segments of the UK population. Nonetheless, as a way of thinking about the various motives that people have for joining an organisation, VALS can be a highly useful stimulus for any kind or size of membership scheme. The next exercise asks you to create a written metaphor of your typical member(s) by using VALS as a starting point but tailoring it by adding your own insights.

### Exercise: Create a written profile of your typical member(s)

What does your typical member look like? Or, since most membership schemes address people with subtly differing attitudes and needs, what do the typical subgroups of your target audience look like?

The following case study of Anytown Nature Trust illustrates how the exercise works. The director is concerned that the charity's one-size-fits-all approach to structuring their membership scheme is holding back the Trust's potential to grow their support. To create her pen-portraits, she has drawn on a number of sources: such as replies to past questionnaire surveys, the charity's postbag and her encounters with members at the Trust's sites.

**Typical member 1:** is closest to the VALS believer personality type. Aged 55+ and retired. Has lived in Anyshire since childhood, or long enough to see modern industrial blight encroach into once wholly green local spaces. A routine visitor to Trust sites. Conservatively minded, seeking order and stability in a fast-changing world, their support for the Trust is moral and practical rather than intellectual or political. Loyal members who, if prompted, are open to opportunities to volunteer.

**Typical member 2:** is closest to the VALS achiever personality type. Aged 26–45, typically well educated and professional, well informed about world trends and their implications for the environment. They lead extremely busy lives and so make only rare trips to Trust sites (but make up for it by reading the magazine or making donations). Asset rich and time poor, key motivations are to protect Anyshire's green spaces from desecration and to give something to the cause.

**Typical member 3:** is closest to the VALS experiencer personality type. Is in full-time education, has most likely been introduced by a third party (parent, teacher or Trust volunteer). They seek entertainment, and savour the offbeat and scary. Still in the process of forming deeper philosophical attitudes to nature but responsive to clear messages about right (protecting species) and wrong (litter and pollution). At this stage, their interest is fun seeking and opportunistic.

On completing this exercise, the Trust's director starts thinking about how the Trust can move away from its traditional one-size-fits-all approach. In the past it had only

one membership category. Now it recognises that perhaps that in addition to its standard membership category, at least three additional options are needed – one for each of the above personality types.

From these personality types, the director and her colleagues considered some possible new membership categories:

Typical member 1 may value an attractively priced Life Membership to reward the long-term loyalty of its older and more conservative members who would appreciate free entry to the Trust sites for life, and the Trust's public recognition of their deep-rooted beliefs about the local countryside.

Typical member 2 may value a new Gold Membership that enables people to combine the standard membership benefits with additional financial support for the cause via direct debit (and to be rewarded with special privileges such as attending an annual Gold Event to meet the management and its celebrity patrons).

For Typical member 3, a Youth Membership category might be more appropriate with a more funky welcome pack and special open days at the Trust sites where young people can get involved with fun activities and handle animals under supervision.

In doing this exercise, it is very important to avoid writing wishful descriptions of your prospects and members. Remember that the objective is to narrow your focus to those personality types who are most likely to be interested in your membership offer, not to broaden your focus so much that it includes the entire UK population.

As far as possible, your own profiles should be evidence based, using formal market research or your own internal knowledge and observations, or both. The profile can be as simple or as detailed as is useful. When you have written it, don't keep it to yourself. Circulate it! Get your organisation to adopt it as part of their strategy (see Chapter 3). Carry out market research to confirm and elaborate on it (see Chapter 4). Use it to guide your marketing mix (Chapter 5) and your promotional copywriting (see Chapter 6).

## Action points

✓ To pursue a relationship marketing approach to membership success, you must first know what your members need and want.

✓ Know the five levels of individual need and want: physiological, safety, social, ego and self-actualisation.

✓ From formal market research to reading the postbag; gather as much data and insight as you can about your members and what makes them tick.

✓ Make sure everyone in your organisation is aware of the need to capture data or insight into your members.

✓ Know the six most common membership benefits sought, but don't try to deliver them all at once. Find out which one(s) best match your audience's needs.

✓ Gauge whether your members are predominantly givers or takers.

✓ Create your own pen-portraits of your typical member(s).

✓ Circulate your pen-portraits and use them to guide your membership strategy and activities.

✓ True relationship marketing means one size doesn't fit all. Consider whether your pen-portraits give evidence of a need to segment your target audience into distinct personality types and, if so, how you might serve them by creating different membership categories and tiers.

1.Maslow, A H (1970) *Motivation and Personality*, Harper and Row
2.Alderfer, C P (1972) *Existence, Relatedness and Growth: Human Needs in Organisational Settings*, Freepress
3. Mitchell, A (1983) *The Nine American Lifestyles: Who We Are and Where We're Going*, Macmillan

# 3 Mission and strategy

Whether you have 100,000 or 100 members, regardless of how many relationships your scheme manages, long-term success can't be left to chance. Good planning is vital. As the catchphrase says: fail to plan = plan to fail.

> *Strategic planning sounds very grand but it isn't. If you go on an important journey, a holiday, for example, you want it to be a success. So what variables are involved in a successful holiday? Destination? Duration? Cost? Who is going and their needs or wishes? Purpose of the holiday (not everyone enjoys the same things)? It helps to think in the same way when embarking on strategic planning.*
> (John Harris, *The Good Management Guide*, NCVO, 2002)[1]

In Chapter 1 about relationship marketing, we discussed the six stages of the membership journey – from prospect to member, from supporter to advocate, from renewed to lapsed. As the above quote from John Harris implies, any journey involving a group of people needs some kind of agreement. This applies just as much to the local group in a draughty village hall as it does the national head office-run scheme.

From the outset, the journey must flow out of a shared understanding by the key stakeholders as to precisely why the membership scheme exists at all, what is the destination, and so on.

**If the ultimate goal is to provide your organisation with friends for life then you must develop the ability to scan change in the outside world.**

If the ultimate goal of relationship marketing is to provide your organisation with friends for life then you must develop the ability to scan change in the outside world: What's going on out there? What are the trends? How will they impact on the members and on our relationship with them? Taking all this on board, every membership scheme must ask itself on a regular basis: What are our natural strengths and weaknesses? What are the opportunities and the threats? And how can we assimilate all this into a well-costed business plan?

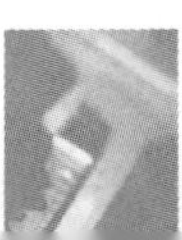

The objectives of this chapter are:

- to explore how being a learning organisation is a crucial prerequisite to membership success;
- to use a PEST analysis to assess developments in the outside world and link them to your own unique situation;
- to use a SWOT analysis to identify your strengths, weaknesses, opportunities and threats;
- to know the membership product life cycle;
- to refresh your membership products using the Ansoff matrix, mind mapping and other aids to creative thinking;
- to set out the key building blocks of the written business plan – the vision, mission etc.

## Being a learning organisation

Why does your membership scheme exist? Even if the answer seems obvious to the people involved in the scheme, no one can be complacent. The time is past when long-established membership bodies (such as the steadily declining Working Men's Clubs) could go for decades without reviewing their purpose. The global economy has dramatically speeded up change in the outside world. People's lifestyles, needs and priorities change; membership schemes don't always keep up. History is littered with the remains of those that failed to adapt. In the 1990s, trade unions had to reinvent themselves in the wake of changing social attitudes and new legislation. Those that did are still around, but many that didn't simply went to the wall.

**The ability to ask questions, gather data and act on the results are healthy characteristics of any learning organisation.**

Good membership schemes are good at learning. The ability to ask questions, gather data and act on the results are healthy characteristics of any *learning organisation*. The importance of this concept has grown for private, public and third sector bodies alike in response to the outside world's increasing pace of change and growing competitiveness. For the purpose of this guide, the definition of a *learning membership scheme* is a scheme that involves continual learning – the organisation continuously learns from the members and vice versa.

### Exercise: Is yours a learning membership scheme?

On a scale of 1 to 5, rate how well your membership scheme follows these principles:

1. We regularly monitor the political, economic, social and technological trends that affect us and our members.
2. Our members' life experiences feed into our strategy and policies.
3. We always acknowledge members' input into our work, we thank them and feedback on the consequences of their input.
4. Our membership benefits package is flexible and changes in response to their evolving needs and wants.
5. We value complaints from members as free consultancy.
6. All our staff understand and support each other's role in delivering the membership strategy.
7. Our staff and volunteers are encouraged to learn new skills that will contribute to membership success.
8. We have appropriate reward or recognition systems for good membership work, wherever it is achieved in the organisation.
9. People are not blamed for bearing bad news.
10. We refresh our membership scheme by experimenting with new services and products or refinements to existing ones.
11. We test ideas on a sample of members before implementing them on a wider scale.
12. Information technology is used to help us to deliver a better service to the members, not merely to automate it.
12. People understand the importance of money and resources and use it wisely.
14. The IT or financial consequences (negative or positive) of all membership activities are fed back to those concerned.
15. People are encouraged to come up with different ways of meeting the needs of members.
16. There are several channels of communication for collecting and sharing information from and to the members.
17. We often meet other membership bodies to share good practice and ideas.
18. We share ideas, experiences and skills to create win–win situations of mutual benefit to trustees, staff and members.

(adapted from The Learning Company by Pedler and Aspinall in *The Experience of Managing* by Legge, Clegg et al, Macmillan, 1999)

What new learning processes can you introduce? Can you improve some existing processes? Implementing some of the ideas in Chapter 4 about market research will also help.

## Scanning the outside world for change

As John Harris (NCVO 2002) points out, the concept of the learning organisation stems from a way of looking at organisations which is biological or organic. Biology teaches us about how organisms need to learn to adapt in order to survive in a hostile environment. The survival of the fittest principle applies to charities and voluntary bodies just as it does to microbes and animal species.

Learning organisations factor time into their daily routine and scan the outside world for the social, political, economic and technological factors that may impact on them and their members.

Public opinion Politics

Fads and fashions Pollution Competitors

Shopping trends Consumer debt Popular media stories

Medical research Public services The role of charities

Quality of life issues The internet Funding sources

What women want Postal costs Climate change

Mobile phones Email Education Employment

War and conflict Other membership organisations Poverty

The housing market Disability legislation Youth culture

The third world Mortgages The arts

Market research The EU Available leisure time

The ageing population

We often overlook these kinds of macro events in the outside world either because they feel beyond our control or appear too far removed from the day-to-day reality of running a membership scheme.

A helpful way to link them to your own situation is to organise them into a PEST analysis.

## Exercise: A PEST analysis of your own situation

P = Political, E = Economic, S = Social, T = Technological. You can swap around the order of these factors. For example, if your membership scheme is about serving first social concerns, then technological ones, there's no reason why it can't be rejigged into a STEP analysis.

This pro-forma template offers a straightforward way to organise your own scan of the outside world.

In the example below, the PEST analysis has grouped together the most significant external factors impacting on the work of the charity One Parent Families and on its members.

| **Political** | **Economic** |
|---|---|
| • Child tax credit and other benefits<br>• Government's new deal for lone parents<br>• 04/05 Government poverty reduction target to halve child poverty by 2010<br>• Access to childcare | • Inflexible working practices<br>• National minimum wage<br>• CSA child support maintenance<br>• Improved housing conditions |
| **Social** | **Technological** |
| • Relationship breakdown and child contact arrangements<br>• Work/family life balance<br>• Public stigmatisation<br>• Loneliness, depression | • Wider access to advice and support via different channels – telephone, email, internet |

Of the multitude of national issues, these are most relevant to the One Parent Families' 04/05 Manifesto which subsequently informs the charity's membership strategy and benefits – the handbook, magazine and information helpline.

Carry out a PEST analysis for your situation. What are the key issues? For each item consider:

- Is it just a short-term effect or a long-term trend?
- What are the implications for your members?
- What needs to be done? By others? Or by your organisation?

Having gathered these signals from the outside world, the next step is to assess how your organisation and membership scheme should respond. Cue another classic assessment technique: the SWOT analysis.

SWOT is: S = Strengths, W = Weaknesses, O = Opportunities, T = Threats. It links the factors you've identified in your PEST analysis to your organisation's internal situation.

- organisation's philosophy (vision and mission)
- membership structure and categories
- organisation's policies
- board of trustees
- funding sources
- properties and sites
- equal opportunities
- new legislation
- internet, email
- internal databases
- demographic factors
- psychographic factors
- membership survey results
- your managers, staff, volunteers
- other stakeholders (service users, donors, external funders)
- strategic alliances (with companies, public services, other voluntary groups)
- your other services (information, advice)
- new initiatives or directions

The following case study illustrates how SWOT can be used to review the purpose and strategy of a membership scheme and to revitalise relationships between the key players.

## Case study: Anytown Fell Walkers (AFW)

Founded in 1954, the membership strategy of the AFW has now reached a crossroads. The trustees – mostly veterans of the cause – want to hold a private 50th anniversary dinner to celebrate their heritage.

Some of the younger members think the idea of a private dinner is a waste of time and money. They are more concerned about the threat to the group's existence with the lack of new members coming in.

An argument is brewing about the cost of the event. The factionalism always latent in the group is beginning to stir once more. The AFW chair suggests that they do a SWOT exercise together. She hopes this will allow the different factions to think outside the box and come up with fresh ideas that everyone can unite behind.

| Strengths | Weaknesses |
|---|---|
| • A wealth of accumulated know-how of local routes and resources<br>• A core of experienced fell walkers who, if persuaded, could pass on their skills to another generation<br>• Five younger members keen to do outreach to potential new recruits<br>• A surplus of financial reserves and therefore a generous budget for the 50th anniversary event | • Age differences have split the AFW into uncooperative factions<br>• Anytown's population shift towards minority ethnic groups is not reflected in the Association's membership<br>• There is clarity about its past but not its future place in the world<br>• The AFW cannot do justice to the public awareness-raising potential of the 50th anniversary without all trustees pulling together |

| Opportunities | Threats |
|---|---|
| • There is a lot of energy in the group that could be better channelled to a common objective<br>• The 50th anniversary might aim both to celebrate its heritage and attract new recruits<br>• Young people's concern about green issues could be translated into an interest in fell walking<br>• IT might also be used to reach new audiences (email/internet) | • The age split threatens to send the AFW into permanent decline<br>• The AFW's ability to move forward is compromised by the reluctance of members to talk to each other<br>• A sharp drop in future sponsorship and membership fees if the AFW does not increase its membership and make it more culturally diverse<br>• Possibility of a breakaway group |

With sensitive handling by the AFW chair, the SWOT helped the trustees to acknowledge the need to stem the mission drift away from the charity's original purpose – to introduce people to fell walking. There was an urgent need to embrace the town's changing population, in particular young people and the minority ethnic population. The previously conservative trustees were fired by the idea of taking a senior role in refreshing the charity's membership – one even offered to organise taster walks for local school parties and youth groups.

The SWOT analysis can be used on a macro level, taking in the whole aspect of your organisation's vision, mission and membership strategy, or on a micro level to focus on a specific problem or opportunity that significantly affects your membership scheme. Sometimes, focusing the analysis on a specific issue – as the AFW did on their 50th anniversary – can open up wider issues that touch upon the fundamental workings of your scheme.

## Exercise: SWOT analysis of your project, group or organisation

The SWOT grid below can be used to organise your perceptions of the strengths, weaknesses, opportunities and threats as they appear to you regarding your membership scheme. Try doing it by yourself, with a colleague or a small group. Alternatively, assign the letters (S/W/O/T) to four separate groups, asking them to focus just on that letter and, afterwards, reconvening to share and discuss the results.

You may find that some issues appear in more than one area: for example, some of your strengths may appear as weaknesses too, while some external threats might also create an opportunity to introduce a new membership benefit or service. The aim is to produce a one-page summary of your organisation's strategic position and the implications for your membership scheme.

| **Strengths** | **Weaknesses** |
| --- | --- |
| | |
| **Opportunities** | **Threats** |
| | |

- Ensure that the SWOT inputs are based on actual evidence (for example, concrete unbiased data from membership surveys, new local government policies, etc). Avoid over-relying on the subjective impressions of the people involved (or the exercise risks becoming a set of platitudes and opinions).

- An initial SWOT may contain many more items than you can fit onto a single flipchart or sheet. This is fine – you can use the closing session to edit them down to the highest priority issues.
- Don't just file the SWOT away. Use it. Circulate it and use it as a prompt for focusing your creative thinking and problem solving as you move into the next stage of the strategic planning process.

**The membership scheme life cycle**

A typical membership scheme's life cycle has five stages of development:

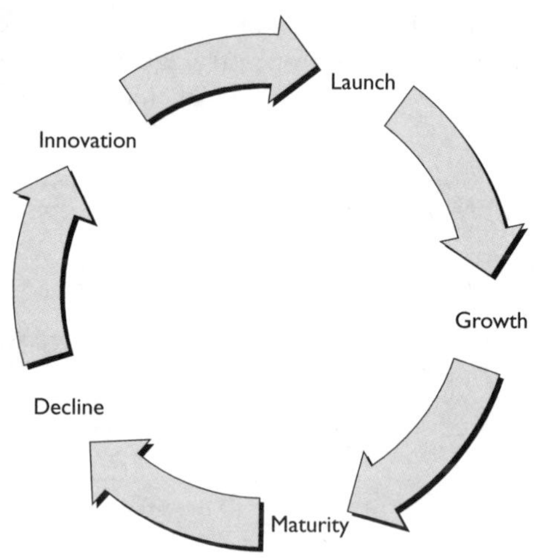


- **Launch**: the service begins based on the organisation's mission and an understanding of its prospective members' needs.
- **Growth**: the service is promoted, demand increases, its reputation becomes more widely established.
- **Maturity**: the membership is meeting a need but growth levels off.
- **Decline**: the target audience moves on, demand levels off, members lapse in greater numbers, new competition or new trends draw people away.

- **Innovation:** in response to actual or potential decline, the organisation innovates a new product or service, or adds a new feature to an existing one.

These stages work on two different levels – the overall membership service, and within that, the individual features of the service. For example, five years after the launch of an organisation's new scheme, its membership base is still increasing by 10 per cent a year (the scheme is in *growth* stage) but for the original members who joined in the launch year, the magazine is starting to look tired after five years of an identical format and needs a revamp (a *mature* product needs to stave off *decline*).

**The Ansoff matrix**

A useful aid exploring the strategic options for the different stages of the membership life cycle is the so-called *Ansoff matrix*, named after its developer, Ivan Ansoff. Adapted for this guide, the matrix shows the four possible combinations of membership products and target audiences.

1. Promoting existing membership products to existing target audiences (audience penetration)
2. Promoting existing membership products to new target audiences (audience extension)
3. Developing new membership products for existing target audiences (product development)
4. Developing new membership products for new target audiences (diversification)

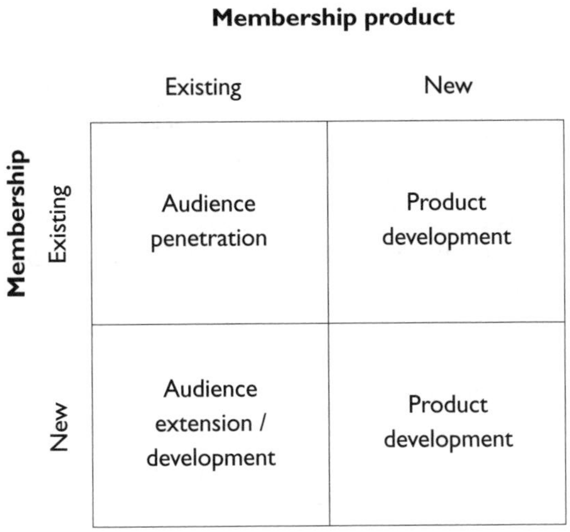

**Membership product**

| Membership | Existing | New |
|---|---|---|
| Existing | Audience penetration | Product development |
| New | Audience extension / development | Product development |

In this context, the term *membership product* relates to the total experience that you are offering to the member, including the brand, the membership categories you offer, the benefits involved and so on. (For further details, see the Product section in Chapter 5.)

### Audience penetration

This strategy involves retaining your existing members while finding new ones in the same target audience without changing your membership product. In the third sector, this approach is the most widespread as it has the fewest unknowns and represents the least risky option.

> Example: *Anyshire Nature Trust already has a good membership product (a quarterly magazine and free access to local nature reserves). It mostly recruits through word of mouth and by volunteers handing out leaflets at Trust reserves. This approach carries no risks and costs next to nothing (volunteer expenses and leaflet printing costs only) but each year it only brings in as many new members as those who lapse. The Trust is operating in a comfort zone but is not growing or widening public support for a vital cause.*

### Audience extension/development

This assumes that your organisation has either the capability to open up new marketing channels to your existing target audience or to innovate new uses for the existing membership product.

> Example: *Anyshire Nature Trust already has a good membership product (see above) but it wants to widen public support for the cause. It decides to seek a new audience by doing presentations in local schools. Pupils are given a brochure about the Trust's work to share with their parents. The visits successfully recruit new members who would not have been sourced by the Trust's existing word-of-mouth networks.*

### Product/service development

This strategy involves adapting your current membership product to boost recruitment within your existing target audience, increase income or reduce costs. This implies that your organisation has the resources and skills to make the proposed product change viable.

Example: *After a year of promoting Anyshire Nature Trust's work to local schools, recruitment is still modest. Feedback indicates that the children view the Trust as 'worthy but dull', and insufficient fun to warrant families signing up. The Trust decides to consolidate its access to this new target audience by tailoring a new membership product to it – family membership. The benefits include a welcome fun pack plus four family days a year at their sites where the children may feed and handle the animals.*

**Diversification**

This involves developing both a new membership product and taking it to a new target audience (or a new segment of your existing target audience). It may imply that new resources and skills will have to be developed. As both products and audience will be new, it is a higher risk approach. The element of dealing with the unknown makes this a more risky strategy, so it demands very careful research, testing and planning. Get the delivery right and significant growth may follow – get it wrong and it will cost your organisation both time and money.

Example: *The Anyshire Nature Trust wants to reach a new target audience of affluent working people who are sympathetic to local 'green' issues but who lead busy lives and have little time to visit the sites. So the Trust innovates a new product: a gold membership that enables them to financially support the cause via direct debit and to be rewarded with special privileges (such as regular email updates with animated images of the Trust's work and the opportunity to meet celebrities at an annual Gold Trust event).*

As 90 per cent of our work is pure routine, Ansoff is a useful tool for rethinking what we do in membership schemes. It can help us to review our work and open up new areas of development.

Another stimulus to creative thinking is mind mapping, as adopted by Tony Buzan (*The Mind Map*, BBC Books, 1993)[2]. While Ansoff looks at the broad thrust of future membership strategy, mind mapping can help you to visualise ideas within each area of the matrix.

## Exercise: Visualising the future

A mind map is like an organic flowchart that mimics the way the brain thinks. It can have many creative uses.

In this context, it is a way of visualising the infinite options of your membership scheme's future work.

In this example, Norma Sweeny of the Brains Trust visualises a *diversification* scenario: the conception, birth, infancy, nurturing and growing pains and the spread of their brain clubs to new overseas territories, especially the Arab nations. She sees the Trust as being like the nucleus of a brain cell with its synapses connecting it to people in different countries and situations:

Draw a similar mind map for your membership scheme. Try doing one for each of the four areas of the Ansoff matrix.

Initially, do not include too much detail – just visualise your ideas and see where they lead.

Mind mapping is just one of a whole a range of methods for generating ideas for refreshing your membership scheme – from techniques for prompting flashes of inspiration (the eureka moment) to more formal analytical methods.

**Organise a brainstorming session**
Book an away day for your managers, staff or volunteers. Do some blue sky thinking on totally new products or new ways of using your existing products. Use a flipchart and list all the ideas that come up. Don't allow knee-jerk judgements: "That would be too expensive", "There's no demand for that", "You must be joking!" The aim is to generate as many ideas as you can – big or small, expensive or cheap, sensible or offbeat, exciting or dull. Judgement should be suspended until there is time for reflection to savour the ideas and see where they lead. Remember that for every one idea that works, you need about 30 that fail. So the more ideas the better. One may in time become a new product, but it might not be the most immediately obvious candidate.

**Lateral thinking**
Lateral thinking uses new ways of looking at old habits, processes etc – turning them inside out to see what happens. A famous example of lateral thinking is Rod Dyson's vacuum cleaner. Among other technological advances, it boasts a transparent casing that allows the user to see the rubbish being sucked inside. Suggest that in a brainstorm session and you'd be labelled crazy. But as a marketing device it worked a treat by differentiating this product from all the others in a very visible and tangible way. For more information on lateral thinking see the books by Edward de Bono and Tony Buzan listed in the further reading section.

**Talk to your members**
A very cheap and underrated technique: talk or listen to your members, those who have lapsed or people who have not yet joined. This can be done anywhere: on the telephone, in the reception area, at conferences and field events.

**Technological advances**
Keep abreast of technological advances – scan magazines, review scientific literature, think about the internet, mobile phones etc.

**Scan legislation**
Scan forthcoming legislation (for example, that which has implications for social care, health or disability). Non-profit organisations, particularly those with research, policy and campaign teams, will be keenly aware of white papers, draft bills and Acts coming on-stream. These may harbour all sorts of opportunities to innovate new services or products – be it an advice line, publication or seminar.

**Ideas scheme**
Operate an ideas scheme with all your staff and volunteers. Allocate an email address or noticeboard where ideas can be posted. Make yearly or periodic appeals through your intranet or staff newsletter.

**Attribute listing**
Itemise the attributes of a product or service and then consider how these can be modified or improved. For example, if a magazine carries ad hoc directory listings in each issue, could these be combined into a handy year-book?

**Market gap analysis**
Where are the gaps that lie between your work and public services and business? Is there a need somewhere that no one is filling?

**Your competitors**
Monitor the activities of your direct and indirect competitors.

**Futures group**
Create a futures group to look at demographic, social and technological trends in the next three, five or 10 years.

## What opportunities exist?

**Revisit your membership surveys**

Revisit your past surveys to see if any of the suggested ideas which, though not appropriate then, might now be timely. This often happens with new technology such as the internet. We are aware of their potential sometimes years in advance yet when the window of opportunity comes we can easily miss it.

**Forced relationships**

Creating forced relationships – this is a technique of presenting existing or new products in different combinations. Surprisingly effective new products can be created. For example, an internal database of useful services for use by information officers could be loaded onto your members' only website area with a search engine to allow online searches.

**Market research**

Carry out new market research (see Chapter 4).

**Customer complaints**

Rather than feeling resentful when people complain, think of it as a form of free consultancy. Someone who is giving you a hard time might have touched upon an opportunity that's waiting to be exploited.

Whichever route we take for dreaming up new membership products or services, some general principles apply:

**You need 30 unused ideas for every one that makes it into the marketplace, so the more ideas the better.**

- Few ideas get much further than a marker pen scribble on a flipchart. You need 30 unused ideas for every one that makes it into the marketplace, so the more ideas the better. Try to generate them more systematically – in other words, don't just leave it until the last minute when you're desperately putting together next year's budget!
- Keep a file of unused ideas and review and update it at least twice a year. Ideas from earlier sessions that were premature back then might well be opportune now.
- There's a lot of fun to be had with creative thinking techniques, but be aware of their limitations. They tend to produce product-focused ideas rather than market-focused

ones. Whenever possible, test ideas through market research (see Chapter 4).

- Allow time for reflection. Shortlist ideas that merit further investigation, then test the ideas to destruction with this checklist of questions

- ❑ What is the evidence that members actually need the new product or service?
- ❑ Is it meeting a short-term or long-term need?
- ❑ Will the demand be high or low?
- ❑ Will it service existing members or introduce new ones?
- ❑ Are these new members actually reachable?
- ❑ How would the new product fit within our existing range?
- ❑ Do we have the budget and know-how to develop the service?
- ❑ Is someone else already delivering a similar product or service? Can we improve on it?
- ❑ Would it be profitable or require a subsidy?
- ❑ Is it appropriate to our organisation's mission and values?

## The building blocks of membership strategy

When you have scanned the outside world and have a membership journey and destination in mind, the next step is to produce a map or strategic plan. Given a broad degree of agreement about aims and objectives, strategic planning can unite all the key people – trustees, staff, members, volunteers, funders and strategic allies – and determine the direction they are travelling in.

Different schemes are inevitably subject to the varied planning processes of their respective host organisations, but a good plan will include:

### Key components of a membership strategic plan

**Executive summary**
A shortened one or two page version of the plan listing the key points.

**Vision and mission**
Your host organisation's vision and mission statement.

**Membership aims and objectives**
In the context of the mission, the specific aims and objectives of your scheme.

**Key performance Indicators**
The key measures for evaluating whether or not the plan has been achieved.

**Target audience/segments**
Your target audience and the segments within it (eg individual, organisational, family, bronze, silver, gold and so on).

**Desired relationships**
Description of the relationships sought from your target audience (and the segments within it).
Prospects > members > supporters > advocates > renewed > lapsed.

**The marketing mix**
Philosophy, product, price, promotion, place, people and processes.

**Financial plan**
The detailed financial plan including:
- fixed cost and variable cost analysis
- break-even analysis
- income forecast
- cash flow forecast

## Appendix

**PEST/SWOT analyses**
A condensed version of your PEST and SWOT analyses summarising the key issues that trustees and decision makers need to be aware of.

**Research basis for plan**
The research evidence to back up the recommendations in the plan.

## Vision and mission

**A good membership strategy should include a clear and up-to-date mission statement.**

Would you join an organisation that was unsure of its vision or mission? At best, you'd be unsure. A good membership strategy should include a clear and up-to-date mission statement. Many schemes lack an explicit written statement to guide them. The host organisation may have been born out of idea or belief that has since become an implicit mission that is not discussed or written down but has become 'the way we do things'. Refreshing the organisation's purpose and setting it down on paper becomes especially important when:

- the organisation grows and takes on more activities;
- the growing number of people involved – trustees, staff, volunteers, members – risks the core purpose and beliefs being diluted or lost in a multitude of conflicting activities and communications;
- the organisation lacks an agreed purpose and pulls in different directions.

Are your host organisation's vision and mission statements up to date? Are they clear enough to steer your membership strategy?

### Exercise: Creating or updating your vision and mission statement

#### The vision

If you don't already have a vision statement, the easiest way to conjure one is to imagine it as being the desired future for the organisation's users, the members and for the world at large. It is commonly phrased with sentences like 'Our vision is of a world in which ...' For a local group it could just as easily start with 'Our vision is of a village which ...' or 'Our vision for autistic children in Anyshire is ...'

- **NCVO** – Our vision is of a fair and open society, which encourages and is supported by voluntary action.
- **Diabetes UK** – Our vision is to set people free from the restrictions of diabetes.
- **Greenpeace** – Our vision is to ensure the ability of the earth to nurture life in all its diversity.

The vision doesn't have to include an explicit reference to the members. If it is carefully worded and inclusive, it will encode an implicit acknowledgement that the organisation is unlikely to achieve the vision on its own without the help of others (including the members).

**The mission**

If the vision expresses an idealistic view of the future, the mission statement (often called a *statement of purpose* or *our aims*) details in a more prescriptive fashion the host organisation's role in achieving that future. It should:

- Define the agreed role of the host organisation in securing the vision.
- Set down the reason for being.
- Give clarity and focus.
- Make choices.
- Be concise.
- Be the product of an inclusive and participative process, not the product of leaders or managers working in closed session.
- Be agreed by the wider organisation.
- Underpin the ethos of the people who recruit and serve members.
- Be inspirational to the members or to people thinking about joining.
- Be inclusive of all stakeholders, including the members, briefly spelling out their value and their role in the organisation.
- Be reviewed or updated once every five to 10 years, or more frequently if significant external change demands it.

Often an otherwise powerful mission statement can be interpreted as having been written by senior managers within a bunker. This can make the host organisation appear hermetically sealed off, giving the (hopefully unintended) impression that achieving the mission is the sole prerogative of the managers and staff, and that the members are merely beneficiaries of it. In the case study below, the British Association of Adoption and Fostering (BAAF) effectively integrates its vision, mission and membership strategy so that each feeds into and in turn gains strength from the other.

## BAAF

BAAF is the leading national membership organisation in the UK for professionals and organisations working in adoption, fostering and childcare. We work with our members and partners to:

- promote and develop high standards in adoption and fostering for childcare, medical, legal and other relevant professionals;
- promote public and professional understanding of adoption and fostering, and of the life-long implications for children separated from their birth families;
- ensure that the developmental and identity needs of looked-after children are respected and addressed by social, health, legal and educational services;
- inform and influence policy makers and legislators, and all those responsible for the welfare of children and young people.

BAAF values and respects the commitment made by foster carers and adoptive parents and believes that a wide range of support services is essential to enable families to parent children separated from their birth families.

BAAF will work in a child-centred, multidisciplinary and anti-discriminatory framework, with individuals, statutory agencies and voluntary organisations.

BAAF will work in partnership with its members and with others to achieve common goals, believing in the value of openness and honesty and that a powerful voice for children will best be heard by working together.

## Membership aims and objectives

In the context of the vision and mission, the membership strategic plan will then detail your aims and objectives.

- An **aim** will specifically describe the impact that you seek to achieve.
- The **objectives** describe in general terms how you will achieve this.

In Chapter 1, we saw that the ultimate aim of any membership scheme is to create a two-way flow of value. Members derive real value from their relationship with the organisation which converts into value for the organisation.

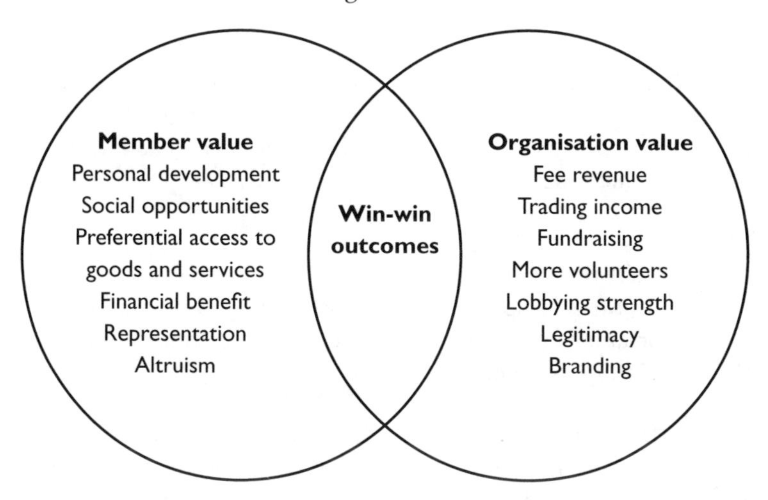


Too many organisations make the mistake of setting one-sided aims and objectives that focus narrowly on organisational value with little or no detail about offering the members value. You can avoid this pitfall by producing two parallel sets of aims and objectives, one for member value and another for organisation value.

## Case study: Anytown Alzheimer's Support Group (AASG)

**Mission/purpose**
To improve the quality of life for
Anytown people with Alzheimer's and their families

| Member value | Organisational value |
|---|---|
| ↓ | ↓ |
| AIM<br>To create social and IT networks that empower local families to help each other | AIM<br>To strengthen AASG's work via an active membership base of supporters and advocates |
| ↓ | ↓ |
| OBJECTIVES<br>To offer 12 social opportunities via monthly group meetings | OBJECTIVES<br>To secure £500 in donations for a local campaign fund |
| To offer IT networking via 20 second-hand home computers | To secure active support of 20 volunteers to lobby the health authority |
| To deliver two self-advocacy training courses | To secure 10 case studies for media use to raise AASG's profile locally |

The classic formula for setting objectives is SMART:

SPECIFIC

MEASURABLE

AGREED

REALISTIC

TIME-RELATED

The greater the value that offered to members, the greater the return in value for the organisation – and the greater the likelihood of a win–win outcome of mutual benefit to both parties. Your strategic plan will include some permutation of the values demonstrated in the table below (plus some of your own).

| Member value | Organisational value |
|---|---|
| Social opportunities<br>Access to networks<br>Time saving and convenience<br>Privileged access to goods and services<br>Financial benefits<br>Value for money<br>Advocacy support<br>Representation<br>Kudos and self-esteem from altruism to others<br>... and so on | Donations<br>Volunteer time and help<br>Case studies for media use<br>Campaign support<br>User feedback<br>Market research survey information<br>Legitimacy<br>Word-of-mouth advocacy<br>Introduction of new members<br>Strength in numbers<br>Enhanced brand image<br>... and so on |

Yet few schemes will deliver all these values at once. The key is to prioritise the values desired by your members and match these with the values sought by your organisation. The following away-day exercise may help you to do this.

**The key is to prioritise the values desired by your members and match these with the values sought by your**

## Exercise: The value Christmas tree

Lay out eight small pieces of paper. On each of these pieces jot down one of the values that your members seek (for example, for a professional lecturers' association these might be networking opportunities, career advancement, financial benefit, workplace representation, and so on). Organise people into small groups and task them with prioritising the eight values into the shape of a Christmas tree.

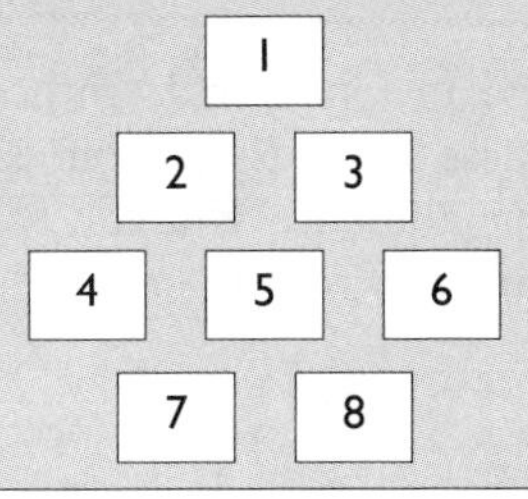


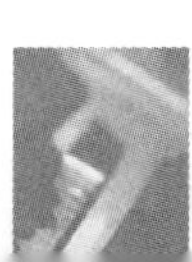

The star value at the top of the tree is the value the group feels is the one most desired by your members now and in the near future – for example, to gain financial benefit. The next tier comprises those values that are the next most desired, for example, to gain social opportunities and representation and so on.

Now repeat the same exercise for your organisation values. What is the 'star' value most sought by your organisation? Is it to generate revenue or achieve campaign support? The answer to this question should be consistent with the strategic purpose of your membership scheme.
Once each group has created their two Christmas trees, ask them to report back to the whole team to discuss the results.

(Exercise adapted from Joe Saxton, *What are Charities For?* Third Sector, 1997.)

It is important that the answers to the above exercise are consistent with your vision and mission, and based on robust market research about your members needs and wants (see Chapter 4) otherwise there is a risk that your choice of value and the benefits that flow from that will be based on wishful thinking rather than what is achievable.

## Target audience and segmentation

Your membership strategic plan will also specify your target audience. At first, this will be fairly easy.

| DEAF PEOPLE | ART GALLERY VISITORS |
|---|---|
| TEACHERS | LOCAL VOLUNTARY BODIES |

However, as discussed in Chapter 1, rather than treating your target audience en masse and basing a one-size-fits-all scheme on it, by segmenting your audience you can tailor a more personal service for different subgroups of members.

| DEAF PEOPLE | ART GALLERY VISITORS |
|---|---|
| Deaf people<br>Hard of hearing people<br>Their families<br>Health professionals who serve them | Adult visitors<br>Young visitors<br>Overseas visitors<br>Corporate hospitality users |
| **SCHOOL WORKERS** | **LOCAL VOLUNTARY BODIES** |
| Fully qualified teachers<br>Student teachers<br>Classroom assistants<br>School administrators | Health and welfare groups<br>Social groups<br>Environmental groups<br>Arts groups |

## Membership categories and tiers

Once you have identified your target audience segments, the plan will need to detail whether a single membership category is sufficient to address their needs or whether you need segmented (multiple) categories or a membership tier.

### Segments

Segmented membership categories are horizontal and non-hierarchical:

| INDIVIDUAL | FAMILY | CORPORATE |
|---|---|---|

### Tiers

Tiered membership categories are vertical and hierarchical:

| GOLD MEMBERSHIP |
|---|
| SILVER MEMBERSHIP |
| BRONZE MEMBERSHIP |

With such a huge variety of membership schemes in the UK serving different niches, there is no golden formula for segmenting your membership categories – each organisation must adopt the right mix for its own unique situation. The most common ways of dividing up a target audience are concessionary, age-related, family status, corporate, geographical, occupational or professional and duration.

### Concessionary

Many organisations with a social purpose are concerned to avoid excluding people on low incomes and so offer concessionary rates to young people and senior citizens. Before you do this, make sure you know the demographic profile of your target audience; for example, if the largest proportion of members are retired then the notion of concessionary rates may be costly for your organisation in lost income.

### Age-related

Frequently a young person's category is offered as a fun introduction to the organisation or the cause, tailored to match young people's interests and to sow the seeds for a long-term relationship once the member comes of age and is eligible for adult membership.

#### The Poetry Society

The Poetry Society exists to help poets and poetry thrive in Britain today. Established in 1909, it has a membership of around 4,000 teachers, librarians, booksellers, journalists, readers, and writers of poetry from all over the world.

The society encourages young people to take up creative writing, so in addition to its full membership at £35, it also has secondary school membership at £50 and primary school membership at £30 – both of which enable schools to benefit from the work of the society's dynamic education department which for 30 years has aimed to bring poetry to life in schools.

There is also a youth membership at £15 designed for young writers aged 11–18 with tailored benefits including a young writers pack with full-colour poetry poster, a Young Poet of the Year anthology, access to a Young Writers Network and to Youth Pages on the website, plus invitations to readings and workshops for young writers.

Age-related categories for adults may also exist in schemes oriented around social opportunities for people who enjoy meeting and mixing with others of broadly similar age. For example, sports clubs may have junior, adult and veteran membership categories.

### Family status

Family membership can also widen interest in your organisation, for example by encouraging the whole family to visit a heritage site or nature reserve, not just the individual member. Introducing this category is not always as straightforward as it may seem. In the early 20th century, the typical family consisted of Mum and Dad who were married and had 3.5 children. The household often included extended family members. By 1998, half of all families were divorced and remarriage was increasing.[3] Allied to the rise in cohabitation, this means there is no golden rule for defining family membership – each organisation must arrive at its own practical solution. Here are some examples of family membership rates in 2004:

- Family membership of the **Barnsley Family History Society** is for a maximum of four people, others must register as additional members.
- The **National Association for Bikers with a Disability** states that family membership includes two adults and two children up to the age of 16.
- The **Inland Waterways Association** includes two adults and all children up to the age of 18.
- At the **Cambridge Astronomical Trust,** family membership covers all members of a household.
- For the **Young Jains UK** a family member currently resides with others in the same house, but could move elsewhere in future, retaining their Young Jains UK family membership status.

### Corporate

According to a 2004 Charity Commission report, 11 per cent of charities with a membership scheme now have an additional corporate membership category. This is a potentially valuable way of widening public support for your cause and is usually offered with one or more of the following goals in mind:

- boosting fundraising support for the cause
- promoting your cause's objectives to the company's staff and users

- creating wider alliances for the advocacy and representation of your cause
- a channel for offering endorsement or quality marks to the company

Today, many company chief executives understand that cause-related marketing can bring commercial benefits for their company – for example, research shows that the majority of consumers are more likely to buy a product associated with a cause (price and quality being equal).

## The Wildlife Trust

A day out at one of the many Wildlife Trust reserves is a popular family pastime but membership fees from individuals and families alone are not enough to cover all the Trust's costs. So it launched a fundraising-driven corporate membership aimed at attracting companies with the promise of improved customer loyalty, enhanced brand value, increased sales and market share, motivated staff and heightened loyalty. The Trust offers a range of options including: sponsorship, donations, grant management and consultancy, employment schemes. From BP to the National Grid, from IKEA to Vauxhall cars – in return for its financial investment in the Trust, a company will gain the Trust's cooperation in maximising the payoff for its brand, PR and sales opportunities (see the Further reading section for more information on cause-related marketing).

Other membership schemes may use corporate membership as a key channel for raising awareness, delivering training and consultancy, and providing goods and services. Some of those services will be available to non-members but the process of engaging them as corporate members brings them closer to the organisation and affords special privileges such as discounts.

## 4Children

4Children (formerly known as Kids' Club Network) is a charitable pressure group and after-school club service provider with a vision to see up to 10,000 centres established for children in or around schools – backed up by joined-up cooperation between various professionals working with children and one major funding stream from the government.

4Children has a range of membership categories that allow different people and organisations to choose the kind of relationship they would like to establish with the cause including individual membership, club membership, local authority membership, and charity/voluntary membership. Its standard package of benefits includes a free subscription to a quarterly *School's Out!* magazine, discounted insurance, a dedicated helpline, regular briefings, and discounts on publications and events.

In September 2004, the charity launched corporate membership as a childcare and work-life information and support service for employers, with additional benefits over and above the standard package, including:

- a quarterly email childcare policy bulletin
- a free diagnostic consultancy tailored to the organisation's human resources needs
- major discounts on consultancy rates
- a dedicated Childcare Helpline Service
- free club membership for the organisation's childcare scheme

**Geographical**

Some UK organisations offer membership categories that reflect the nation or region in which the membership resides. Within the context of a standard UK package, it may offer specific national/local voting rights or a regional newsletter giving details of local services and events. Schemes that centre around a publication or website may have an overseas membership to include people who wish to compare the UK situation with their own (for example in science or medical affairs). Friends' schemes that support major arts or cultural institutions may have an international category of membership for visitors who have enjoyed their visit and wish to show their appreciation through a regular financial contribution. Some overseas schemes link up to similar organisations in other countries to offer reciprocal benefits.

- **The Elgar Society** recognised that it was not practical for its widely dispersed overseas members to attend UK meetings. So it set up an email list on its members' website to allow people of different nationalities to correspond with each other.
- Overseas membership of the **British Lichen Society** confers the chance to apply for grants from a travel fund for overseas members to enable them to visit the UK and collaborate in laboratory or field research with UK members.
- Reduced-rate overseas membership is available for the **Old Fairfieldians Society** for alumni who live abroad but who may wish to keep in touch via a reduced package of just receiving the annual newsletter.

### Occupational or professional

Often a scheme aimed primarily at individuals will incorporate an additional occupational or professional category. For example, a scheme for disabled people may empower them with full membership and voting rights, however, it may be more appropriate to assign the social and health professionals who work with them the chance to support the cause through a separate associate and perhaps a non-voting category.

Conversely, a professional scheme may have a niche for people who are not qualified professionals but nevertheless have a personal interest in that field, as with the case study below.

## British Complementary Medicine Association (BCMA)

Formed in 1992, the BCMA is the leading authority in the field of complementary medicine. The BCMA's primary target audience is complementary therapists but it has also harnessed the wider public interest with a range of membership categories that allow people different levels of engagement with the cause.

| Category | Criteria for membership | Annual fee |
|---|---|---|
| Full member organisation | Open to all organisations with members practising complementary medicine | £100 (+ £15 per therapist up to six people, free thereafter) |

| | | |
|---|---|---|
| Corporate member organisation | Open to all organisations involved in complementary medicine which do not have full member status but wish to have an association with BCMA | £200 |
| Independent school/college | Open if fulfilling BCMA membership criteria | £100 |
| Affiliated school/college | Open if belonging to full member organisation and sponsored by it | £50 |
| Independent clinic | Open to all clinics passing BCMA inspection | £100 |
| Practitioner register | Open to any therapists if full member of full member organisation | £15 |
| Student member | Open to all students of complementary medicine | Free |
| Friends of the BCMA | Open to all people with a personal interest in complementary medicine and wishing to support the BCMA | £20 minimum donation |

**Prices correct as of 2003**

**Duration**
Some schemes offer a choice of one or two-year memberships with the latter being designed to secure the member's loyalty – or at least defer the date when they are asked to renew (see Chapter 7 on loyalty and retention). Then there is the widely used life membership category, often segmented into life membership for younger working people, say under 55 (higher priced because the benefit will usually be consumed for many years to come and so the service costs will be higher for the organisation), with life membership for senior citizens, say 55+, priced at a lower rate (and so often more profitable as shorter life expectancy may imply a donation to the cause). Some membership schemes that collect their dues on a fixed date each year may offer half-yearly discounted rates if someone joins at a later date, for example, halfway through a cricket club's season.

### Tiered categories

A tiered membership scheme is a vertical form of segmentation. Generally, these begin with a standard benefit package for an affordable fee. The next tier up will have an enhanced benefits package for a higher fee with a top tier of full benefits for a premium price. The tiers may be differentiated by titles such as bronze, silver and gold. In turn, each tier may comprise differential fees to reflect age, family, concessionary status and so on. Sometimes tiers may be labelled affiliate, associate and full member whereby the distinction is that certain categories have voting rights and others don't.

Be wary of creating too many tiers with subcategories within them as they are more labour-intensive to administrate and market. Whether your scheme is segmented or tiered, it is essential that the structure is logical, fairly priced and clearly explained in your marketing literature. You will certainly need a membership database to manage it. Below are some examples of how tiered schemes may be structured:

- **choice of benefits** – from entry level to comprehensive benefits;
- **desired level of fundraising commitment** – with higher tiers offering progressively more benefits in return for the member's increasing generosity of fee/donation;
- **professional or occupational grade or educational qualification** – the more advanced the qualifications, skills and experience, the higher the tier.

### Chartered Institute of Marketing (CIM)

CIM aims to enable marketers to do a better job, at whatever point they are at in their career. It has a core benefits package available to all members that spans a magazine to an internet-based knowledge hub to networking opportunities. The tiered structure is primarily a means of recognising different levels of attainment in academic qualifications and working experience. The higher up the tier the member travels, the more esteemed the public recognition for their professional competence.

| Category | Category | Annual fee |
|---|---|---|
| Affiliate member (studying) | To study for a CIM qualification, students require study membership | £105–£185 depending on the level of qualification sought |
| Affiliate member (professional) | Basic entry level for people active or interested in marketing, for those who do not qualify for a higher grade | £80–£85 |
| Associate member | Membership for those meeting specific academic criteria or having a specified number of years of marketing experience | £100–£130 |
| Full member | As above but for those meeting a higher set of academic criteria or having a greater number of years of marketing experience | £100–£130 |
| Fellow (FCIM) | As above but with a proven expertise and strategic responsibility; must be an FCIM to be eligible to go forward for election | £115–£145 |
| Chartered marketer | The highest tier, only open to full members or FCIMs who have completed two consecutive years of continuing professional development | Unpriced |

**Prices correct as of 2003**

## Desired relationships

Having defined your mission, aims and objectives, your target audience and the segments (or tiers) within it, your membership strategic plan can now set out in more detail the kind of relationship your organisation is seeking with its members.

As discussed in Chapter 1, a relationship marketing approach to growing your membership support entails nurturing the members on a six-stage journey – as illustrated by the idea of a membership trapezoid.

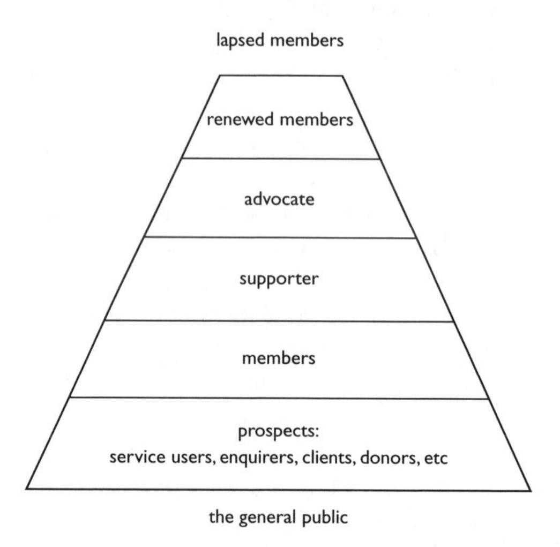


To make this happen, the strategic plan should spell out in some detail how your organisation proposes to take people on a journey.

- Define who your prospects are and the recruitment activities you will use to convert a percentage of them into members.

- Define who your members are (and the segments or tiers) and the internal marketing you will use to convert a percentage of them into supporters and/or advocates.

- Define how you will convert a percentage of your members/segments/tiers into supporters (those who contribute further to the cause) and the type of support you seek (for example, purchases, donations, volunteering).

- Define how you will convert a percentage of your membership/segments/tiers into advocates (those who actively promote your organisation and its cause to others) and the type of advocacy sought (for example, introducing new members to your cause, action in support of your campaigns, etc).

- Define how you will renew your membership/segments/tiers and any plans for reactivating lapsed members.

Nurturing your members from one level of commitment to a higher one requires the forward planning of a sequence of marketing communications – from the recruitment to the subsequent internal marketing aimed at stimulating further support (for example, via direct mail appeals or through your newsletter). We will explore this process in more detail in Chapter 6 on recruitment and Chapter 7 on loyalty and retention.

Your strategic plan can summarise the relationship marketing process at a glance by setting it out as a flowchart. In the following example, the relationship marketing plan summarises the use of both segmented and tiered membership categories to recruit members who will financially support a dream holiday of choice for terminally ill children and upsell the members to higher levels of support and advocacy.

The flowchart also illustrates the so-called 'Pareto principle', which expresses an almost universal truth that whatever the area of your business – retail, licence trade, bookmaking, fundraising etc – around 80 per cent of your sales will come from around 20 per cent of your customers. Examine your own scheme and if this is true it is a fair clue as to where you should be concentrating your resources. It also illustrates the principle that moving your members up the relationship marketing trapezoid increases their loyalty to the cause and so they renew at higher rates (see top layer: 92 per cent of advocates renew, 84 per cent of supporters, while 67 per cent of members).

**Around 80 per cent of your sales will come from around 20 per cent of your customers.**

### Dream Holiday Campaign (DHC) relationship marketing plan

| | |
|---|---|
| **375 renewed**<br>46 advocates (92% renewed)<br>126 supporters (84% renewed)<br>235 members (67% renewed) | **Eight renewed**<br>(80% renewed) |
| ↑ | ↑ |
| **50 individual advocates**<br>Members who lobby businesses and attend events to recruit new members<br><br>*Standard benefits, invite to DHC celebrity gala evening, plus advocacy skills training* | **One corporate advocate**<br>Travel firm sponsors £5000 and donates display space in all branches for one year<br><br>*Standard benefits plus 25 staff invitations to top table at DHC celebrity gala evening* |
| ↑ | ↑ |
| **150 supporters**<br>Members who commit a further monthly donation of £10–£50<br><br>*Standard benefits plus invitation to DHC celebrity gala evening* | **Three corporate supporters**<br>Members upgraded to supporters after donating an additional £500 each<br><br>*Standard benefits plus five staff invitations to top table at DHC celebrity gala evening* |
| ↑ | ↑ |
| **300 members**<br>Join at £20<br><br>*Thank you letter plus quarterly newsletter* | **10 corporate members**<br>Join at £100<br><br>*Thank you certificate plus staff circular* |
| ↑ | ↑ |
| **50,000 prospects**<br>40,000 travel firm customers<br>5,000 attendees at school festivals<br>5,000 voluntary group members<br><br>*500 people recruited via displays at travel firm branches, school festivals and local voluntary groups* | **250 prospects**<br>One major travel firm, plus<br>200 local businesses<br>25 local schools<br>25 local voluntary groups<br><br>*Members recruited via telephone marketing campaign plus personal contacts* |

## Exercise: Sketching out a relationship marketing process

Research and analyse your target audience and their needs and then define:

1. Who is your target audience?
2. How is the target audience segmented?
3. Do you need a single membership category or a segmented one?
4. Do you need a tiered membership structure?
5. Who are your prospects?
6. Who will become your members?
7. What form of support do you desire?
8. What kind of advocacy do you desire?
9. What internal marketing processes (newsletter, bulletins, direct mail appeals, emails, etc) must you carry out to nurture members to become advocates and supporters?

Summarise your plan into a flowchart (see above) and circulate and test your ideas.

## Performance indicators

Without performance indicators of success, a membership scheme will have little by which to measure its value – to either the members or the organisation. On their own, platitudes such as 'we've had a very successful year' don't help much. Performance indicators are vital because they:

- focus people and resources on the achievement of strategic objectives
  - *rather than allowing effort to be spread too thinly across too many services and activities*
- provide information on the nature of your relationship with the members
  - *so you know how and why they become supporters and advocates*
- give the host organisation feedback on members' views
  - *so you know what to improve*
- identify trends and allow comparisons with other similar schemes
  - *so you know how you compare with internal and external benchmarks*

Some performance indicators will be descriptive and qualitative; others will be statistical and quantitative in nature. They should measure:

- the value of the membership to the organisation
- the value of the organisation to the membership

The more successful membership schemes surveyed for this guide utilised at least a dozen of the following indicators and often many more.

## Organisational value

- Key performance indicators, including:
  - The size of the membership base
  - The number of new recruits joining
  - The number becoming supporters
  - The number becoming advocates
  - The number renewing or lapsing
  - The overall profit/loss of the membership scheme
  - The profit/loss per member
  - Membership satisfaction rates
  - The average lifetime of the membership in years/months
  - The average £ lifetime value
- Other fiscal indicators, for example:
  - £ spent by members on other services, products and merchandise
  - £ donations over and above the subscription fee
- Participation indicators for supporters and advocates, such as:
  - The number of members recruited as volunteers
  - The numbers involved in campaigning/advocacy
  - The numbers attending projects or events involving members
  - Voter turnout in trustee elections
  - The number of member complaints logged and resolved/unresolved
- Evaluation of the wider value of the membership to the organisation, for example the benefit to the organisation's brand (such as being seen by politicians and funders as a representative body).
- Impact measurements to define outcomes caused in whole or in part by the activities/presence of the members, such as a change in the law or delivery of a volunteer project to improve local conservation.

Some organisations break down the above measures by segments – eg by membership categories – so that comparisons can be made between individual and organisational members, ordinary and life members, and so on.

## Membership value

**Membership values are often linked to outcomes that are more difficult to identify.**

Of the organisations surveyed, few had explicit measures to define the membership scheme's value to its members. This partially reflects the fact that membership values are often linked to outcomes that are more difficult to identify. For example, a member might use an organisation's membership magazine article on legal rights to subsequently go on to win a legal case without the charity's knowledge of the outcome. In cases like this, the host organisation can appeal to its members to inform them of outcomes that are attributable to information or support provided by the membership scheme. In most instances, if asked, members are happy to report these.

The most common channel for membership value indicators was the membership survey. By asking closed questions, usually with multiple choice options, you may compile data on membership satisfaction issues, such as:

- Membership renewal rates
- Perceptions of value for money
- Willingness to recommend membership to other people
- Perceptions about whether membership has achieved the member's desires
- Membership participation indicators (see above)

## Research basis for a plan

As we saw in Chapter 2, there is a whole range of intrinsic motivations behind people's reasons for becoming a member. Without some good solid market research, risky gut assumptions are made about why people might join. For example, we can't take it for granted that someone who has pledged a bequest to a charity will want to make any other commitment to the cause. That person may be happy with just having an arm's-length relationship. Likewise, just because a member has joined a scheme it doesn't automatically mean that they will respond to a donor appeal (some might even object to receiving appeals). A good membership strategy should be evidence-based via market research (which doesn't have to cost huge sums of money). In support of its recommendations, the strategy should include, as an appendix at least, any evidence you have for the kind of people who will join and the benefits they desire (see Chapter 4 for further discussion on common research methods).

## The marketing mix

Any kind of membership scheme needs a marketing mix that includes the so-called eight Ps. It means making sure that your target audience truly understands and empathises with your **philosophy** (the vision, mission and your values). It means that for each and every membership category or tier, you are clear that your **product** (the brand, the membership service and benefits) is in the right **place** at the right **price**. It means effectively telling people about it (**promotion**). It means providing **physical evidence** of the benefits. It means being confident that all your organisation's **people** are fully behind it and that you have a user-friendly **process** for joining.

If any one of these ingredients, or the mix between them, is wrong, then your organisation will be severely compromised in its ability to form relationships with prospective members. We will further discuss the marketing mix in Chapter 5.

## Membership finance

**Whatever the cause it represents, no membership strategy can ignore the financial realities.**

Whatever the cause it represents, no membership strategy can ignore the financial realities. What follows is not intended for finance directors or accountants, but sets out the key elements of a typical financial plan for membership schemes. It is best read in conjunction with this guide's sister publications, *The Good Management Guide* and *The Good Financial Management Guide*. Depending on your set-up, the membership financial plan may include:

- **Income forecast:** reasonable assumptions for the next year and beyond.
- **Capital expenditure:** larger, one-off costs, for example, property, computers, photocopiers, vehicles, office furniture.
- **Revenue expenditure:** ongoing costs of the organisation, for example, the apportionment of central costs such as salaries, rent, heat and light.
- **Cost analysis:** the membership-based fixed and variable costs for the next year and beyond.
- **Break-even analysis:** the number of members/the amount of income needed to reach break-even point (where all expenditure is recovered).

- **Cash flow forecast:** the flow in of income and the flow out of expenditure at monthly intervals across the financial year.

## Exercise: Developing an income forecast

Different schemes will have different income streams, but typical questions to be answered when making your forecast will include:

- What is your membership fee structure for the year ahead?
- Will you apply a flat or tiered fee structure for different membership categories (see Chapter 5)?
- What level of inflationary price increase will you apply?
- How many new members will you recruit (in each category)?
- How many existing members will you renew (in each category)?
- How many subscriptions will be gift aidable (worth up to 28 per cent of the fee, paid back to you in reclaimable tax (see appendix)?
- What other income is available (eg membership magazine ad sales, donations, publications/merchandise sales, proceeds from membership events, etc)?

If the membership service is offered free at the point of delivery, your income forecast must demonstrate how the cost is recovered through fundraising or other income streams.

It is very easy to be idealistic about income earned. As far as possible, you must base your reasonable assumptions on hard evidence. So think about the probability of different income streams. Some income may be *definite and confirmed* – for example, when a scheme is funded by a grant or contract that has already been agreed for the coming year. If your scheme is funded by membership fees, some income may be probable, for example:

- **New subscriptions for existing membership products and for existing audiences:** when the outcomes are predictable – for example, if year on year the number of visitors to a nature reserve is fairly constant at 10,000 and typically 5 per cent are converted into members for your existing product (which will not change in the year ahead), then you might reasonably forecast 500 new members (assuming that visitors will not all be the same people as per the previous year). Getting this kind of forecast right depends on rigorous monitoring and evaluation of all your recruitment activities (for further details, see Chapter 6 on recruitment).

- **Renewed subscriptions:** with all things being equal, income from renewing members can be forecast using the previous year's results – assuming that you are collecting year-on-year data on the renewal rates and are aware of any variables that might affect next year's rates (for further details, see Chapter 7 on loyalty and retention).

Some income streams will be *possible*, for example:

- **New subscriptions from existing recruitment channels:** when new members are recruited from new activities and the outcomes are less predictable, a more conservative forecast should be made.

- **New membership products or audiences:** when outcomes cannot be predicted except via careful market research and testing.

The sample income forecast below cites the average renewal rates (row A) for two existing membership products (individual and families) and uses this to calculate the probable number of renewed members (row B). Probable forecasts are made for new members in existing categories (row C) along with a possible forecast for new members in a new category (professional). New and renewed members are totalled (row D) and multiplied by the planned pricing policy (row E) to generate total forecast income (row F).

**Sample income forecast for 2003/04**

| | | Individual | Family | Professional (new) | Total |
|---|---|---|---|---|---|
| A | Renewal rate (%) | 80% | 70% | 0% | 75% |
| B | Renewed members | 6,000 | 1,500 | 0 | 7,500 |
| C | New members | 1,700 | 500 | 300 | 2,500 |
| D | Total members | 7,700 | 2,000 | 300 | 10,000 |
| E | Price (£) | £10 | £20 | £35 | |
| F | Subscription income (£) | £77,000 | £40,000 | £10,500 | £127,500 |

## Expenditure forecast

To be able to make effective strategic decisions about our membership schemes, we must have a thorough understanding of our cost base.

Use the checklist below to ensure that you have accounted for all your capital and revenue costs before performing the other exercises in this section.

### Exercise: Have you accounted for all your expenditure?

Every membership scheme will have its own unique cost base. Use the checklist below to ensure you have accounted for your costs before carrying out the exercises below. A typical cost base will include capital costs; human resources; IT/computers; promotion and products. This list is not exhaustive and you should add other items as relevant.

**CAPITAL COSTS**

- ❑ Premises
- ❑ Office furniture (desks, chairs, etc)
- ❑ Fixtures and fittings (lights, carpets, etc)
- ❑ Recruitment costs
- ❑ Computer
- ❑ Photocopiers
- ❑ Vehicles

**REVENUE COSTS**

**Human resources**

- ❑ Salaries
- ❑ National Insurance
- ❑ Pensions
- ❑ Recruitment costs
- ❑ Travel
- ❑ Subsistence
- ❑ Training/development
- ❑ Volunteer expenses

**IT / computers**

- ❑ Membership database software
- ❑ Other software
- ❑ Consumables (ink, paper, etc)
- ❑ Maintenance
- ❑ Peripherals (printer, cables, etc)
- ❑ Internet/email

**Membership promotion**

- ❑ Materials (leaflets, envelopes, etc)
- ❑ Collation (mail merge, packing, etc)
- ❑ Postage (direct mail)
- ❑ Exhibition costs
- ❑ Advertising costs
- ❑ List rentals
- ❑ Reciprocal marketing

**Product costs**

- ❑ Magazine (print, packaging, post)
- ❑ Website (server, firewall, etc)
- ❑ Venues/sites
- ❑ Courses
- ❑ Merchandise
- ❑ Other product (1)
- ❑ Other product (2)
- ❑ Other product (3)
- ❑ Other product (4)
- ❑ Other product (5)

## Revenue budget

The revenue budget is the working budget for the membership scheme, showing both the running costs and the project-related costs (such as printing the membership magazine, recruitment campaigns, etc), totalling them together with the aim of matching income to expenditure. In addition to a detailed revenue budget for the year ahead, you will need outline budgets for the following three to five years. The revenue budget *forecasts the amount of membership income earned less the membership costs incurred*. It displays the surplus (profit) or the deficit (loss) which arises if the financial plan is achieved.

### Sample revenue budget for 2003 to 2006

| | | 2003/04 | 2004/05 | 2005/06 |
|---|---|---|---|---|
| A | Subscriptions | 100,000 | 147,000 | 176,000 |
| B | Other income | 10,000 | 12,000 | 14,000 |
| C | Total income | 110,000 | 159,000 | 190,000 |
| | | | | |
| D | Membership costs | 45,000 | 46,350 | 47,740 |
| E | Capital expenditure | 5,000 | 0 | 2,500 |
| F | Central costs allocated | 10,000 | 11,000 | 12,000 |
| G | Total costs | 60,000 | 57,350 | 62,240 |
| | | | | |
| H | Surplus income over expend | 50,000 | 101,650 | 127,760 |

## Fixed and variable costs

A crucial element of good membership finance is understanding the fixed and variable costs.

*Fixed costs* do not alter in proportion to the number of members – for example, capital expenditure items such as property, salaries and computers.

*Variable costs* change in proportion to the number of members – for example, if you have 1000 members your magazine print costs will increase when you reach 2000 members and then again for 3000 members, and so on.

The next table shows a typical relationship between fixed and variable costs. As the number of members (row A) increases, the fixed costs (row B) and fixed cost per member (row C) stay the same. Meanwhile, as the membership grows from 1000 to 5000, the variable cost per member (row E) decreases from £5.00 to £4.30. This is due to economies of scale (for example, as more magazines are printed the unit cost per copy charged by the printer goes down).

### Sample fixed and variable membership costs

| | | | | | | |
|---|---|---|---|---|---|---|
| A | No. of members | 1,000 | 2,000 | 3,000 | 4,000 | 5,000 |
| B | Fixed costs | £5,000 | £5,000 | £5,000 | £5,000 | £5,000 |
| C | Fixed/member | £5.00 | £5.00 | £5.00 | £5.00 | £5.00 |
| D | Variable costs | £5,000 | £9,500 | £13,650 | £17,600 | £21,500 |
| E | Var./member | £5.00 | £4.75 | £4.55 | £4.40 | £4.30 |
| **F** | **Total costs** | **£10,000** | **£14,500** | **£18,650** | **£22,600** | **£26,500** |
| **G** | **Cost/member** | **£10.00** | **£7.25** | **£6.21** | **£5.65** | **£5.30** |

**Break-even analysis**

The fixed and variable cost analysis can be used to work out how many members you need for your scheme to break even on income and expenditure.

In the table below, the subscription fee amounts to £7 per member (row G). With a membership of 1000 the cost per member is £10 (row F) so the organisation incurs a loss of £3 per member (row H). The variable cost per member decreases until, with a membership of 3000, the scheme shows a profit (with a 79p contribution per member).

**Sample break-even analysis**

| | | | | | | |
|---|---|---|---|---|---|---|
| A | No. of members | 1,000 | 2,000 | 3,000 | 4,000 | 5,000 |
| B | Fixed costs | £5,000 | £5,000 | £5,000 | £5,000 | £5,000 |
| C | Variable costs | £5,000 | £9,500 | £13,650 | £17,600 | £21,500 |
| D | Total costs | £10,000 | £14,500 | £18,650 | £22,600 | £26,500 |
| E | Cost/member | £10.00 | £7.25 | £6.21 | £5.65 | £5.30 |
| F | Total income | £7,000 | £14,000 | £21,000 | £28,000 | £35,000 |
| G | Income/member | £7.00 | £7.00 | £7.00 | £7.00 | £7.00 |
| H | Profit/(loss) | (£3,000) | (£500) | £2,350 | £5,400 | £8,500 |
| **I** | **Profit/member** | **(£3.00)** | **(£0.25)** | **£0.79** | **£1.35** | **£1.70** |

You can use spreadsheet software to explore different break-even scenarios. For example, what happens to the break-even point if:

- Membership fees are held, increased or decreased?
- Your fixed costs are increased (eg the cost of an additional staff member)?
- Your fixed costs are decreased (eg moving to cheaper premises)?
- Your variable costs are increased (eg more promotional spend)?
- Your variable costs are decreased (eg the magazine printing is competitively tendered to achieve lower costs)?

**Exercise: Analysing your income, costs and break-even point**

What are your membership scheme's fixed costs? What are its variable costs? What is the relationship between the two? At what level of membership does your scheme break even?

Use and adapt the models in this chapter to forecast your membership income and expenditure.

**Ultimately, good membership finance is an art, as well as a science.**

Ultimately, good membership finance is an art, as well as a science. So, take some time out to play around with your figures on a spreadsheet. Always be sure that they are based on hard evidence so they are realistic and achievable. But be alert to the different configurations of income and costs and how you can manipulate these.

In doing so, you will enrich your ability to understand and control the financial implications of different strategic options for your membership scheme.

## Action points

✓ Remember: fail to plan = plan to fail.

✓ Be a learning organisation. Ask questions of the outside world, gather data and act on the results.

✓ Annually review your membership scheme's Strengths, Weaknesses, Opportunities and Threats.

✓ Ensure that your host organisation's vision and mission and your scheme's purpose are synchronised.

✓ See change as an opportunity as well as a threat.

✓ Launch – Growth – Maturity – Decline – Innovation: know the membership life cycle and, if you need to, be prepared to refresh your purpose.

✓ Develop the ability to think in terms of both existing and new audiences, existing and new products and services (the Ansoff matrix).

✓ Mind map your ideas and visualise the future.

✓ Use market research to assess your target audience and its desired benefits.

✓ When developing your membership strategy, aim for a two-way flow of value between the organisation and its members.

✓ Make sure you have a clear idea of what success looks like; compile performance measures to evaluate whether you are achieving it.

✓ No membership strategy can ignore financial realities. Collect hard evidence to underpin your income forecasts, and understand your fixed and variable costs.

---

1. Harris, J (2002) *The Good Management Guide,* NCVO
2. Buzan, T (1993) *The Mind Map*, BBC Books
3. Evans, E and Saxton, J (2003) *Five Key Trends and their Impact on the Voluntary Sector*, nfp Synergy

---

# 4 Market research

This chapter covers:

- Understanding the six stages of the membership journey
- Gut assumptions versus hard evidence
- Why do market research?
- Justifying the cost of market research
- Some common research methods
- Sharing your findings with the members
- The limitations of research
- Putting research into practice

In Chapter 1, we looked at how relationship marketing calls for us to understand our members as people who have embarked on a six-stage journey. Ideally, your market research will encompass the following stages of the journey:

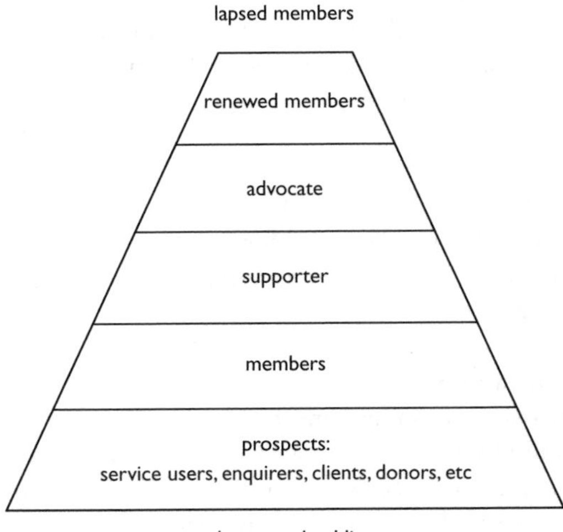

**Know your prospects**

True relationship marketing begins with understanding your prospects.

True relationship marketing begins with understanding your prospects; those who are your users, enquirers, donors, etc, who have not yet joined but who have made a one-off or infrequent transaction with your organisation and are most likely warm to your cause.

At this first stage, the key question is: What will persuade them to join? Are they concerned with taking benefit from your scheme or with giving benefit to it? Do all your prospects want the same thing or will they need to be segmented into different groups and with different benefits tailored accordingly? (For further discussion of segmentation see Chapter 5 on the marketing mix.)

**... and your members, supporters and advocates**

We also need to ask some fundamental questions of people who are still in their first year of membership. What motivated them to join? What inspired them/stopped them from being a supporter (who further engages with your cause, by purchasing a product, donating or volunteering)? What compelled them/put them off being an advocate (who goes one step further and actively promotes your cause to others, eg by supporting a campaign or recruiting new members)? What do these subgroups of your membership base like/dislike? What works for them and what doesn't?

This is a key group of people who have not yet reached the end of their first year of membership and who may have not yet decided to renew. Will they renew? If so, why? If not, why not? How do the answers to all these questions vary between people on different tiers of your membership scheme (eg individual, family, professional)?

**... and your renewed members**

We should also be concerned with the mindset of those members who have renewed. They've rejoined for another year but for how much longer will they stay on board? What will keep them active and from going stale?

**... and your lapsed members**

Finally, we must seek to understand our lapsed members too. We have to ask (politely) why they chose to go their own way. What might tempt them to come back? From the feedback we can try to improve the future odds on our existing members not lapsing in the future for similar reasons.

**Gut assumptions versus hard evidence**

Some trustees, managers and group leaders neglect to invest in market research out of a belief that they already know their members' needs anyway. Yet this knowledge often turns out to be assumptions based on personal experience. One individual's experience will rarely be the same for each and every member.

As a random example, a trustee of a multiple sclerosis charity might say "I've had MS since childhood, what our members need is ..." (But that person may not have such a clear view of someone who has only recently acquired MS.) Or a staff member might say, "Based on my ten years of professional experience ..." (But lay people view MS from the other end of the telescope.) Or a volunteer might say "In my local MS group, we all think that ..." (But group members may not empathise fully with people who prefer to get their information in the privacy of their home.)

When a board of trustees or a management team has in-depth knowledge of their field, then gut instinct is a valuable way of generating ideas. Yet as the following case study demonstrates, it is invariably wise to do some research before rolling out a new membership product or service.

**Market research is a process of under-standing your members and matching your services to their needs at a cost that you can afford.**

Market research is a process of *understanding your members and matching your services to their needs at a cost that you can afford.*

Analysing your members' needs

⇩

Generating ideas to meet these needs

⇩

Preliminary analyses of these ideas

⇩

Positioning selected ideas in terms of member needs

⇩

Field study to test the concept on your members

⇩

Analysing response (understanding, reaction, benefits)

⇩ Negative

⇩ Positive

⇩

Introduction of new product or service

## Case study: Using research to make member-driven decisions

The chairman of Anyshire Nature Trust had been on an internet course. You could tell because at the next board meeting he demanded the Trust immediately roll out a members' website with an electronic news service. "Printed newsletters are for dinosaurs," he declared. "Once we've met the website's start-up costs, we'll keep our members up-to-date without the usual print and postage costs draining our valuable resources."

The director was a little more cautious. Their members were mostly over 50 and she felt not all would have a home computer let alone access to the internet. "Pah!" the chairman retorted. "All my friends have one. I can't see what's stopping us. We'll be voluntary sector trailblazers. Soon everyone else will think 'why didn't we do that before?'" (The chairman was ambitious.) Ever the pragmatist, the director suggested testing the idea first with some market research. The chairman agreed reluctantly to set aside a budget for some market research but said he could think of better ways to spend the money.

When the results came back, the Trust found:

- just 40 per cent of members had access to a home computer;
- 30 per cent had an account with an internet service provider (ISP);
- 25 per cent were considering buying a computer and accessing the internet in the next one to two years;
- of those members who already had an internet account, 33 per cent would consider giving up their traditional printed newsletter to receive news by internet and email only.

Then the director piloted a website-based news service. A letter was sent to the 30% of survey respondents with an ISP inviting them to visit the site and provide feedback via an electronic questionnaire. The results were fed into an improved screen layout that was easier to navigate.

When these members' subscriptions came up for renewal they were given a choice: to continue receiving the printed newsletter or to switch to the electronic version. A third chose to go electronic for two reasons: for the convenience and on the understanding that it saved the Trust money thereby allowing a greater portion of their membership fee to be ploughed back into conservation work. In the year ahead, a steady trickle of new members also opted for the electronic version as soon as they joined.

Had the website service been imposed on all the members with immediate effect, as the chairman at first wanted, over 60 per cent of the members would have been cut off from news and information and the impact on retention and fee income would have been disastrous.

The chairman's vision had not been frustrated but market research had tempered it. The result: a relationship marketing-driven strategy for enabling each individual to stay in control of how they continued on their membership journey. They could elect to go electronic as and when they were ready or willing to do so. The director's financial projections indicated that within five years, half of all their members would be using the electronic version and the net financial saving to the charity would be in the region of £50,000. The modest £5,000 cost of the research had been more than recouped. Many members were delighted with being offered the choice of a printed or electronic newsletter.

This case study shows the power of market research to inform planning and budgeting decisions. Yet too few third-sector bodies do it. Some perceive only the expense and so don't budget for it. In the commercial sector, it is taken for granted that a percentage of each year's budget is put aside for market research. Companies know that good data is the first step to profitability. Without that insight, profitability is vulnerable to the subtle shifts in customer attitudes and trends. The same principle applies to membership bodies too – whether or not the profit motive exists.

The non-commercial application of market research is increasingly applied in the public sector. Both national and local government bodies rely on it to guide policy work in a wide range of areas, such as local transport planning, social services provision and the development of schools and universities.

## Justifying the cost of market research

As the above case study demonstrates, the real question is not 'can we afford to do without market research?' but 'can we afford not to truly understand our members?' From there, the next step is how to justify the cost to the people who approve or reject expenditure plans. The vital case for market research is:

- With solid research data you can test your assumptions, track shifts in your members' attitudes, discover which future membership offers are the most appealing, what people think of your organisation, whether or not your strategy is in tune with your members' priorities, and so on.
- The more intimately you know your members, the more relevant your membership strategy will be to their ever-changing lives.
- Some basic research doesn't have to cost the earth and can be carried out within a tight budget or even at zero cost (see common research methods below).
- In the long term, research is an investment providing that the costs don't outweigh the financial gains. For example, is it worth spending £250 on a piece of research that will only gain you £100?
- For a non-income-generating membership scheme, a thoughtful cost-benefit analysis – with the costs of the research weighted against the benefits received – can justify the investment.
- The hidden costs of not doing research may lead to poorer quality decision making and the loss of members or income.

Your organisation is more likely to perceive market research as being affordable if it is made part of an annual plan and budget rather than as a one-off activity. This way you will not only deduce where you are now but also set a benchmark for future surveys to which you can refer back.

## Some common research methods

### Qualitative and quantitative research

Market research seeks to answer six basic questions: Who? What? When? Where? How? Why?
The two main types of market research are:

- **Quantitative** – concerned with hard statistics: the size of demand for your membership scheme, the percentage of those who like/dislike a particular product or service, and so on.

- **Qualitative** – explores the softer issues behind the numbers: the intrinsic motives for joining or not, why people like/dislike a particular product or service, and so on.

Some researchers prefer to do qualitative research first; teasing out people's attitudes – such as probing the reasons why they might or might not join – and then consolidating it with quantitative research to put some hard figures on the softer issues. For example, a focus group of architects discusses three potential membership benefits – a quality assurance manual, an internet bulletin board and discounts for publications. Funds are limited, so the organisation has to consider which of these ideas would generate the most popular interest. A postal survey indicates that 66 per cent would welcome a quality assurance manual, 28 per cent the publication discounts and 24 per cent the internet bulletin board. The quality assurance manual is introduced, while the other two ideas are shelved for possible introduction in future years.

Or, qualitative can follow quantitative research as a way to probe your survey results in greater detail. For example, a charity membership survey indicates 71 per cent are satisfied with their membership, 15 per cent are neither satisfied nor dissatisfied, while 14 per cent are dissatisfied. The charity could hold a focus group to investigate why some people were dissatisfied and see what lessons could be applied.

Here are some common research methods and their respective pros and cons:

| **Approach** | Pros | Cons |
|---|---|---|
| **By post** | Postal surveys can be done fairly cheaply<br>Simple questionnaires can be done in-house<br>Specific data<br>Popular and non-intrusive | Detailed surveys need professional support<br>Leading questions may appear if you write your own script<br>Only the committed members respond |
| **By telephone** | Quick response<br>Few will decline<br>An opportunity to listen and ask probing questions | Needs professional help<br>High cost of obtaining phone numbers<br>Perceived as intrusive |

| | | |
|---|---|---|
| **Face to face via individual interviews** | Allows for detailed and probing conversations<br>Omits leading questions<br>Reliability of answers can be quickly verified | Demands a lot of pre-preparation<br>Requires professional interviewers so high cost per individual<br>Attracts mainly committed members |
| **Face to face via focus group** | Full and frank<br>You can listen in<br>Reliability of answers can be quickly verified | Requires professional interviewers so high cost<br>Attracts mainly committed members<br>Outspoken people will dominate the shy ones |
| **By meeting your members** | Low cost<br>Motivating to do | None so long as treated as qualitative information only |

**No one single piece of research can present a full picture of your members.**

**Mixing your research channels**

No one single piece of research can present a full picture of your members. Individuals are affected by so many variables – the economy, technology, social attitudes etc. All this points to the need to mix your research channels.

Each of the following methods has its own inbuilt pros and cons – some will work better with certain audiences than others.

*Questionnaires*: Traditionally a postal questionnaire survey, but now frequently an internet or email survey. They have the value of being non-intrusive and can be sent to a statistically valid sample of your target audience. These can be relatively cheap if you draw up simple questionnaires in-house but more complex ones should usually be scripted by professional researchers. Either way, for large samples you will have to pay for the counting and tabulation of the results.

The majority of your respondents will be your committed members, so the results will be slightly skewed. For example, if 90 per cent of your members indicate that they will renew their membership this year it should be no surprise if the subsequent renewal rate turns out to be, say, 80 per cent. This is because those people who lapsed were also less likely to have completed your questionnaire and the results will have to be viewed in this light. Be aware of this factor when interpreting your results. Your unhappiest members may not be responding.

Before carrying out your survey, think about your target audience. If your results are to be statistically valid and truly representative of what the broad spread of your members are really thinking, then select a representative cross-section of respondents – by age, gender, geographic location, type of membership, etc – to avoid bias towards one particular group.

***Telephone research***: Telephone research is not widely used as a membership tool – a probable reaction to the fact that many of us loathe being on the receiving end of telemarketing. Yet this overlooks the fact that response rates to the telephone are superior to postal mailings.

A pre-prepared script is drafted to open the call and explain the purpose of your research. The questions should be professionally scripted and delivered to avoid the pitfalls of leading questions (introducing bias by exerting pressure towards certain answers). Time is money, so the call has to be skilfully closed within a time limit and without undue pressure. Tact and diplomacy are essential. The call is an opportunity to reinforce loyalty to your organisation, but handled inappropriately it may lead to a loss of friends too. Be aware that older members, who are also proportionately more likely to have some hearing loss, may dislike using the telephone to speak to someone they do not know well. If you listen in to the calls you will certainly get some fascinating insights.

***Focus groups***: These are an excellent way to scratch beneath the surface to discover what your members really think and feel. Always remember that you are paying money to test your assumptions, not to have them confirmed irrespective of people's responses. Sit in on the discussions but don't influence them.

Some research houses offer rooms with customised and unobtrusive recording facilities and two-way windows that enable you to observe unseen, but focus groups can often be just as effective held in hired or rented local halls.

Avoid holding focus groups in your office (as respondents will tend to be more polite on your territory). Professionally convened focus groups are relatively expensive but they can be very rewarding. They can identify areas of debate that you may not have anticipated and so alert you to factors vital to your marketing or service activities that you have overlooked.

A single focus group may comprise of a representative cross-section of your target audience, or separate groups can split your target audience into segments – for example, disabled people, their relatives, carers, professionals – in order to assess both common and differing values.

Focus groups are best led by trained, independent facilitators with the skills to draw out participants' views without giving an opinion themselves. The optimum size for a focus group is no larger than six to eight people.

*Face-to-face interviews*: Holding one-to-one meetings with a prospective or actual member also offers qualitative analysis but on a deeper level than generally permitted by focus groups (where two or three strong personalities will sometimes influence the behaviour of others). The same caveats apply as for focus groups – the high cost and the need for a professionally neutral facilitator – but the insights can be both very detailed and very specific.

*Meet your members*: In practice, you should meet with your members regularly – at group meetings, conferences, AGMs and so on. Consider holding an open day at your head or regional office, or local branch or service. It is both informal and inexpensive. Mingle with your members; ask them what they think of the current benefits and what they recall about the most recent magazine. Is there something that your organisation could or should be doing to provide an even better service? Keep a log of all the ideas and comments to share with your colleagues and feed the information into meetings and reports.

*Read your postbag*: This astonishingly underrated research method costs nothing and can provide food for thought in the most unexpected ways. For sure, the complainers are much more likely to reach you through this channel than people who are happy, but that is precisely why the postbag is important. Complaints offer free consultancy – an inkling of what might be on the minds of a lot of other unhappy members who haven't been in touch.

**In-house or external research agency?**

For some types of research – especially focus groups, telephone research and more complex postal surveys – it is invariably a good idea to employ the help of an external research agency. It is not just a matter of using their experience on sampling issues and questionnaire scripting and design – it is about ensuring that your research has a degree of independence. One important pitfall to avoid is asking leading questions: for example, 'Which section of our membership magazine do you like best?' These tend to lead towards a certain answer and so produce an unrepresentative response – it excludes respondents who might not like any sections of your magazine.

On the other hand, if you do choose to carry out the research in-house, first test the script on a wide range of typical respondents. Share it with your work colleagues or volunteers and ideally with some outsiders who are not so intimate with your work. This will help you to check whether the questionnaire is clear and logical to all and not just to you.

## Exercise: Scripting a membership questionnaire

Make a list of all the questions that could be included in a membership survey. At first, come up with as many factors as you can even though some may not make it into your final script. The list should include questions about:

- extrinsic factors: facts such as age and gender
- intrinsic factors: perceptions and attitudes

There is no one-size-fits-all template and this sample is only a guide to get you thinking. The most important thing is to start out with some clear objectives. For example, in the sample below the objectives were to probe:

- people's motivations for joining
- their in-depth perceptions of the scheme's core benefit – the magazine
- how they rate the other benefits
- their customer service experience
- key demographics such as age and gender
- attitudes to the internet and email
- their readiness to recommend membership to others

The actual multiple choice options you offer will, of course, vary from one organisation or target audience to another. The example script below, for asthma charity XYZ, uses a mixture of closed questions (that ask the respondent to choose a multiple choice answer) and open questions (that allow the respondent to say what they want).

**How you joined us**

1. **How did you first hear about our membership scheme?**
   By letter / by visiting your website / by word of mouth / by attending an exhibition / by reading your magazine / by telephone / by other means (please describe) ______

2. **My key reasons for being a member of XYZ are: (tick a maximum of three)**
   I wanted to support XYZ financially / I wanted to get my own regular copy of the magazine / I wanted to get regular information about asthma / I wanted to volunteer / I wanted to vote in the elections / I wanted to get discounts on XYZ's products and services

**Your membership magazine**

3. **How much of XYZ do you usually read?**
   From cover to cover / Most articles / A few articles / I just flick through the magazine / I don't read it but place it somewhere it can be read by others / I dispose of it as soon as it arrives

4. **In your opinion, which of the following statements best describe XYZ magazine? (please tick one)**
   It's informative / It's easy to read / It's interesting / It's useful / It gives a clear view of asthma issues / It's irrelevant to my needs / It's boring

5. **Looking at XYZ magazine, please indicate your view about the amount of: (tick as appropriate)**
   Information features – Too much / Just about right / Too little
   Human interest stories – Too much / Just about right / Too little
   Features about the work of XYZ – Too much / Just about right / Too little

6. **How many people read your copy of XYZ magazine? (please tick one)**
   Just me / Two / More than two / I pass it on

7. **Tick the statement that most applies to you (please tick one)**
   I feel that XYZ magazine is best suited to professionals who work with people who have asthma

I feel that XYZ magazine is best suited to people who directly experience asthma
I feel that XYZ magazine is equally suited to individuals and professionals concerned with asthma
I feel that XYZ magazine is suited to anyone with an interest in asthma

8. **Ideally, how frequently would you like to receive XYZ magazine? (please tick one)**
   Monthly / Bi-monthly / Quarterly / Twice a year

**Your membership service**

9. **In the past year which membership benefits have you used? (tick as many that apply)**
   The magazine / The welcome booklet / The telephone helpline / The website members only area / Publication discounts / Free access to sites / My membership vote in trustee elections

10. **The membership helpline exists to help you with your application and renewal, enquiries and complaints. How do you feel about the helpline? (please tick one)**
    Very satisfied / satisfied / neither satisfied nor dissatisfied / dissatisfied / very dissatisfied

11. **If you have made a complaint in the past year, how satisfied were you with the way it was resolved? (please tick one)**
    Very satisfied / satisfied / neither satisfied nor dissatisfied / dissatisfied / very dissatisfied

12. **Compared with last year, do you feel that the practical value to you of membership of XYZ is: (please tick one)**
    Greater? / The same? / Less?
    Please tell us the reason for your answer ____________

13. **Is there anything about your membership that you would like to see improved?**
    Yes / No
    (If yes, please describe) ______________________

14. **Overall, how satisfied are you with your membership of XYZ? (please tick one)**
 Very satisfied / Satisfied / Neither satisfied nor dissatisfied / Dissatisfied / Very dissatisfied
 If you wish, please tell us your reason_______________

15. **Do you feel that your present membership of XYZ is: (please tick one)**
 Excellent value for money? / Value for money? / Poor value for money?

16. **At this time are you likely to renew your membership of XYZ?**
 Yes / No

17. **If your answer is no, can you suggest any change that would make you reconsider? (please describe)**________

**Please tell us about yourself**

18. **Your age?**
 15–24 / 25–34 / 35–44 / 45–54 / 55–64 / 65–74 / 75+

19. **Are you?**
 Male / Female

20. **What is your occupation?**
 I am retired / I am in full-time education / I am in part-time education / I am in full-time employment / I am in part-time employment / Other (please describe) ______

21. **What is your interest in XYZ? (please tick one)**
 I am asthmatic / I am professionally concerned with asthma / I am not asthmatic but I am related to someone who is / I have a general interest in asthma

22. **If you are asthmatic, at what age did it begin?**
 From birth to 15 / 16–35 years / 36–50 years / 51–70 years / 71+ years

**The internet**

23. **Do you own a home computer?**
 Yes / No

24. **Do you have an account with an internet service provider (such as AOL or Hotmail)?**
    Yes / No

25. **Would you be interested in receiving further news from XYZ by email? (please tick one)**
    Yes / I would consider it / No

26. **If XYZ magazine were made available online in the future, would you consider receiving it electronically rather than by post (to save XYZ money and allow more of your subscription fee to be devoted to campaigning)?**
    Yes / I would consider it / No

**Your relatives, friends and acquaintances**

27. **If we provide information about XYZ for you to pass on to other people who might be interested in joining as a member, would you be able to help? (please tick one)**
    Yes / I would consider it / No

## How to maximise the responses to your survey

Naturally, your market research is going to be ineffective if there are too few participants. Some tips for boosting the response:

- Include a covering letter that explains fully why you are asking the questions and how the results will be put to use.
- Offer incentives – eg a prize draw.
- Avoid overlong surveys – 30 questions maximum, if your script is longer, a smaller number of people will complete it.
- Design it to look user-friendly and easy to complete. Allow sufficient space for people to write their responses. Use a clear layout that is easy for the eye to scan and navigate. Don't squeeze things in by using tiny eight-point text – making it hard to read will lower your response.
- Avoid including the about-you type questions (age, gender, etc) at the beginning of the survey – many of your respondents may have taken part in other surveys and will not be too thrilled if you begin with questions they will be answering for the nth time.
- Ensure there is a logical flow to the question script.
- If you can afford it, offer a FREEPOST postal response

device. It will lift response. But if you explain that using a stamp will save you costs, you'll be amazed how many will helpfully affix one.

**Explain yourself**

If you are sending a postal questionnaire do ensure that your covering letter explains clearly why you are contacting them, why the questions are vital to your cause and how the results can benefit the service that you provide; this also applies to focus groups, face-to-face interviews and particularly to telephone research because you only have a few moments in which to get your message across.

**Share your findings**

No matter which research method is undertaken, if you are committed to relationship marketing you will see research as a vital cog in maintaining a rapport between your organisation and its members.

**If you are committed to relationship marketing you will see research as a vital cog in maintaining a rapport between your organisation and its members.**

After the research is completed and the report has been finalised, don't keep the findings to yourself. Having given their personal time, people are naturally curious to learn the results and will be genuinely delighted to hear the outcome. It is a great way to interest the prospective member or to reinforce the commitment of an existing one. Share the findings and invite feedback – the feedback will become another source of qualitative data.

## Interpreting research data

There are lies, damn lies and statistics. There's some truth in this catchphrase. For example, the act of telling a market researcher that you will join this or that organisation is not the same thing as actually going ahead and doing it. The answer 'yes' only represents what the respondent believes that they would do in a given situation at a point in time in the future. In real life, people behave differently.

The motivations for joining as a member may be logical, emotive, impulsive or irrational. Even the most professionally conducted research will not pin down all the variables underlying these behaviours. That is one reason to give at least some value to your assumptions or gut instincts rather than simply allow them to be overrun by the more tangible but still possibly biased, research data. Interpreting good market research is not a science – it's an art. The general public instinctively knows this whenever politicians or vested interests flaunt their statistics and presume uncritical acceptance of them. This so-called 'hidden flaw' in market research does not invalidate the results; it simply requires you to interpret them with this factor in mind.

## Putting research into practice

Most of us know of a piece of lovingly crafted and detailed research whose inch-thick report goes straight onto the office shelf and gathers dust. For some, the thrill lies in conducting the research, in the kudos of producing the report. Sometimes the problem lies not in the pudding but in the eating of it. People may skim the report and find the results at best inconvenient or at worse threatening. (Membership satisfaction is slightly down. Insufficient numbers of people liked the idea of your proposed own-branded credit card. Your new 'improved' magazine is only attracting the same ratings as last year.) Or it is just that the results seem to require more thought to extract the underlying lessons and so it gets filed away for future reading. All this is self-defeating. *Research only pays if you put it into action.*

We looked earlier at how relying on trustee or staff assumptions can be misleading and how research can be used to qualify them. Just as dangerous is the act of selectively misreading the results in search of data that confirms those assumptions, while overlooking or screening the bits that (inconveniently) challenge them. As a rule of thumb, when drawing up a research brief, get the agreement of trustees, managers and other stakeholders that the results will be used honestly.

## The PR value of good research

Not only should research never be hidden in a drawer, it can have powerful uses, both internally and externally, as a PR tool. One organisation that had reason to be grateful for researching their members' views is Girlguiding UK.

### Girlguiding UK

Since 1909, the Girl Guides – now called Girlguiding UK – has been a pillar of British society. For 90 years and more it has offered girls an eight-point challenge: to be friendly; keep healthy; help at home; do their best; lend a hand; make things; have fun out of doors and be wide awake.

Such is the value that some people place on the membership's time-honoured rituals or insignia, that attempts to modify or update it can attract national media comment. So much so that when the Brownies section revamped its badges in 2003, the first such exercise in 35 years, it attracted the not unpredictable wrath of the *Daily Mail*.

Under the sensational headline of "PC badges for the new-age Brownies", the newspaper complained that "Britain's 300,000 Brownies will be tackling politically correct subjects such as disability issues, discovering faith and learning about the environment." In opposition, the Daily Mail quoted the chairman of the Campaign for Real Education: "I would think most parents would be horrified ... The trendy people controlling the organisation seem to be throwing the baby out with the bath water."

To show a token degree of balance, the journalist was obliged to acknowledge that the changes were based on a huge national consultation exercise. A Girlguiding UK spokesperson said: "We asked 40,000 members what they liked and didn't like about the badges they could try for. They felt a lot of the more old-fashioned things just weren't what they wanted. Brownies is about getting girls to do things, not forcing activities on them, so we decided to drop some things as specific badges. We are not telling them that they cannot learn knots, knitting or bell-ringing. It is about choice, not political correctness. We are left with a much more modern and relevant set of badges."

In spite of the negative tone of the *Daily Mail* story, any objective reader is left in no doubt that Girlguiding UK had the support of its members. It carried out market research and consulted widely. It checked that both Brownies and their parents endorsed change and were ready to move with it. In contrast, the only evidence against it that the *Daily Mail* could muster was a spontaneous quote from the Campaign for Real Education.

As Girlguiding UK knows, market research is far from being an optional extra. It is a vital tool for survival in a changing and often hostile world.

## Action points

✓ Research isn't an optional extra. It helps you to understand your members and to make your scheme relevant to them.

✓ Work out the costs of research versus the benefits. Ensure that your trustees or management understand the cost of *not* doing research.

✓ Make an annual plan to include research and you'll be able to track even subtle shifts in your members' needs and wants over time.

✓ Even if you have plenty of personal knowledge about your members, don't just rely on gut assumptions. Test your thinking with some unbiased research.

✓ Remember the six basic questions: Who? What? When? Where? How? Why?

✓ Ask these fundamental questions of people at all stages of your relationship with them – prospect, new member, renewing member, long-term member and lapsed member.

✓ Meet your members as often as possible – at clubs, events, AGMs – and seek their views on the issues that matter.

✓ Take a regular interest in your member postbag – another source of qualitative data.

✓ Be transparent. Always explain clearly why you are doing the research and how it will help you to provide a better service.

✓ Always share your key findings with your members. It motivates them and increases the feeling of being truly involved in your organisation.

✓ Beware of the filing cabinet syndrome. Once you've commissioned the research, act on the findings.

✓ Remember the hidden flaw in market research. What people say they will do and what they actually do are two different things. Interpret your research data with this in mind.

✓ Be alert to the PR value of your membership research when dealing with external audiences such as the media, business or politicians.

---

# 5 The marketing mix

## This chapter covers:

- Why marketing?
- The marketing mix and the eight Ps
- Philosophy – make your cause a reason to join
- Product – the brand, the benefits, the unique reason to join (URJ)
- Physical evidence – making your cause tangible
- Pricing – how to set the right fees
- Place – positioning your membership where it will be seen
- Promotion – the key to successful recruitment
- Process – making it easy for people to join
- People – your trustees, staff and volunteers and how to get them to support your membership scheme

In the first chapter, we saw that the ultimate purpose of any kind of membership scheme is to manage relationships for the mutual benefit of the members, the organisation and the cause they represent. A key theme of this guide is to explore how relationship marketing can help you to achieve long-term support for your cause.

The term *relationship marketing* has two words in it – you can't have one without the other. We know what relationships are – we have them with relatives, friends and colleagues – but what is marketing and why is it often regarded with suspicion in the third sector by people who run membership schemes? One chief executive told me: "We don't do membership marketing – we recruit. We get out and network with people. If they're sufficiently impressed with how we advance the cause they will join us." He was not alone. In fact, a majority of non-profit organisations 'don't do marketing' – they just recruit. But at what cost to their membership growth?

All too frequently, third-sector bodies view marketing as a commercial activity geared to *selling people something they don't want or need*. As many non-profit bodies are campaign or service

**A good membership strategy treats the marketing plan as an inclusive document.**

driven and so attract like-minded trustees and staff, it's quite understandable that this misconception flourishes.

One way around this mental block is to see marketing for what it really is: a process of building relationships – both inside and outside your organisation. A good membership strategy treats the marketing plan as an inclusive document. It should:

- link all your marketing activities to your organisation's vision statement or governing document: the reasons why it exists in the first place;
- factor in detailed research on both your prospective and existing members' needs and wants;
- explain how your membership service will meet those needs;
- make the business case for delivering the service profitably (or with a subsidy your organisation agrees it can afford);
- present quantitative information on targets, costs and income;
- identify the win–win situation: how your plan's success mutually benefits both the cause and your beneficiaries' lives;
- get your colleagues on your side by showing them how membership support benefits their activities too – research, campaigns, services and fundraising.

Looked at this way, relationship marketing is the opposite of selling people something they don't want. It is responsive to member needs. It is inclusive and empowers your staff. And if you make a profit it doesn't enrich shareholders – it gets reinvested in the cause. A good relationship marketing plan (see Chapter 3) will inspire your trustees, staff and volunteers. After all, who else will be the vital ambassadors for your scheme? You will maximise your membership support only when everyone – from the chairman to the receptionist – is directly or indirectly involved in recruitment. Your marketing plan is the roadmap for spelling out their role in the big picture. The more people who can input into the marketing plan – in large or small ways – the greater the sum total of your organisation's commitment to helping your scheme grow.

Within this context we'll look at the *marketing mix* – a holistic approach to marketing that looks both at the product you are promoting and the people who will deliver it. Calling it a mix reminds you to try to get the balance right. For example, if take-up of a newly priced membership scheme is poor, an answer could be to deliver it in a way that is more convenient to the prospective member (rather than cut the price).

All kinds of membership schemes will find the marketing mix an essential tool for building relationships. It derives from McCarthy's classic theory of the four Ps[1]:

- Product
- Price
- Place
- Promotion

The four Ps were originally proposed during an era when the embryonic 'marketing industry' was driven by the need to sell fast-moving consumer goods (FMCGs). So if you feel, not unnaturally, that these four Ps sound a bit too hard-edged for your liking, one way around this is to rethink them as the four Cs developed by Robert Lauterborn[2] and put forward by Philip Kotler[3]:

- Product becomes **Customer needs and wants**
- Price become **Cost to the user**
- Place becomes **Convenience**
- Promotion becomes **Communication**

These Cs reflect the growth since the 1980s of the service-based industries (of which membership is one). They are useful reminders to bear in mind the needs of the members when using the marketing mix. As marketing texts still tend to use the Ps to describe the elements of the mix, we shall continue to use them here. Furthermore, in recent years the four Ps have been expanded to seven to reflect the growth of the service-based industries, by adding:

- **People** (good services are not likely to be delivered by unmotivated people)
- **Process** (the way the service is conveniently accessed, for example at a local church or through the internet)
- **Physical evidence** (the things that you have and hold, such as a magazine, which make your membership benefits tangible)

In 1998, the then RNIB chief executive, Ian Bruce, proposed an eighth P specifically for third-sector organisations:

- **Philosophy** (the mission, vision and values of your charity become part of the reason why people join)

In short, good relationship marketing means ensuring that your target audience truly understands and empathises with your **philosophy** (the vision, mission and your values). As stated in Chapter 3, it means ensuring that your **product** (the membership service and benefits) is in the right **place** at the right **price**. It means effectively telling people about it (**promotion**), providing **physical evidence** of the benefits (a newsletter or other product), being confident that all your organisation's **people** are fully behind it and ensuring that your **process** of joining is user-friendly. Your organisation will be severely compromised in its ability to nurture your prospects into a relationship with your cause if any one of these ingredients, or the mix between them, is wrong.

## The first P is for philosophy

Public trust in institutions has been falling steadily for decades. In 2003, just 18 per cent of the public felt that political parties were "relatively well trusted" and 20 per cent felt the same about the press. At the same time, over 60 per cent saw voluntary organisations as trustworthy.[4]

**Your philosophy, and the way you make it tangible, is a priceless asset to your marketing plan.**

With these trends in mind, your philosophy, and the way you make it tangible, is a priceless asset to your marketing plan. Your vision is for a better world for your target audience. Your membership subscription serves a need, not to generate profit for shareholders. Don't hide your light under a bushel. As noted above, Ian Bruce suggested that third-sector organisations should add **philosophy** to the already well-established seven Ps of the classic marketing mix.[5] As most non-profit bodies are founded out of a missionary zeal to pursue an idea or a belief, this guide places it first in the mix:

*Greenpeace's goal is to ensure the ability of the earth to nurture life in all its diversity.*

*Scope believes that everybody is entitled to share in the opportunities and responsibilities of everyday life.*

*Through membership of the National Women's Register, many individuals discover the ability to face new challenges.*

Anyone who joins one of these membership schemes knows that they are getting much more than just a magazine or a benefit – they are buying into a vision of a better world. Good membership schemes don't bury their host organisation's philosophy in a mission statement and then forget it.

Your mission and your values should be implicit in all your communications. Each and every time a user contacts your organisation, they should be able to see or feel your philosophy in the way your staff and volunteers act, in the design and wording of your publications, and so on. In the next section, we'll explore how your mission and values can be integrated with the more tangible benefits of the membership *product*.

## The second P is for product

For many people, the term 'product' has associations with mass-manufactured goods – cars, baked beans and the like. This guide equates it to the *totality of what your organisation is offering to the prospective member* – your philosophy, your organisation's brand, the cause that you represent, the membership benefits and so on.

It can help to deconstruct your organisation and its membership scheme into a series of *product attributes*:

The cause
⇩
The brand
⇩
The unique reason to join (URJ)
⇩
**THE MEMBERSHIP PRODUCT**
⇧
The incentive to join
⇧
Added value
⇧
Segmentation and choice
⇧
The benefits

We'll now look at how to get these attributes to work together and maximise the appeal of your membership product.

### The cause

As we saw in the previous section on the first P (philosophy), your cause can be a powerful magnet to attract new members. For cause-led organisations such as Anti-Slavery International it will be the primary reason to join. For benefit-led schemes, integrating the cause into the benefits package will boost long-term loyalties.

Once members take the benefits for granted, the cause acts as an incentive to renew.

At RNID, I found that initially most deaf and hard of hearing people joined specifically to get information through the *One in Seven* magazine. We discovered that one reason some of our members were lapsing at the end of their first year was that they had used it to work out a solution to a specific problem – for example, whether to get their hearing aids on the NHS or to buy them privately. So we refined our product attributes by giving greater prominence to our campaigning work. "So much achieved, so much still to do," we said. That way, our membership was repositioned as a long-term proposition, not just a short-term fix. We developed a slogan "supporting us, supporting you" which reminded all our members that their continued support gave RNID the strength in numbers it needed to challenge the outside world to match its vision of a world where deafness and hearing loss is no barrier to opportunity and fulfilment.

**The brand**

Another membership product attribute is your brand. Joe Saxton[6] defines 'brand' as:

> *That nebulous bundle of perceptions that floats in most people's heads about virtually every person and every organisation they come into contact with. That bundle of perceptions, whether justified or unjustified, whether conscious or unconscious, help each of us make decisions every day of our lives.*

**Your brand is the intangible way that your organisation's vision and values come across to the public.**

Saxton likens an organisation's brand to a personality and its brand identity to the clothes that it wears.

In practical terms, your brand is the intangible way that your organisation's vision and values come across to the public – taking in everything from your chief executive's appearance in the media to the way your receptionist handles the calls. The brand identity is the tangible aspects of your name, logo and strapline, your mission statement, your key messages, and the publications house style.

Ultimately it is all about *how other people see you*. The questions that people must ask of their membership scheme are: Does our host organisation have the kind of brand that makes people want to join us? Are we perceived as open, inspiring, accessible or dull, unapproachable and backward looking? For better or worse, the answer will form one of your key membership product attributes.

We all know who the big UK brands are: BBC, Sainsbury's, David Beckham *et al.* The largest membership bodies have concerted programmes to develop strong brand identities – for example, the National Trust and the RSPB. Others, such as the WWF and Amnesty International, are internationally known brands. Yet enjoying a strong brand isn't just about how many £ millions you have. My local corner shop has a strong brand – it is always well stocked, the staff are always polite, helpful, reliable, friendly and they open until late. The sign above the front door isn't particularly sophisticated but it denotes a brand strong enough to attract local shoppers even when nearby supermarket giants offer vastly greater choice and lower prices.

Girlguiding UK is not known as an advertising big spender yet it has a very distinctive brand. Traditional, adventurous, fun, open, welcoming, a reassuring presence at the heart of the community; the brand image now updated with tastefully modern kit and merchandise and made accessible to all in a multicultural society.

Good schemes strengthen their recruitment activities by integrating the fact of having a membership into their overall brand image. Everybody knows the National Trust is a conservation body that welcomes and involves its members. That is partly why so many people join it. Would the National Trust have three million members if its membership scheme were more like a well-hidden secret, as it sometimes is with less brand-savvy organisations? In all too many brands, the very fact that there is a membership scheme at all is subsumed by a mess of conflicting images – of the organisation as a researcher, a service provider, fundraiser or whatever else it does – so that membership seems (and possibly is) peripheral to the mission.

## Exercise: Is your brand attractive to members?

Good brand management is about proactively controlling how the public perceives your organisation, not leaving things to fate. So here are some issues for people who coordinate membership schemes to consider:

- What kind of brand (personality) does your organisation have?
- Is this brand an asset or hindrance to membership recruitment, and why?
- How does your brand identity (the clothes and appearance) fit with your membership product? Think about

your name, logo, strapline, key messages, style of publications, use of written language. Does it all add up? Is it in tune with the kind of image that is attractive to your audience?
- Does your brand identity make membership visible to the outside world – for example via your mission statement, annual report, exhibition stands and the full range of publications?
- Do the key membership people in your organisation have any input into the wider brand strategy? Or, if you don't have anything so grand as a brand strategy, can you influence your trustees or key people on how your organisation is perceived – and maximise your attractiveness to prospective members?

**Find your URJ**

Once you are absolutely clear about the nature of your cause and the brand, you can then focus your prospect's attention on a convincing reason for joining. The marketing industry is awash with jargon – so here's one I invented earlier: the URJ, which stands for unique reason to join. It is, of course, a pastiche of another classic term, the unique selling proposition – USP.

If the term USP is unfamiliar to the average layperson, the practice is omnipresent in their daily lives. A couple of random examples: one of the best-selling factual books of recent times was Stephen Hawking's *A Short History of Time*. It was read by millions of otherwise scientifically illiterate readers, not out of any special interest in quantum physics or quasars, but because a bold campaign persuaded them it was a unique chance to "know the mind of God". On a more earthbound level, Ronseal, caught the popular imagination by promising to do "exactly what it says on the tin!" In both cases, the advertisers' skilful use of USP catapulted their client's product into the public's awareness over hundreds of others jostling for similar attention.

So how do you make your membership scheme stand out from all the other claims on your prospect's time and money? A fine example of how the URJ can be applied with great success is offered by Amnesty International. The charity's mission requires a mental effort to get your head around it. It campaigns on the death penalty, torture, extra-judicial punishments, the rights of refugees and asylum seekers, fair trials and much more. From the Tibetan Buddhists to Nigerian minorities, its remit is worldwide. But its URJ is not human rights – there are plenty of other voluntary bodies with a claim to be active here. The URJ for a great number of its one million plus members was the idea of the pen as a sword of justice. People join not because of any esoteric knowledge of human rights legislation but because joining gives them the chance to fight injustice by writing letters from the relative safety of their home.

Another charity with a beautifully expressed URJ is Gingerbread, which brings lone parent families together. Its URJ is not the network of clubs, the quarterly magazine or the free handbook about bringing children up alone. It is the proposition: "You may be a lone parent but you are not alone."

### Exercise: What is your unique reason to join?

Invite key people to a brainstorming session and list all the attributes of your membership product – the brand, the cause, and the various other benefits that you offer (see below). All these product attributes are among the key reasons why people join your organisation. Now consider which factor(s) stands out above all. Shortlist your candidates for the URJ and test them out on your members, prospective members, staff and volunteers.

Which one exerts the most unique attraction that sets your membership apart from the rest?

**The benefits**

As we saw in Chapter 2, the range of benefits that membership schemes can offer include:

- social opportunities
- access to networks
- time saving and convenience
- privileged access to goods and services
- financial benefits
- value for money
- advocacy support
- representation
- kudos and self-esteem from altruism to others

To be truly user driven, your marketing mix will select and prioritise those benefits which deliver the best fit between the organisation's mission and its members' needs. For example, Amnesty International's mission is *altruistic* – to advocate for human rights. Its members join to help others and to get the benefit of personal satisfaction and self-esteem from helping other people. Because Amnesty's strategic purpose is so clear, its benefits package can be constructed and marketed with the end in mind: to attract altruistic people who seek the personal fulfilment of helping others. There would be no point in Amnesty selecting, say, a financial perk as their primary benefit as this would attract people with motivations at odds with Amnesty's mission.

Even a membership scheme with a strong cause, brand and URJ will invariably need to offer some kind of tangible benefit. As we explored in Chapter 2 on intrinsic motivations for joining a membership scheme, even when giving is the primary motive of the member (for example, to donate to the cause) there is also invariably an expectation of taking some kind of benefit in return. This benefit may be tangible (such as a magazine) or it may be intangible (such as an enhanced feeling of self-esteem for having supported a cause).

Good schemes organise their benefits into a hierarchy. At the apex will be the core benefit such as the membership magazine or yearbook or access to facilities. Secondary benefits are services or products that you include to enhance the overall value of your membership scheme and which are exclusive to your members, but which don't form a primary reason why people join (eg access to a telephone helpline, a welcome pack or voting rights).

### Added value products

Increasingly, good membership schemes are including *added value* products. These benefits are not exclusive to your members, they are also available to other people such as your enquirers. Their inclusion in your membership product acts as a reward for their loyalty. Good examples are affinity goods and services such as own-branded credit cards or discounts on popular brands such as supermarket goods or coach tickets. Many added value products have a financial value and so must be made available to non-members to avoid compromising your membership scheme's Gift Aid status (see Appendix).

### Segmentation and tiers

*Segmentation* divides your overall target audience into different groups so a personal choice can be offered. Membership benefits and fees are then tailored to meet specific needs and wants. For example:

- Individual
- Joint
- Concessionary (unemployed/retired/on state benefits)

- Family
- Life
- Senior citizens
- Young people
- Corporate
- Overseas
- Clubs/branches/societies
- Upgraded (eg committed givers)

Some non-profit organisations are now beginning to tailor packages more sensitively by personal need or by creating tiers that reflect the desired level of commitment to the cause, for example:

- Diabetes UK asks joining members to cite whether they have type A or type B diabetes. Each group receives information specific to its own needs.
- Soil Association has a higher tier of membership plus for people to enjoy standard benefits at the basic rate while also further donating to the cause via monthly direct debit.

**The incentive**

Sometimes known as the 'special offer', you can create an *incentive* by isolating a product attribute and giving it added prominence.

The incentive can range from a handy information booklet to an elegant charity-branded key ring to a 10 per cent discount off the subscription fee if the respondent joins within three weeks of the offer. A well-chosen special offer can boost recruitment by making the prospect feel that he/she is getting something special. You can test different offers and see which work the best.

**Making your product attributes work**

As the following Royal Society for the Protection of Birds (RSPB) case study demonstrates, good membership schemes have a very acute grasp of their product attributes and they underpin their marketing mix to brilliant effect.

## RSPB

In 1889, a society was founded by a small group of people worried about the great crested grebe – threatened with extinction by the millinery trade's habit of removing its head frill feathers for decorating ladies' hats. The feathers could only be taken by killing the birds. It might be hard to credit but that same group today has over a million members.

From its humble origins, the RSPB has grown into an internationally renowned charity with over 180 nature reserves and a huge programme of research, conservation and public campaigns. Its success is no bizarre fluke but a lesson for any membership scheme – large or small – on how to maximise its resources. Consider RSPB's membership product attributes (as promoted in the 2003 Save Our Songbirds campaign) and you'll see how it makes conscious use of all the product attributes listed above.

**The cause**

The RSPB isn't just about birds. It's also about the natural world and how you and future generations can survive and thrive in it.

**The brand**

The traditional and rather tongue-tripping full name (the Royal Society for the Protection of Birds) is now superseded by the elegant short acronym, RSPB. The stylish logo based on the avocet appears on all its key communications, often supported by the strapline *for birds, for people, for ever*. The insertion of *people* in the strapline brings <u>you</u> into the picture (the implicit message; this isn't just about our feathered friends but about meeting <u>your</u> needs too).

**The URJ**

**Join the RSPB and we'll help <u>you</u> turn your garden into a haven for wild birds.**

As a URJ this has all the benefits of combining altruism – the conservation of birds – with the self-interested act of making your back garden a more exciting place to look at. It takes a potentially esoteric cause and brings it right into your back garden. As a URJ, it is simple, memorable and persuasive.

**The benefits**

**From your armchair you can marvel at a breathtaking world of wildlife – anything from the imperious, soaring eagle to a nest of tiny, fluffy blue tits.**

The *core benefit* is surely the quarterly *Birds* magazine – a window to another world for urban dwellers feeling hemmed in by overcrowding, pollution and other ills. You are promised over 100 fascinating pages, award-winning photography, top-name writers. Even if not all of the RSPB's million members actually get out of the armchair and get down to the nature reserve, this is a core benefit that all can have and hold.

The *secondary benefits* include a welcome pack full of information and activities for the family: full details of their 180 reserves; updates on conservation; a gift catalogue; special events; a chance to join the thousands of volunteers supporting the work, and more.

**Segmentation and tiers**

The RSPB has worked hard to segment its package by age, income, geography and the degree of commitment each individual member feels about the cause. The result is an inclusive scheme that offers people a feeling, not of being squeezed into a one-size-fits-all package, but of real choice. People may join as an individual, joint or family member. There is the option to be a fellow – which enables you to support conservation at a higher subscription level or as a life fellow. There is a concessionary rate for up to two adults who, for whatever reason, cannot afford standard rates. Members living in Northern Ireland, Scotland or Wales can opt to receive their own country newsletter. There is also RSPB Wildlife Explorers, the junior section with a dedicated magazine for each of three age groups – *Wild Times* for under eights, *Bird Life* for eight and over, plus *Wingbeat* written by and for teenagers. Finally, there is gift membership to allow members to nominate a relative or friend.

**Added value products**

The RSPB adds value to its core and secondary benefits with a range of special offers – from discounts on leading brand leisure wear and birdwatching equipment negotiated with companies such as Canon (cameras) to green electricity and gas at competitive prices from Scottish and Southern Energy.

**The incentive**
"Join us now and we'll send you this RSPB bird feeder plus enough nutritious seed to fill it. It's got four seed ports so there's room for a crowd of hungry visitors. We'll send you a free guide when you join that will help you identify the wild birds you are helping." The incentive offers instant gratification, the chance to have and hold something tangible that can be used with immediate results.

As the Save Our Songbirds campaign makes clear, the RSPB isn't just about birds. It never was.

## Exercise: Identifying your product attributes

**What are your membership scheme's product attributes? How well do they work together?**
Visualise your product attributes and organise them into a flowchart like this. Do any of the attributes need fine tuning to make them fit better into the overall package? Are the individual attributes sufficiently visible in all your membership promotions?

The cause
⇩
The brand
⇩
The unique reason to join (URJ)
⇩
**THE MEMBERSHIP PRODUCT**
⇧
The incentive to join
⇧
Added value products
⇧
Segmentation or tiers
⇧
The benefits

## The third P is for physical evidence

The idea behind physical evidence is quite simple. It means offering something tangible in return for joining. If a scheme is benefit-led it will usually have very tangible products. When the reason for joining a scheme is more intangible, such as the opportunity to attend discounted training courses, then offering a course brochure, pencils and notepaper for members to keep, a certificate of attendance, are all ways that the benefits can be made more tangible and lasting. When a scheme is primarily about giving rather than taking (see Chapter 2 on intrinsic motivations to join) the immediate benefit may be an intangible one, such as self-esteem or inner satisfaction felt by the member when donating to the cause. However, a well-written and sincere thank you letter sent as a follow-up to the donor equates to physical evidence that augments the intangible benefit.

## The fourth P is for price

Getting the price right is one of the most important issues you will face. Your membership fee has a vital bearing on:

- the strategic positioning of your organisation
- the number of members you recruit
- the size of your profit or loss (or the subsidy)

Yet many non-profit organisations go on little more than gut instinct when setting membership fees and keep them low for fear of alienating the less affluent. This section sets out some of the tools for taking a more objective approach to membership fee structures that maximise your income while keeping your cause accessible to all.

### The cost-plus method

The cost-plus approach aims to set a price that will:

- recover an agreed percentage of the costs
- break even, or
- generate an agreed level of profit/surplus

Which objective is chosen depends on the purpose of the scheme. If it is designed to achieve loyalty and raise commitment, it may be acceptable just to recover an agreed percentage of the costs. The fact that it makes a loss does not undermine its purpose. But if your scheme is aimed primarily at revenue generation, then it clearly needs to make a profit, either by setting fees as high as you can without depressing demand or by keeping costs to a minimum. You can use a spreadsheet package to customise a cost-plus approach and analyse different cost and income scenarios.

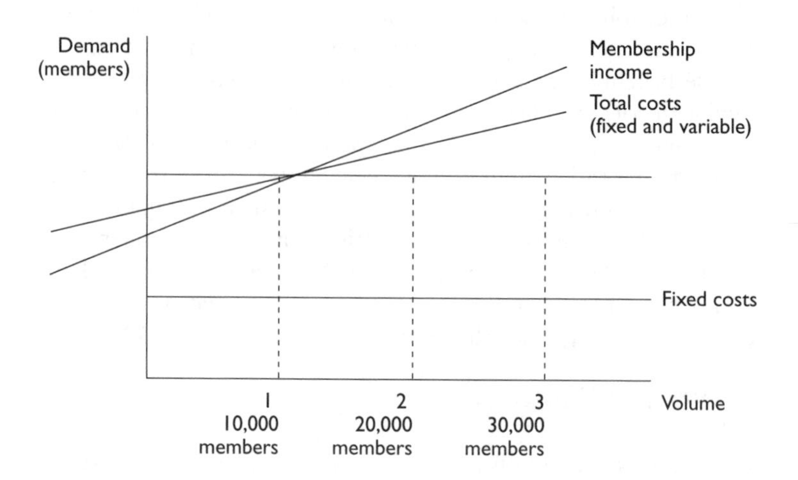


In this example, 1 marks the point where fee income recovers the fixed costs (such as staffing and computers which don't change whatever the number of members recruited). At point 2, all costs are met including the *variable costs* (eg magazine printing and postage costs which increase in line with the volume of members). At point 3, a profit target has been set. This model can be used to ask all sorts of questions such as what happens if we raise the fee by £1, or will we reach break-even faster if we print four magazines a year rather than six?

Many non-profit bodies use the *cost-plus* approach simply because it is easier for them to just measure the costs and take it from there. The pitfall of this approach is that it may fail to take account of a host of other important factors. For example, if a £30 fee is set merely in order to recover the cost of servicing 20,000 members, it overlooks the question of whether members can actually afford it or if they perceive it as good value for money.

**Ideally, membership fees should be reviewed annually.**

Ideally, membership fees should be reviewed annually and include the following inputs.

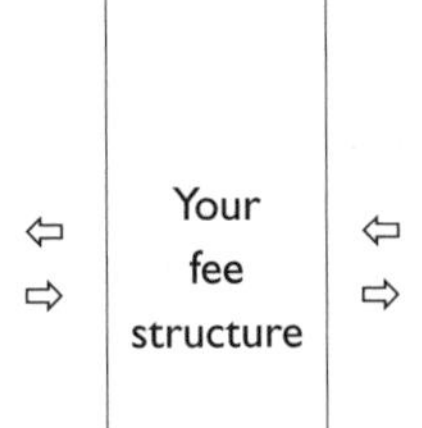

| **Organisational factors** | | Your fee structure | | **Market factors** |
|---|---|---|---|---|
| • Strategic positioning<br>• Marketing objectives<br>• Membership categories<br>• Your other services | ⇦ ⇨ | | ⇦ ⇨ | • Price elasticity<br>• The economy<br>• Perceived value for money |

In determining your membership fees there are two sets of factors to be considered: those directly within your control, the *organisational factors*, and the others outside of it, the *market factors*.

## Organisational factors

### Strategic positioning

If your fees are too high you may be seen as overly exclusive by the very people you wish to recruit. But set them too low and some will wonder whether you really have anything much of value to offer. For example, if a professional membership scheme is to be taken seriously it must be seen as a high quality product for people in a pressurised work environment. The British Association for Adoption and Fostering (BAAF) supports people taking critical decisions on child welfare. In 2003, it set an appropriate price of £67 with a discount for individuals at home. Charging that same price for a scheme that seeks to involve disabled people on low incomes would be self-defeating. The onus here may be on using trading income and fundraising to subsidise the fees.

### Marketing objectives

How do your membership fees sit with your organisation's overall marketing strategy? High prices depress demand; artificially low prices may bring in more members than you can afford to serve. If the objective is to recruit a large supporter and advocacy base to boost your organisation's lobbying clout, then high fees may be counterproductive. But if, like a friends' scheme for a prestigious arts institution, your aim is to maximise income from a small, affluent and highly committed membership, then charging a high price from the outset makes good sense.

### Your membership categories

Another factor in your control is the pricing of different categories in a way that seems logical and fair to your members. There are no golden rules, but in a 2003 survey of 30 organisations carried out for this book, I found that:

- Reduced rate membership (whether for the unwaged, students, retired, etc) was priced at between one-third to just over half of the standard basic rate. The cheapest basic fees had no discounted rate.
- Joint/family membership was 25–100 per cent over and above the individual fee, the most common hike being around a third. At the lower end, this reflects the minimal cost of additional members – for example, the granting of additional voting rights but no other benefit. At the higher end, doubling the price was justified by the more generous nature of the benefits on offer, such as allowing unlimited free entry to heritage or nature sites.
- Life membership was priced at 13 to 27 years' equivalent of a one-year individual membership fee. At the lower end, the average age of members was 50+ and so the actual duration of the life membership itself was shorter and cost the organisation less to service. At the higher end, the members' average age was lower and so the corresponding fee was set higher.

When pricing tiered structures, be careful to differentiate clearly between the fee for each tier: set them too close and people may not perceive them as a tier, set them too far apart and the leap from one tier to the next may be perceived as so great that almost everyone settles on a lower rung.

### Your non-membership products and services

If your organisation also has non-membership goods and services, ideally there will be a coordinated pricing strategy. For example, some non-profit organisations use a free information service to promote uptake of a paid-for membership scheme which is charged at a market rate. Others may price membership as a loss leader – the fee is subsidised – while using it to cross-sell other goods and services that bring in trading income or fundraising revenue.

## Market factors

*Market factors* are those that lie outside your organisation (and so are beyond your immediate control).

### Price elasticity

Classic marketing theory equates monopolies as enjoying inelastic prices (demand for the product is not greatly affected by the price). When businesses face competition, prices become elastic (the higher the price, the lower the demand and vice versa). A good example is how BT was forced into price cutting by deregulation of the telephone market to open it up to new companies. While many non-profit membership schemes enjoy a monopoly within their own field, it is usually more realistic for them to think of competition as being an *alternative source of benefit*. For example, Diabetes UK is the only UK-wide membership body for people with diabetes but it is not the only information provider. It complements the NHS primary care sector and there are many medical websites and commercially published guides to contend with. Among a host of other pricing factors, Diabetes UK's £20 basic rate for 2003 reflects that whatever added value it offers over and above NHS primary care, it is not the sole information provider and like most non-profit membership schemes, its fees are therefore elastic.

### Perceived value for money

Fees should reflect the value of the benefits to members, not just the costs. When economists speak of 'utility' they are referring to the idea that price must reflect the financial value that customers confer upon the product. So think about how your members perceive:

- the *value for money* of the benefits you offer
- the *value of your cause* and how your organisation advances it

The £76 fee charged by the Consumers' Association for *Which?* magazine works well because its subscribers perceive it as good value for money. Its superbly well-researched guides on choosing and using products – from cars to fridges to computers – will save money on household bills over and above the cost of the actual subscription itself.

**Understanding how much the benefits are worth to your members is a good gauge for setting fees.**

Understanding how much the benefits are worth to your members is a good gauge for setting fees. For example, like hundreds of thousands of parents, in 2003 I paid £45 for my daughter to attend her local Girlguiding UK Brownies group. I did so because it seemed an acceptable price in return for enabling my daughter to join her friends and for promoting her confidence and personal development.

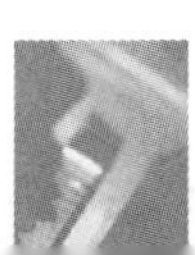

Against this, certain cultural factors affect people's perceptions of value for money. Many people would blanch at paying £45 to join a medical or disability-related membership scheme given the traditional perceptions that their schemes should be cheaply priced, irrespective of their life-transforming value to their members.

### Economic factors

As membership prices are generally elastic, levels of disposable income in your target group may have a significant impact on your recruitment levels. As was apparent during the 1980s and 1990s, cycles of economic boom, wider trends in inflation, state pensions and mortgages can impinge on membership fees as much as they do on charitable donations. When setting your membership fees, you will invariably have to take some account of your members' earnings, the state of the economy and its impact on your members' disposable incomes.

### Donations

On your membership application form, or renewal form, you can facilitate the opportunities for your members to be generous and donate a sum over and above their membership fee. Many members do donate as a way to show their appreciation for the benefits or for the organisation's work for the cause.

### Gift Aid

The UK's voluntary sector received a major financial boost with the government's introduction of the Gift Aid scheme. The scheme applies to all charitable donations from tax payers. On average, it allows the charity to reclaim up to 28 per cent of the donation.

The Inland Revenue has subsequently clarified that membership subscriptions can be treated as a 'donation' providing that the benefits received by the member do not equate to more than 25 per cent of the financial value of the membership subscription. Remember that this is not necessarily 25 per cent of the cost, but 25 per cent of the value. If you qualify, it can increase your membership fee income by nearly a third. Further information is given in the Appendix.

### Conducting an annual fee review

Ideally, all membership schemes should review their fees on an annual basis, irrespective of whether they believe they will actually raise them. This has the virtue of avoiding the price hike syndrome where fees are frozen for several years, either from inertia or caution, and then when costs rise, members are alienated by a sudden price hike.

## Exercise: Annual membership fee review

As can be seen from the above range of variables, there is no magic formula for pricing membership fees. But using the following checklist will help you to structure your own fee review and explain your reasoning to your trustees, staff and members.

You may not be able to fully answer all these questions, but the more you can address the more objective your price review will be.

### Organisational factors

1. When was the last time your fees were increased, by how much and what was the rationale used to justify the rise?
2. Do the fees reflect the strategic positioning of your organisation?
3. Are you clear about the marketing objective of your fee structure? Is it to generate revenue or to facilitate involvement and loyalty?
4. Have you tiered your membership categories to maximise income from the more affluent and committed while still recruiting others?
5. Is this to maximise recruitment or income? Or both?
6. Do you actively manage your members' perceptions of value for money? Do you communicate clearly how their fees support the cause or fund the benefits?
7. Do you, or should you, offer members the opportunity to top up their fees with an optional donation?

### Market factors

8. What is the socio-economic split within your membership base (whether based on informal observation or market research data)?
9. What economic trends impact upon your members and their ability to pay – inflation rate, state benefits, pensions, mortgages, employment status, etc?
10. Who are your direct or indirect competitors? How do they impact on the elasticity or inelasticity of your membership fees?

11. Can you benchmark your fees against others in your field? Are you cheaper or more expensive? How can you justify this?
12. Do your members perceive your service as good value for money? If so, how highly do they value it? Is it a necessity or a luxury for them?

**Gift Aid**

13. Are the membership fees eligible for Gift Aid and if not, why not? What percentage of your members are taxpayers and how many of these have signed a Gift Aid declaration?

The case study below is an example of how the different elements of the marketing mix can be adapted to changing circumstances.

## Soil Association

Soil Association is the UK's leading campaigner for organic food and farming. Founded in 1946, the Association had a low public profile for many decades and was viewed as a niche interest group. Most people weren't even aware that they could join as an individual. It had two basic packages. For individuals, the basic membership package priced at £18 included a quarterly magazine *Living Earth*, recipe ideas, member offers and invitations to special events. Producer membership empowered farmers and suppliers with the quarterly *Organic Farming*, seminars, training events and a helpdesk.

Then in 1999/2000, opportunistic marketing saw a dramatic growth in its public support. The impetus came from two directions. First, the steady rise of public interest in organic food – by 2000 the market was growing at 40 per cent year on year with some 75 per cent of households purchasing some organic food that year. Manufacturers such as Unilever, Heinz and Mars expanded their organic ranges and three of the major supermarkets – Waitrose, Tesco and Sainsbury's – each stocked over 1,000 organic lines. Secondly, the Association's public profile grew rapidly as it contributed to the genetically modified (GM) food debate.

It was an opportunity too good to be missed. The Association altered its marketing mix to maximise fee income and capitalise on its higher profile. The standard membership fee was increased by a third to £24 while a new category was introduced; an upgraded 'membership plus' that combined basic membership with committed giving – priced at £3 or £4 a month (grossing up to £36 to £48 annually).

While the price increase significantly boosted the average income per member, the numbers of new members fell and dipped under the numbers lapsing that year – the Association finished the year 2000/01 with 9,500 members.

By fine tuning the marketing mix once more, the Soil Association recovered from this temporary blip. The product was refreshed with an additional incentive to join: an accessible and thought-provoking booklet *The Truth About Food*. The price remained the same but a drive to boost the numbers of both existing and new members converting to Gift Aid increased the value of two-thirds of subscriptions by a further 28 per cent. A direct debit conversion drive succeeded in boosting retention rates by 6 per cent to 81 per cent. Moreover, the Soil Association increased its membership base to 15,000 by thinking out of the box and rolling out an innovative range of new recruitment vehicles:

- A joint promotion with the ecological cleaning company Ecover (who covered the costs) via 400,000 washing-up bottles that generated 50,000 responses. Ecover saw its sales double during this period while the association recruited 1,900 new members.
- Ongoing cross-promotions with some of the 2,500 food brands licensed to carry the Soil Association kitemark. These brands have a vested interest in turning organic dabblers into committed consumers and saw promotion of the association as a way to foster and strengthen that commitment.
- Inserts in targeted publications at the height of the foot and mouth outbreak.

By now, the Soil Association had learnt that not all people want to join. So it extended the choice of products on offer by introducing a new supporter scheme aimed at those who wanted to support the cause, but didn't want to become a member or receive a regular magazine. These supporters will contribute from £3 to £5 a month, or more if they wish, while receiving only the campaigning newsletter produced for the membership plus category. The income is high but the cost per supporter is lower.

In summary, the Soil Association has transformed its membership and supporter activities into a flexible (and profitable) enterprise that enables people to engage with the cause at different levels of commitment.

## The fifth P is for place

The fifth ingredient of the marketing mix is *place* – the physical location where you actually recruit your members. The art lies in knowing your prospect's lifestyle and values and then prioritising the locations – be it a trade exhibition, doctor's surgery, sports centre or at home, or wherever else they are most likely to be reached. With the growth of direct marketing, place also equates to the internet, email, telephone and post. Many include an organisation's customer service points under the heading of place, so the way your reception, call centre, regional office, etc, handles your membership prospects also has an impact on recruitment.

### External channels

Sometimes the best places to recruit are the most obvious ones, eg a professional teachers' association will naturally recruit through schools and educational conferences. Charities tend to recruit primarily from a captive warm audience of enquirers and service users. But year on year, overdependence on the same channels can limit the scope for membership growth. A little lateral thinking about external channels for recruitment can really help to raise your organisation's profile and reach new audiences.

Take Diabetes UK: while it has always recruited its enquirers and service users, its most significant growth was kick-started in the 1980s when local GPs and practice nurses were encouraged to recommend the charity to their patients. This was no fluke but the result of a long-term strategy to build a long-term relationship with the health sector via a judicious mix of research, policy, awareness campaigns, training and professional seminars. In 2003, Diabetes UK widened its outreach through another third party, the national pharmacy chain, Lloyds, who positioned leaflets on their shop counters – an opportunity that initially arose through the charity's corporate fundraising department.

## Exercise: Where are the best external places?

Think about the different places where your membership promotion could be positioned so people will see it. Here are some examples. Can you add to them?

- At home (via direct marketing – post, email, telephone or personal visit)
- Special interest groups who cover related interests of relevance to your members
- Reciprocal promotions via other organisation's membership schemes
- Shops and shopping centres
- Sports and leisure centres
- GP's surgeries, health centres, hospitals
- Drop-in centres or social services
- Schools, colleges and universities
- Churches
- Public libraries
- Public transport – buses, trains, tubes and stations
- Local or regional newspapers
- Special interest magazines
- Local or regional newspapers
- Nightclubs

In Chapter 6, we will further explore recruitment methods that can be used in these places – from advertising to face to face, from direct marketing to exhibitions – and the pros and cons of forming partnerships with public and private sector bodies.

### Internal places

Are the majority of your offices, services and projects fully accessible to your membership prospects and ready at all times to recruit? This isn't always as straightforward as it might be. Consider these hypothetical scenarios at the Anyshire Nature Trust:

> *A local group of GCSE biology students is due to visit to the Trust's bird reserve. The volunteers have run out of membership leaflets. They are not sure how to order more. A message is left on the head office answer machine. No reply is received.*

*People who ring the Trust's helpline are not informed about the possibility of joining. The information officer says: "It's not in my job description, I don't work for the marketing team. All they want to do is pickpocket other people's money."*

*A busy professional makes a lunchtime call to the switchboard of a charity she wants to join and is placed in a queue. After ten minutes she rings off exasperated. She wonders why the leaflet doesn't show a dedicated phone number for membership applications.*

*In a local charity shop, a prospect sees a membership leaflet in a plastic dispenser on the wall behind the counter. He cannot reach it without asking for help. The counter assistant avoids making eye contact. The prospect is too shy to ask.*

Each of these scenarios represents an internal barrier to joining. In this light, place must take into account:

- the internal distribution of membership materials so that they are in the right place and at the right time;
- internal clarity about the roles and responsibilities of your staff and volunteers to augment your recruitment drives;
- the degree to which your customer services build membership recruitment into their work;
- the physical appearance and convenience of your internal locations and how membership materials are made accessible in them.

The internal places you use might include, but need not be limited to:

- reception areas (in your head and regional offices)
- your customer services
- your organisation website
- your annual report
- your publications
- your annual conference or AGM
- at your open days or events
- your organisation's local branches or group
- at volunteer activities

### Exercise: Where are the best internal places?

Review your organisation's use of internal places to recruit members:

- Do you have a combined plan for positioning your membership product in the maximum number of internal places?
- What are the internal barriers to joining and how can they be overcome?
- Do other head office departments/regional offices/local branches/project workers have the opportunity to suggest other internal activities that might be used to recruit people?
- What are the implications of using more internal places? Producing additional materials? Staff or volunteer training?

This exercise can be surprisingly rewarding and can identify places that you had previously not thought of as recruitment areas. When I worked at RNID, we sent out an internal appeal for ideas; our finance department told us they were happy to attach organisational membership details to invoices and bills to our external clients and companies. For minimal effort, we recruited some new members.

We were contacted by field staff in the more far-flung corners of the UK who attended local events of which we, in our London ivory tower, were simply unaware. These appeals yielded a steady flow of new members because people had been given the chance to proactively suggest ideas and so became recruitment agents themselves.

We will further explore the people aspect of recruiting in external and internal places when we reach the seventh P – *people* – later on in this chapter.

## The sixth P is for promotion

The sixth P, promotion, is how we let our prospects know what we have to offer. A good membership promotion will build on the work done on the first five Ps – philosophy, product, physical evidence, price and place. So before you start writing copy and designing your promotion, gather all the facts together.

## Exercise: Before you draft your promotional copy

**1. Who is your target audience?** For example: Is it deaf people? Or is it all people with a hearing loss including deaf, deafened, hard of hearing people? Are you seeking a broad church or a specific niche group? Will your audience(s) be served by a single member category or by segmented multiple categories or tiers? The answer will affect how you draft your copy.

**2. What are your audience's intrinsic motivations?** Refer back to Chapter 2 and our discussion of the five levels of individual needs and the six most common benefits sought by prospective members.

**3. Who are you?** People don't just buy into a scheme, but into a relationship with your cause. Be clear in your own mind about who you are, your vision and mission, and how you impact on people's lives (see Chapter 2).

**4. What are the benefits of joining?** List all your membership product attributes (see this chapter's section on product). Always remember the difference between your membership features and benefits.

**5. What are the disadvantages of not joining?** How will the prospect lose out by not joining? Can you spell out these disadvantages in an implicit way without alienating people?

**6. What is the unique reason to join (URJ)?** List all the key reasons why your prospects might join. Now organise them into a hierarchy and choose your URJ, the unique reason to join (see this chapter's section on product).

**7. What might be the objections to joining?** List all the possible reasons that your prospect may have for not joining and how your promotion will overcome them (see copywriting section below).

**8. Why might some people object to your fees?** Consider what conscious or subconscious objections people might have to your fees and how to overcome them (see copy-writing section below).

**9. How do you differentiate your organisation from your competitors?** What benefits can you offer that others don't?

**10. Who has benefited from your membership and why?** Can you get quotes from celebrities or specialists to endorse your scheme? Anecdotes from ordinary people can be just as powerful.

**11. What is the reason to believe?** What is your evidence for proving that your membership scheme benefits people's lives? Can you dig out statistics from your market research? Do you keep a happy file of positive emails and letters? A log of campaign successes?

**12. What special offers can you make?** Make a list of inexpensive but attractive ideas (see this chapter's section on product).

**13. How can the risk be managed?** A powerful way to diffuse resistance is to show that there's no risk in joining. Can you do this? (see copywriting section below).

**14. How will it be illustrated?** Some messages may be articulated in writing; others are best communicated visually. How will the text and pictures fit together?

**15. What marketing channels are you using?** Writing promotional copy for a direct mailshot is different from writing it for a website. The way people read a letter is subtly but crucially different from the way they scroll information on a computer screen (Chapter 6 will explore some of these differences in greater detail).

## Copywriting your promotional material

Creativity is fun but your overriding goal is to *get people to join*. Strive too hard for a creative writing award and you may end up writing for the wrong audience. Wrongly chosen puns or too much purple prose may distract your readers and lower the response. You will maximise your recruitment only if the promotion explains the benefits clearly and directly, with no superfluous distractions at all.

**Always communicate with your prospects on their terms, not yours.**

Another key principle is to always communicate with your prospects on their terms, not yours. It isn't what you write, but what your prospect reads that makes the difference. You will already be intimate with your organisation, its cause and the benefits of joining. But don't assume that the prospect is automatically tuned into your wavelength. If your initial question is "How can I create a jazzy promotion and achieve my annual recruitment target?" then theirs will be a very different one: "What do *I* get out of it?"

### Sharpening your promotional copywriting

The following four mini-exercises are all aimed at getting you to see your offer from your prospect's point of view.

### Communicate the benefit

As soon as your prospects look at your recruitment material, they will ask "What and why?" If the answer isn't delivered within seconds, your lovingly crafted materials will be put to one side or binned. So get your benefits across as quickly as you can. All too frequently, third-sector bodies undersell their membership scheme because their promotion only describes the features not the benefits. Your membership magazine, for example, may have 80 pages and be printed in full colour, but this is a feature of the magazine not a benefit to your members. You need to describe how the feature supports the benefit. For example: "80 full colour pages in our handbook make it easy to identify your favourite trees, flowers and shrubs."

## Copywriting exercise (1)

Make a list of the *features* of your membership scheme then write down how you might communicate the *benefits* in a way that is inspiring to your prospects. Here are some examples of how good copywriting has transformed a droll feature into an exciting benefit.

**We have a national network of 300 branches**

*Gingerbread's national network of 300 self-help support groups offers you and your children a welcoming place to meet others in the same situation as you*



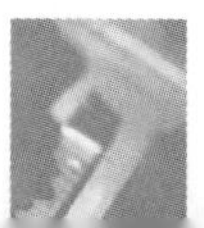

**Our national telephone helpline is open daily from 9am to 5pm**
*Subscribers to Which? also get access to our Members' Helpline – open daily between 9am and 5pm – a telephone service offering up-to-the-minute Best Buy information*

**You'll get a free 92-page membership handbook**
*The ARP/050 free 92-page handbook is packed with authoritative information about the key issues affecting all over-50s*

**Membership gains admittance to the Annual Conference**
*At our Annual Conference, you can hear leading experts or visit over 60 exhibitions with up-to-the-minute technological solutions*

**Stress the disadvantages of not joining**
To help the sale along, commercial marketing often capitalises on the fear of missing out on something vital: "Without life assurance, your family could lose all the comfort of ..." Obviously great care must be exercised before using this kind of hard sell for a third-sector cause. But sometimes it is warranted; for example, without the support of its members the WWF would find it much harder to tackle the grave threat to rare species. In other cases, it is better to state the disadvantages of not joining in an implicit manner, eg by clearly stating the benefits that are unique to a scheme for disabled people, the reader can deduce the disadvantages of not joining.

## Copywriting exercise (2)

Consider if and how the disadvantage of not joining your scheme can be stated explicitly:

*Without the support of people like you, Britain's natural heritage faces catastrophic decline ...*

Or, implicitly:

*We'll ensure that you're kept right up to date about the latest treatments for asthma*

**Removing the objections to joining**

Most people have an inbuilt set of predetermined responses to promotions of any kind. Your materials will trigger them to think: "Do I really need this?", "My problem is not that great.", "I live in Newcastle: what do Indian elephants have to do with me?", "I don't join trade unions/charities." How well you deal with these gut reactions can make the difference between a recruitment success or flop.

## Copywriting exercise (3)

Consider the possible objections that people might have to joining your organisation and how to diffuse them as best as you can. For example:

**It is not worth it to me to join just to get your magazine**
(There are over 500 cameras on the market. Reading our consumer guides saves you time and money when shopping around)

**There's no cure for my medical condition**
(While there is no present cure for X, you'll find our dietary and lifestyle tips can make a big difference to the quality of your life)

**It's too far to visit your caravan sites**
(Whether travelling near or far, we have 800 caravan sites all over the UK)

**I'm not sure this will benefit me – it doesn't seem worth risking the fee**
(If you are not satisfied, you may cancel your subscription at any time in the first six months for a full refund)

**Overcoming price objections**

In our daily lives, we are constantly exposed to demands on our wallet or purse. Exhortations to spend pour out of newspaper advertisements, our television screens, our mailboxes, in shop displays and so on. Our response to all of this has been to develop a natural defense mechanism against any offer with a price tag on it.

Our intuitive reactions on seeing any goods, service, proposition or offer, is "It isn't worth that much to me", "I can't afford that right now", "I've got other things to spend my money on".

Your membership promotion needs to be alert to these intuitive responses and try to disable them. Removing the price barrier is a key goal often best approached by focusing on value for money.

## Copywriting exercise (4)

Consider your membership fee structure and how you can explicitly or implicitly get around people's intuitive objections to paying to get your benefits.

**Can you accentuate value for money?**

For £12, your organisation offers a quarterly magazine about your medical condition, right? Wrong!

*£12 gets you a magazine written by some of the UK's leading experts who have the most up-to-the-minute knowledge on your condition and offer practical advice*

**Can you tap into the prospect's altruism? Even if you have a benefit-led scheme, can you accentuate the cause?**

*In addition to our great magazine and access to local wildlife parks, your fee will support our campaigns to stop industrial development in Britain's green spaces*

**Can you point out any savings to be made? Deflect the reader's mind away from what they will pay by drawing attention to the savings.**

*Our comprehensive guide can help you make the right choices and save you £££*

**Can you quote a weekly or monthly price? If some prospects might baulk at a £30 subscription, then break it down. For example:**

*It's unbeatable value. For as little as £2.50 a month you will be kept right up to date on ...*

If your organisation charges by instalments or quarterly direct debits then you have even more reason to stress this.

**Scanning for ideas**

Another way to sharpen your promotional skills is to observe how others recruit their members. Build up a personal collection of third-sector membership packs (plus a few commercial and public sector ones too). It is not difficult to collect examples and I have over 100 in my personal collection. It's a good way to broaden your knowledge of techniques that can be used. You can cut and paste ideas into your notebook for possible adaptation for your future campaigns. Invariably, the best ones are those that are repeated constantly – because their repeat use means that they actually work.

The caveat is that you must bear in mind that great ideas don't automatically translate from one field or cause to another. You can't judge a promotion by how glossy it looks or by the use of certain techniques. The writer of another organisation's promotion has not been seeking to impress you. A good pack works because it has been written to appeal to a very particular kind of prospect and the words and images have been chosen accordingly. Their prospect may have different values and needs from yours. So do borrow ideas but adapt them to your own unique situation.

**Borrow ideas but adapt them to your own unique situation.**

The following case study gives you an idea of how other promotions can be deconstructed into their constituent elements so that you can sift through them for ideas you might apply to your own situation.

## Case Study – Woodland Trust

The cover of the Woodland Trust's 2003 leaflet (opposite) features a visual pun. It shows a 50p coin and two £1 coins making up £2.50. This is positioned next to branches from five other well-loved British tree species. The caption states "They're all essential for the regeneration of Britain's woodland."

Upon opening the leaflet, **the cause** is quickly and clearly defined: "Right now all over the country, the UK's woodland is under threat. Golf courses, industrial estates, housing, transport; all compete for land with our precious native woods. In fact the UK is one of the least wooded countries in Europe, and since the 1930s almost 50 per cent of what little remained of its ancient woodland has been lost or damaged."

Betula pendula
BIRCH
Quercus robur
COMMON OAK
Fagus sylvatica
BEECH
Sorbus aucuparia
ROWAN
Pinus sylvestris
SCOTS PINE
Argentum necessarium
£2.50
They're all essential for the regeneration of Britain's woodland
WOODLAND
TRUST


Yet not all of us have the time to go to the woods or feel that we can make a difference. So why should we join? The Trust implicitly **overcomes objections to joining** by insisting that: "There are seeds of hope; for just £2.50 a month you can help the Woodland Trust in its fight to save the country's natural heritage."

The next paragraph then gives you the **reason to believe** its effectiveness in championing the cause. It details the Trust's work since 1971 – securing ownership of 47,000 acres of woodland and caring for 1000 woods. It cites recent victories: "SAVED! Ragpath Wood, Durham. People in the former mining community of Esh Winning contacted us because they were worried that they may lose access to the site. The wood was particularly popular at the local junior school who used it as a living resource for geography lessons. After an appeal, the wood was purchased to secure it for the local community forever." Five more campaign victories at sites across England, Wales and Scotland are cited to give the Trust a feeling of relevance wherever the prospect lives.

It follows this with a reason to believe that **you can make an impact.** "By joining the Woodland Trust for just £2.50 a month, you can help us in so many ways; most importantly, for every new member who joins, we can protect and care for another half acre of woodland." The breaking down of £30 into monthly £2.50 increments makes it look more affordable and so implicitly **overcomes the pricing objections.**

**The unique reason to join** is the chance to have a tree dedicated in your name at the nearest available site. "Normally we ask for £10 to dedicate a tree but to welcome you as a new member we are offering this free". This also works as **an implicit donation request** since some joiners will take note of the £10 value and donate this over and above the joining fee.

The Trust also provides **physical evidence** of the benefits via a free welcome pack for the prospect and his/her family when they join. This includes: a colourful woodland wall chart; a directory of Woodland Trust woods; a window sticker; and the first of their regular copies of the news magazine Broadleaf.

**Your trustees, staff and volunteers must really believe in your scheme, be confident in it, be alert to possible membership prospects and know how to inform and persuade people to**

As we discussed in the section on the fourth P – place – all your trustees, staff, volunteers and other supporters are potential membership recruitment agents. When an isolated membership officer or membership team has to shoulder the entire burden of recruiting members, it is a sure sign that the organisation is underachieving its potential for membership success.

Your trustees, staff and volunteers must really believe in your scheme, be confident in it, be alert to possible membership prospects and know how to inform and persuade people to join. When I worked at RNID we assigned a staff officer to be responsible for internal marketing to key staff at all levels of the organisation. Among the tasks were to:

- regularly visit all corners of the organisation – head office and our regional offices – to debrief key staff on membership;
- coach key staff in face-to-face recruitment techniques;
- ensure that key departments knew how to order membership leaflets, distribute them and to restock when they ran out;
- motivate key staff in England, Scotland, Wales and Northern Ireland with monthly bulletins showing the latest membership figures, successes and recruitment drives;

- encourage staff around the UK to feel a sense of shared ownership of the membership recruitment process;
- hold creative thinking sessions to empower other departments to come up with their own ideas for local recruitment drives via local networks;
- recognise others' success, for example, by using a top level management report to thank the receptionist for signing up ten people in the previous month, or sending a bottle of champagne to the most successful recruiting officer in Scotland.

It was not always easy. Many third-sector bodies have higher rates of staff turnover compared with the private and public sectors; we had to organise regular inductions for new staff. Some departments did not always see membership as a key priority when they had pressing targets of their own. Yet getting other departments to buy in was healthy in that it forced us to continually clarify how membership growth benefited all parts of the organisation – in terms of additional revenue, support and service users. It generated many new leads that we had not previously considered. And giving local teams some ownership of the recruitment process went a long way towards releasing untapped creativity and enthusiasm for signing up new members.

### Exercise: Getting people on your side

You might belong to a multi-million pound charity or a local group staffed by volunteers, but the essential question is the same. Is everyone on side, on message and behind our membership scheme? Ask yourselves:

What should we do to get people on our side and keep them motivated to do their bit to recruit members and keep existing members happy? Training? Debriefings? Updates? Recognition or reward systems?

## The eighth P is for process

The last P is process. In short, is the process of joining as simple as possible? Or are your prospects obliged to endure being passed around different departments? Are they required to fill in a form so complex that they lose enthusiasm before actually completing it? The process of joining is just as vital a stage in the marketing process as the initial promotion.

> *Marketing is like a pantomime horse. Front end or back end – creative or response handling? They are mutually dependent. You can target the right product at the right people but if you let them down on delivery you can forget about a long and loving relationship. These problems adversely affect people's purchasing decisions and give them that great negative story to regale their friends with at social gatherings. If we don't get involved in the back-end processes and customer touch points then response rates will not live up to expectations. It isn't sexy and nobody is going to win a prize at Cannes for doing it. But isn't it time we gave these less glamorous aspects the same focus, time and resources that we do for the front end of the horse?*
> (Andy Akerman, quoted in Marketing magazine, 11 September 2003)

If you're uncertain of how easy or difficult it is to join your own organisation, then why not try a spot of mystery shopping?

## Exercise: Conduct a mystery shopping exercise

Mystery shopping is the act of using your own organisation's services without its staff knowing when or where you are testing them for efficiency and helpfulness.

Ask some people to pose as prospective members and apply to join your own scheme – by phone, fax, post, internet or in person.

Try doing this through different routes – at your reception, head office telephone helpline, via a regional office, the website, by email, approaching different departments by phone to see if they are correctly routed to the membership team. See how long it takes for them to get a reply and receive their first membership magazine or pack.

What are the lessons? How can you improve the process of joining?

## Action points

- ✓ Ensure everyone in your organisation is aware that relationship marketing isn't a tainted commercial activity geared to selling people something they don't need. It creates win–win situations so all parties benefit – the cause, the organisation and the members.
- ✓ Make your marketing plan an inclusive process. Get everyone in your organisation behind it – trustees, staff and volunteers.
- ✓ Know and use the eight Ps of the marketing mix.
- ✓ Your cause is one of your most priceless assets. Integrate it into all your membership marketing.
- ✓ Select the benefits that provide the best fit between your members' desires and the strategic purpose of your organisation.
- ✓ Offer a choice; think about the membership segments and tiers that enable you to tailor your benefits to different subgroups within your target audience.
- ✓ Find the unique reason to join (URJ).
- ✓ Make sure that your organisation's brand and brand identity complements your membership marketing, and vice versa.
- ✓ Setting the right price is one of the most important issues you will face. Don't leave it to tradition or opinion. Hold an annual price review and factor in all the organisational and market issues described in this chapter.
- ✓ Provide physical evidence of the benefits of joining.
- ✓ Position your membership promotion in the right places where your target audience will see it.
- ✓ Communicate with your prospects on their terms, not yours. It isn't what you write, but what they read that makes the difference.

✓ Borrow other people's marketing ideas but don't slavishly copy them – adapt them to your unique situation.

✓ Maximise the number of recruitment agents around your organisation – be they trustees, staff, volunteers, or members – and make sure they understand their role.

✓ Flowchart the process by which people join your organisation, then streamline it and make it as easy as possible.

---


1. McCarthy, E J (1998) *Basic Marketing: A Managerial Approach*, McGraw-Hill
2. Lauterborn, R *New Marketing Litany: Four Ps Passe: C-Words Take Over*, Advertising Age 61 (41) 26, 1990
3. Kotler, P (2003) *Marketing Management*, Prentice Hall
4. Eurobarometer, quoted in *Voluntary Sector Strategic Analysis* 2003/04, NCVO, 2003
5. Bruce, I (1998) *Successful Charity Marketing*, ICSA
6. Saxton, J (2003) *Polishing the Diamond*, nfpSynergy


---

# 6 Recruitment

## This chapter covers:

This chapter covers:

- Cross-marketing via your own services and activities
- Member get member (MGM) recruitment
- Recruitment planning and evaluation
- Direct mail
- E-marketing
- Partnership with public services
- Partnership with private companies
- Media and public relations
- Events and exhibitions

For most membership schemes, no single marketing channel will reach all membership prospects. The widest possible audience can only be reached using a range of different marketing methods. Yet many schemes are still promoted using little more than word of mouth or leaflets given out in face-to-face situations. This chapter surveys a wider range of marketing channels along with the planning and evaluation methods used to justify investing in them.

The most common marketing channels for growing membership support fall into three broad areas:

- **cross-marketing**: using your organisation's other services and products such as your website, publications, customer services, your own members, etc;
- **direct marketing**: contact is made directly with a named individual – for example, using the post, email or telephone;
- **media and public relations**: indirect contact is made using newspapers, magazines, conferences, exhibitions and events. You may not know the individual but will have a good idea of the target audience.

## Cross-marketing

The term *cross-marketing* (or cross-selling) refers to promoting your membership scheme through your organisation's own services and communications. For example:

- your reception areas (in your head and regional offices)
- your customer services
- your website
- your annual report
- your publications
- your annual conference or AGM
- your open days or events
- your organisation's local branches or group
- your volunteers

Cross-marketing has two great virtues. First, it reaches out to the very people who are most likely to join – your visitors, service users, clients, beneficiaries, enquirers, donors and so on. This is your so-called warm audience. People who have contacted your organisation will already be aware of your cause and what you have to offer. They are more likely to be interested in your membership than a cold audience, those who don't know you or your cause and have yet to be educated about it.

Secondly, it is generally the most affordable option too. You will still need to invest in a budget for some good membership materials and you will also need to carry out internal marketing with staff and volunteers to ensure they are appropriately briefed and motivated to recruit (see Chapter 5 on the seventh P for people for more detail on this).

### Your website

According to a *Third Sector* report on 21 January 2004: "a typical charity website recruits only 18 new donors in a year". At the time of researching this book, observation suggested that internet-based membership recruitment was at a much higher level because most websites are information-driven, and information enquirers have always been a warm source of members. For example, a person who logs on to seek enlightenment about a disability, say, is quite likely to want to join to keep up to date.

In the future, internet-based membership recruitment looks set to grow exponentially along with the year-on-year increase in home ownership of PCs (and the spread of faster broadband access). In time, it may even become the dominant recruitment channel. Yet few third-sector websites are as effective as they could be. Many are organised in an insular way, structured by the organisation's departmental boundaries rather than by the user's needs or wants. You'll often find a section on fundraising, one on campaigns, one for services, and so on. In an informal survey for this book, some websites failed even to flag up the membership option on the home page and one required five page clicks to navigate to the membership coupon. That said, website designs are rapidly improving as the third sector becomes more internet savvy. To run a health check on yours, ask the following questions:

- Is it explicitly clear on your website home page that you are a membership organisation?
- Have you ensured that it takes no more than two clicks to get to the membership page?
- Is the membership page laid out in a way that excites people sufficiently to want to join?
- Do your web pages have the same impact as your best piece of direct mail or recruitment leaflets?
- Are hyperlinks placed at strategic points around the website – for example, to lead naturally from the news, information or campaign section through to the membership page?
- Do you place the right amount of information on the site to attract members? If your website contains none at all, your prospects may perceive that you don't have any news or information to offer and will see no point in joining. On the other hand, if you are marketing a paid-for membership scheme and your site is top heavy with hundreds of pages of detailed news and information, it becomes self-defeating; people won't join because they perceive that your website already meets their needs (for free).
- Have you explored links with other websites read by your target audience and negotiated the placement of hyperlinks that lead from these sites straight through to yours (and vice versa)?
- Do you have the resources to keep the website continually up to date? An outdated or rarely updated website with inaccurate details is a real disincentive to join.
- What process do you adopt to handle international enquiries? Lest we forget, the acronym www stands for world wide web. It is an international medium and you may be likely to attract overseas visitors. Do you have an overseas rate for them? Do you need/want them?
- How do you handle the inevitable emails? Your prospects may have questions to ask before they join. With a postal letter they'll expect a few days delay. With email people have

higher – if unrealistic – expectations of a same day reply. Minimise this by pointing visitors to a frequently asked questions (FAQ) section. Add to the list as each new query comes in.

- Do you have a secure server? People won't, nor should you expect them to, entrust credit card payment over the internet without one.

### Member get member

Member get member (MGM) quite simply involves asking each of your members to introduce someone else to your organisation. Depending on the cause or the benefits, you may encourage them to recruit a relative, friend, neighbour or work colleague. MGM is widely used, and for most local groups it is probably their dominant recruitment channel. My son joined his local cricket club because the father of one of his school mates handed me a leaflet about the club. Ditto my daughter when she joined the Brownies. In turn, both of them introduced their school classmates. The beauty of this is that your members can reach out to parts of the community that you cannot. Some tips:

**Members can reach out to parts of the community that you cannot.**

- Place MGM forms in your magazine where they will be seen. Get your chief executive, editor or group leader to back this up with an editorial or appeal to readers to take action.
- If you are a cause-related body make a clear but simple appeal: "each new member you recruit helps to strengthen our lobbying clout".
- Can you appeal to your members' altruism? "Think about how much you have benefited from your membership. Do you know someone else whose life could also be transformed by it? If so, please make their day by handing this form to them and explaining how they could benefit too."
- Some organisations incentivise their appeal by offering a reward for each new member introduced. The reward shouldn't be extravagant – a £5 supermarket voucher or a key ring is fine. If this sounds costly, it might still be justifiable if it is cheaper than other methods such as direct mail.
- Not all your members will know of someone who is a prospect. You can also appeal to them to leave a leaflet where it will be seen – for example, in a doctor's surgery waiting room or site appropriate to your target audience.

## Investment, planning and evaluation

The use of direct marketing, media and public relations to recruit new members is one of the third sector's most underused tools. Outside of the largest organisations, most membership schemes still recruit by little more than word of mouth or by handing out leaflets. Even those schemes that represent a strong cause and have a good product generally don't invest in marketing because it is perceived to be expensive. Fear of failure creates a vicious circle. Without financial investment in marketing there is no growth. Without growth there is no perceived justification for a marketing budget.

The key to unlocking this mental block is to look at marketing as an *investment*. That is, an investment that brings in future revenue for the organisation or an increased level of support and advocacy for your cause.

Your marketing investment might be £10,000 or £100 but there is little point in investing it without some form of ongoing evaluation to measure the *return on investment* – financial or otherwise. So before we explore direct marketing, media and public relations methods in more detail, we'll take a brief look at planning and evaluation techniques.

### Different evaluation models

Any case you make for setting aside a membership marketing budget has to address the question: "Will it pay for itself?" There are three different ways of planning and evaluating your marketing:

- **Return on investment** (**ROI**) which looks at the costs and income of the individual promotion to evaluate its financial cost effectiveness.
- **Lifetime value analysis** (**LVA**) which measures your organisation's costs and income against the lifetime of each individual's membership.
- **Cost-benefit analysis** (**CBA**) which considers marketing costs against the wider benefits (and is more typically used for subsidised membership schemes that make a financial loss).

From a local newspaper advertisement to a stall at a trade exhibition, the key principle is that the data for all your marketing activities must be collected in the same format so that genuine like-for-like comparisons can be made between each activity.

Typically this will include:

- Type of marketing channel used (eg direct mailshot)
- Details of individual promotion
- Size of audience reached (no.)
- Members recruited (no.)
- Response rate (%)
- Cost (£)
- Income (£)
- Profit/loss (£)
- Return on investment (how many £s earned for each £ spent)
- Cost per member (£)
- Income per member (£)
- Profit/loss per member (£)

Once you analyse all your recruitment activities in this way, you can then focus your investment – time, money or resources – wherever it is most cost effective.

**Return on investment (ROI)**

ROI is principally concerned with the financial return on your marketing. In the example below, a charity paid a women's lifestyle magazine to carry its membership flyer as an insert. The magazine had a circulation of 400,000. However, the charity's board, unsurprisingly, considered it too risky. The manager then proposed conducting a test: 40,000 flyers were inserted into a random sample that recruited 200 members. Each joining member paid a £20 subscription and £4,000 income was raised. This equated to a 0.5 per cent response at a cost of £2,000. On this analysis, the promotion generated a 1:2 return on investment, ie for each £1 spent, £2 was earned. Therefore, the insert was profitable.

| Marketing channel | Women's lifestyle magazine |
|---|---|
| Promotion | Membership flyer insert |
| Size of audience reached | 40,000 |
| Number of members recruited | 200 |
| Response rate (%) | 0.5% |
| Cost @ £50 per 1000 inserts (£) | £2,000 |
| Income @ £20 per member (£) | £4,000 |
| Profit/(loss) – (£) | £2,000 |
| Return on investment (ROI) | 1:2 |
| Cost per member (£) | £10 |
| Income per member (£) | £20 |

After this test, the case was made that all things being equal, the charity would recruit 1,800 members and get a profitable 1:2 return if it chose to invest a further £18,000 by inserting a flyer into the remainder of the magazine's 400,000 circulation the following month. Without the test, that decision would have been perceived by the board of trustees as simply too risky and a hugely rewarding promotion would simply not have happened at all.

In the second example below, the same charity attended an exhibition as a prelude to booking into a rolling programme of ten regional exhibitions. As with the lifestyle insert test, the cost of the exhibition was £2,000 but the result was different.

| Marketing channel | Regional exhibition |
|---|---|
| Promotion | Exhibition stand |
| Size of audience reached | 10,000 |
| Number of members recruited | 100 |
| Response rate (%) | 1% |
| Cost for stand, materials, travel, etc | £2,000 |
| Income @ £20 per member (£) | £2,000 |
| Profit/(loss) – (£) | £0 |
| Return on investment (ROI) | 1:1 |
| Cost per member (£) | £20 |
| Income per member (£) | £20 |

This ROI analysis shows that while the promotion broke even, it was not as cost effective as the women's lifestyle insert. The £20 cost per member is twice as high. Therefore the charity's board agreed to the manager's recommendation that the remainder of that year's £18,000 budget be spent on a national rollout of the women's lifestyle magazine insert.

**Lifetime value analysis (LVA)**

Lifetime value analysis (LVA) is a useful tool for assessing the long-term financial case of investing in a promotion. For example, if the ROI analysis shows a financial loss in the first year of an individual's membership, the cost may still be justifiable so long as that same individual's second year of membership is profitable for the organisation. LVA works by extending the ROI to a second year, and beyond, and measuring all the costs and income attributable to each member over the lifetime of his/her membership.

For example:

**LVA for reciprocal charity mailing**

| **Year 1** | |
|---|---|
| Marketing channel | Reciprocal charity mailing |
| Promotion | Direct mailshot |
| Size of audience reached | 10,000 |
| Number of members recruited | 100 |
| Response rate (%) | 1% |
| Marketing cost @ 40p per pack | £4,000 |
| Service cost @ £5 per member | £500 |
| Total year 1 costs | £4,500 |
| Subscriptions @ £20 per member | £2,000 |
| Donations @ average £5 per member | £500 |
| Total year 1 income | £2,500 |
| Year 1 profit/(loss) | (£1,500) |
| Return on investment (ROI) | 0.55:1 |
| **Year 2** | |
| Renewal rate at 90% | 90 members renewed |
| Renewal cost @ 40p per pack | £40 |
| Service cost @ £5 per member | £440 |
| Total year 2 costs | £480 |
| Subscriptions @ £21 per member | £1,890 |
| Donations @ average £6 per member | £540 |
| Total year 2 income | £2,430 |
| Year 2 profit/(loss) | £1,950 |
| | |
| Lifetime profit/(loss) | £450 |

In year 1, the ROI shows that 100 members were recruited at a loss of £1,500. However, in year 2, 90 per cent of the members renewed their subscription at a profit of £1,950. By aggregating the year 1 and year 2 profit/loss figures, the average lifetime value of the 90 renewing members is now in profit by £450. When members are recruited via direct marketing, it is not unusual to see a loss in year 1 of a person's membership and a profit in year 2. In year 1, the promotional costs must factor in the wastage of sending promotions to a very large number of non-responders. In year 2, the much lower renewal cost (where only the actual members are contacted) and the correspondingly higher response rate mean that a profit is generated.

Whether the £450 profit cited in this example makes for an acceptable year 2 lifetime value will depend on the organisation's marketing objectives. For example, if the aim is to build a large resource base of volunteers, the LVA shows this can be done without incurring a long-term financial loss. But if it is to create an income stream, the profit may be too marginal to really benefit the organisation's wider cause. Either way, the LVA analysis is a highly useful aid for taking long-term investment decisions on your membership recruitment strategy.

**Cost-benefit analysis (CBA)**

A third measure for evaluating your ideas is cost-benefit analysis (CBA). This was first used in the USA to inform budget decisions for civil engineering projects such as dams or major roads. Huge or irrecoverable sums of public sector money were involved, so civil servants were concerned to measure the project costs against the value of public benefits they delivered. The same concern applies to free or subsidised membership schemes. When marketing invariably makes a loss, ROI and LVA analyses aren't of much help. A cost-benefit analysis may be more appropriate as it will contrast the costs against both tangible and intangible benefits to your organisation.Tangible benefits may include factors such as increased donations. Intangible relate to things like boosting your organisation's lobbying strength. Public sector CBA models are very complex; this guide offers a simplified version for practical use in evaluating subsidised or loss-making activities. The next example (overleaf) relates to a local group exhibiting at their town's charity fair. On a budget of £500, their marketing objectives were to double their membership figures to 100 individuals with two aims in mind: i) to increase the number of volunteers for a local heritage project, and ii) to make the group more attractive to grant makers.

| Marketing channel | Town hall exhibition |
| --- | --- |
| Promotion | Exhibition stand |
| Size of attendance at fair | 5000 |
| Number of members recruited | 50 |
| Response rate (%) | 2% |
| Tangible costs (£) | £500 for fees, materials, travel, etc |
| Tangible benefits | • 50 new members<br>• £250 in future donations (past trends show that each new member gives an average £5 in the first year)<br>• 25 new volunteers (past trends show that half of all joiners later become active volunteers)<br>• 270 signatories to campaign petition (from non-members)<br>• 14 introductions to local businesses (and potential future sponsors) |
| Intangible benefits | • Doubling membership increases the group's appeal to funders and sponsors<br>• In future, will be seen by local media as a more represen-tional voice |

Against the £500 loss, the CBA shows a significant number of tangible benefits. The group's past records indicate that once people sign up and read the group's quarterly campaign bulletin, they became more committed and go on to donate on average £5 each to the cause. With 50 recruits it forecasts £250 in donations during the coming year, offsetting half of the exhibition cost. Previous results indicated that around half of the recruits would also become active volunteers. The stand generated 270 signatories to the campaign petition and introduced 14 local business contacts as potential sponsors. Doubling the group's membership size brought intangible benefits too: an increase in their attractiveness to local funders and sponsors, plus a boost to their future credibility to local media as a representational voice.

**Whichever method of planning and evaluation you are using, the key principle is that you must apply them consistently across all your marketing methods.**

Whichever method of planning and evaluation you are using, the key principle is that you must apply them consistently across all your marketing methods or the comparisons will most likely be invalid, thus making your investment decisions unreliable.

## Direct mail

Direct mail is a popular and cost-effective channel for recruiting members. The classic A4-sized letter gives you the time and space to explain the benefits and the wider mission of your cause. A typical mailing pack will usually consist of some or all of the following elements:

- an outer envelope
- a covering letter
- a supporting leaflet with the membership offer
- a response coupon
- a pre-paid business reply envelope (BRE)

Direct mail can be ideal for large and small organisations alike because you can:

- contact more people than you normally reach on a face-to-face basis;
- control every aspect of the message;
- target your mailshots by only choosing, or compiling, lists of people who are most likely to be interested in your membership;
- use computer mail merge to personalise messages to different segments of the mailing list;
- test different packs to see what does and doesn't work before committing to significant expenditure;
- immediately measure your return on investment (ROI).

Against this, there are severe challenges to overcome. Marketing messages of all kinds have reached saturation point. The internet, smart shopping cards, sophisticated customer databases, telemarketing equipment, huge data warehouses and cost-effective print solutions have all created tremendous opportunities for commercial, public and third-sector bodies alike. But the onslaught of all kinds of messages has numbed people's receptivity to them. In particular, most direct mail is now viewed as junk mail and most people bin it promptly after barely glancing at it. *The challenge is to make sure that your mailing pack stands out from all the other marketing messages, and goes only to people who would be genuinely interested in your scheme.*

The following tips on good direct mail packs can be read in conjunction with the copywriting your promotional material section in Chapter 5.

Grab the reader's attention within the first few seconds and then take them on a journey – from your organisation's cause to the coupon form – with no distractions whatsoever. Typically, this involves:

- an outer envelope that immediately seizes the prospect's attention
- a persuasive letter that convinces the prospect to take action
- a supporting leaflet to give further details of your membership offer
- an easy-to-complete response coupon
- a handy business reply envelope

**The outer envelope**

When your prospect sees the outer envelope hit the doormat, the next few seconds are critical. The prospect scans it – taking in the image, slogan, the look and feel of the envelope – before deciding whether to open it, leave it to one side or bin it immediately. So first impressions really count. Common attention grabbers used on the outer envelope might include one or two of the following:

- The brand: your organisation's logo, vision or mission
- The teaser: "Opening this envelope will transform your life"
- The proposition: "Don't let asthma rule your life"
- The appeal: "Help save our rainforests"
- The offer: "Join today and save £££"

You also need to decide whether or not the outer envelope should openly communicate the identity of your organisation and the contents of the pack. For example, a pack which carries the proposition "Helping teachers cope in the classroom" will be opened by almost everyone on a list of teachers receiving the enclosed membership offer. Had that same pack carried a teaser: "Opening this envelope will change your life" many of those same teachers would mentally dismiss the pack as junk mail and throw it away without looking inside.

In other instances, it is preferable that the identity of the organisation and the pack's contents are not immediately obvious on the outer envelope. For example, an invitation to join a local gym will be promptly thrown away by people who have an instinctive aversion to the idea. But the use of an outer envelope teaser, such as "How to shed lbs, lbs, lbs without losing £££s" will persuade many recipients to open the pack.

### The letter

Once you have persuaded your prospect to open the outer envelope, you've cleared the first hurdle. The key to a good letter is that it is immediately clear and easy to read. Each paragraph should be kept to a maximum of around six lines in length. The text can be broken up with a number of devices (used in moderation) such as:

- Paragraph headlines
- Indents
- Bullet points
- Italicised text
- Underlined text
- Colour highlights
- Dots
- Dashes

**Take a step back and see it from your prospect's viewpoint.**

Your letter must take the prospect on a clear journey – just one vague instruction and you've lost him or her. How often do you get it right first time when a stranger asks for directions? "When you get to the park, go to the traffic lights and turn left and ... No? OK, we'll start again. If you see that park over there..." You often have to rephrase the instructions because the stranger doesn't have your intimate knowledge of the area – and the same applies to a membership offer. You know your own scheme intimately because it's your job to promote it. But you must also take a step back and see it from your prospect's viewpoint. As you embark on the journey from the unique reason to join all the way to the coupon, you must make yourself clear from the outset and not lose your prospects along the way.

There is, of course, no one-size-fits-all template for a marketing letter. But the sample below, for the fictitious Asthma XYZ, illustrates some of the principles of good practice.

The following sample letter embodies sound relationship marketing principles:

- Mail merging the recipient's name and address into the letter personalises it.
- The use of the pronouns 'you' and 'your' further enhances the feeling of being spoken to on a personal level.
- It shows empathy with the prospect's needs and wants and touches on several levels of Maslow's hierarchy of needs (see Chapter 2).

- It clearly links the prospect's needs and wants to the benefits on offer.
- It appeals to altruism; the prospect's membership will strengthen the wider campaign for a better deal.
- It reduces the risk of joining – the prospect gets two free issues before the membership fee is deducted.
- It incentivises the offer – with a free booklet.
- It carries a deadline – to speed up response and to pre-empt people from thinking about it later.

Common sense tells us that people lead busy lives and can't make time to read long letters, so keeping your membership offer brief, eg to a single-sided A4 sheet, has the best chance of success. However, the direct marketing industry knows that longer letters invariably get a better response than short ones. As with much of best practice, it seems to defy common sense but is confirmed by the widespread testing of any new mail pack against a control pack (your current highest achieving mail pack) to compare the response it gets before making any judgement. The rationale for the success of longer letters is that the more you put in the more your prospect will get out of it. The key principle is not: 'People are too busy these days to read a long letter', but rather: 'How much do I need to put in to really persuade those few genuine prospects who might actually join?'

**Asthma XYZ**

Mrs Smith
2 Acacia Avenue
Anytown AN3 6TJ

1 September 2004

Now you can have independent reports on all the developments about asthma, every two months. Accept a free trial issue of Asthma XYZ today.

Dear Mrs Smith

Breathlessness – wheezing – discomfort. Whether you have mild or severe asthma, we understand the anxiety it can lead to. You may have just recently acquired asthma or had it for many years. Either way, our mission is simple: we're here to make life easier!

You may be familiar with the recent media stories about the causes of asthma and the search for a cure. You've heard the competing claims made for a myriad range of products and services. You may understandably feel that all these highly selective stories simply add to the confusion. More than ever before, there is a need for a more complete picture, a source of independent help and advice – be it in the short term or the long term.

Have you ever thought: "What I need is a source of news, information and practical tips that I can trust absolutely"?

The source needs to look at every single option, not just the ones the media selects. And it must be an expert source that truly understands people with asthma.

Asthma XYZ is that source. Every two months, we can bring you the latest news and stories ... in-depth reviews of medical and lifestyle options – all aimed at helping you make the right choices.

I would like you to have the chance to see for yourself how Asthma XYZ can be your personal source of insight, ideas and inspiration.

So you won't have to take my word for it, we can offer you a free four month trial of Asthma XYZ.

Just complete the offer form enclosed today and we will send you your first trial issue.

You will also get a complimentary copy of *I Did it My Way* written by world-famous race jockey Johnny Castle, who explains how he refused to allow asthma to stop him from leading an active life.

**We're more than just another media story ...**

No one is better placed than Asthma XYZ to give you clear and independent coverage. We have over 100 staff and employ a unique combination of medical experts, researchers and lifestyle columnists - some of whom have asthma themselves and know intimately what it is like. We are independent of commercial interests.

... and much more than just a magazine ...

When you get your regular copy of Asthma XYZ you'll be more than just a reader. You'll become part of a 30,000-strong movement that is championing the cause of asthma. Your membership of Asthma XYZ will give us the strength in numbers that our campaign team needs as we push the government for more research into the causes of asthma and ways of alleviating it. Your membership will help us to keep up the pressure on the NHS health authorities to deliver good services.

... all this for less than £2 per month.

At just £25 a year, your membership of Asthma XYZ works out at less that £2 per month. A small price to pay for the peace of mind which comes from knowing you're not alone.

Send off the enclosed form today to be sure you're not missing out on all the news that the media doesn't cover.

Yours sincerely

Alastair Malone
Editor

PS Reply by 22 September 2004 and you'll get a free copy of *I Did it My Way* by Johnny Castle. It is not available anywhere else in the UK and is yours for free.

**The leaflet**

The leaflet plays an essential supporting role to the letter by:

- illustrating the benefits such as the magazine's cover, booklets, products and services, sites, venues and showing

members already enjoying the benefits
- detailing your organisation's successes
- using testimony from satisfied members

**Last but not least ... the coupon**
Too often the coupon is treated as an afterthought – a box you stick at the bottom of the page. Something to get around to once the creative work is done. In fact, it is one of the most important aspects of your promotion.

It is not unknown for a designer to create a fantastic piece of graphic design and yet allow so little space for the coupon that the prospect has only tiny lines and boxes in which to write. If your prospects see a coupon that looks awkward or daunting to fill in, they'll be tempted to put it aside and deal with it later and then not complete it all.

- **Ease of use:** the coupon should be quick and simple to complete. The longer and more complex the coupon, the more likely it is that some prospects will be deterred from completing it.
- **Only capture essential information:** the only reason for including a question on the coupon is if the answer is absolutely essential to you. If you wish to collect further demographic information such as age and gender, it may be best to try to collect it later by other means, eg a questionnaire form enclosed with your welcome pack or via your annual membership survey. Put simply, the more boxes the prospect has to fill in when joining, the more intimidating the form becomes.
- **Don't forget the email address:** even if you don't do emailings right now, you may want to at some point in the short to mid-term future. It will be a hassle to go back and ask for it again.
- **Print capitals:** a major headache for fulfilment teams is having to interpret spidery handwriting. Ask your prospect to complete the form in block capitals.
- **Limit payment options:** do offer a choice of paying by cash, cheque or direct debit, but be wary of including too many options.
- **Keep the coupon separate:** in a direct mail pack, keeping the coupon separate from the letter will allow the reader to send in the coupon while retaining the pack for information. If the coupon is attached to a leaflet, or the rest of your pack, use dotted lines to indicate where it should be cut.

- **Be transparent:** ensure that your offer is clear and unambiguous, and summarise it within the coupon. For example: "Yes, I would like to become a member of XYZ and get my regular copy of the magazine."
- **Offer an order hotline number:** so that people can ring, fax or email their subscription straightaway. Many people prefer to do this rather than rely on snail mail.
- **Data protection:** ensure your coupon is compliant with relevant data protection legislation and that you are familiar with the latest requirements.

### The reply envelope

In the first few seconds after opening your pack, the presence of a reply envelope sends a subliminal message to your prospect that you are striving to make it as easy as possible for them to join. The evidence is clear and there is no dispute: enclosing a reply envelope will lift your response.

A pre-paid business reply envelope (BRE) is the ideal as it removes the cost of a stamp as one of the obstacles to joining. Some organisations may invite respondents to place a stamp over the pre-printed area with a statement such as "It is not necessary to affix a stamp, but using one will save us money and enable us to devote more of your membership fee to the cause." For smaller groups, even a plain envelope is better than none at all.

### E-marketing

At the time of this guide going to press, electronic marketing – or e-marketing – is full of hype and future promise. It offers many of the traditional features of direct mail, but at a fraction of the cost – you don't have all those print costs, envelopes and stamps to pay for.

## Case study – WWF-UK

In 2003, WWF-UK dipped its toe in the e-marketing water with marked early success. On a monthly budget of £20,000, it paid for banner ads on carefully chosen websites whose content and ethos were appropriate to the WWF brand. It negotiated cost-effective prices through last-minute online space and cut deals with search engine providers to sponsor keywords such as 'wildlife' and 'tiger'. A two-month test yielded 130 new members per week. The email featured a punchy headline – "A quarter of mammals face extinction within 30 years" – superimposed on a bold graphic of a rhino. The subject line – Take Action for a Living Planet – was clearly not an invitation to purchase Viagra. A pale green backdrop instantly differentiated it from the usual domestic or spam emails and the call to action was hyperlinked to a joining coupon. Following the initial test, a wider rollout brought in a further 5,000 new members.

As e-marketing is still a relatively new branch of marketing, best practice principles have yet to emerge. But in essence, the challenge is the same as for more traditional direct marketing routes; you must grab the reader's attention within the first few seconds. The key ingredients are:

**The challenge is the same as for more traditional direct marketing routes; you must grab the reader's attention within the first few seconds.**

1. **Use a clear and transparent address.** This is critical since spamming has made people wary of opening emails from people they don't know.

2. **Choose the subject line with great care.** It should be absolutely clear what the email is about. The use of teasers (You'll love this offer ...) may still work in certain direct marketing contexts but will be fatal in e-marketing – it invites suspicion that it may be from the usual peddlers of get-rich-quick schemes and the like. Some people have preprogrammed detectors to filter out emails whose subject lines contain certain words. This aspect is so critical that some organisations run controlled tests on four or five different subject lines before rolling out their emails to larger numbers of people.

3. **Keep the content short.** Long and wordy emails just won't get read. Traditional direct marketing – letters and leaflets on a double-sided A4 sheet – is fairly easy to scan as your eye runs up and down the sheet and you flip it quickly from front to back, taking in key headlines and messages in seconds. With the same piece of direct marketing on a computer screen, the recipient only sees part of the content and must scroll up and down to digest the whole. It is better to create a journey where the email gives just the headline facts and then prompts the reader to click through to your website to get the detail.

4. **Get the format right.** Use plain text, HTML or Rich Media which allows for rather more lively colours and/or animation. Be sure to establish if your recipients can access your graphics or the impact will be lost. However, the majority of computers will now happily deal with HTML.

5. **Use personalisation.** What chance have you got of persuading your membership prospect to join if you've reduced them to an email address or reference number?

6. **Do repeat mailings at sensible intervals.** Repeat mailings are often more successful than one-off ones. The low cost of email versus traditional print and post creates an obvious temptation to rollout a series of repeat emailings, but don't overdo it. Weekly is too often, once a year means the recipient won't recall the previous one. Monthly or quarterly is probably about right.

E-marketing holds out exciting possibilities, but be sure you're up to speed with data protection regulations. When your prospect clicks on the email he/she must have been expecting it, otherwise you will be in breach of the UK regulations introduced after an EU directive about spamming. This stipulates the principle of informed consent – the recipient must have first opted in to receive your emails.

Many third-sector bodies are now becoming more proactive at collecting opt-ins. There are many ways to do this:

- place enquiry forms on your website that encourage people to leave their email address and opt in to future mailings;
- assure that people who download substantial amounts of information from your organisation's website must first register to do so;
- provide email fields in your direct response coupons in all your printed direct marketing and publications;
- collect emails face to face during field work, at events etc.

Another potentially exciting development is so-called *viral email marketing*. This works by encouraging the email recipient to take action and/or forward the message to other people they know. It can be a very effective form of member get member (see above). Email your members, and encourage them to spread the word – electronically – along with a personal recommendation. Alternatively, when you email a membership offer to your warm contacts ask them to copy the information to others who may appreciate it.

**Partnership with public sector bodies**

If done thoughtfully, most public services are invariably open to approaches from other third-sector bodies, especially if you can demonstrate how your offer will also empower their staff and clients.

Public sector workers – be they teachers, nurses, librarians or social workers – have demanding jobs and cannot always afford the luxury of giving time to your cause, no matter how worthy it may be. Few will just hand out your recruitment leaflets and many have job descriptions or codes of conduct that forbid them to do so without good reason. But if you can find a synergy between their needs and yours, it can make all the difference. For example, a well-produced schools pack about environmental issues – written with the National Curriculum in mind – may be eagerly welcomed by teachers desperate for good quality classroom materials. A good pack can be turned to your advantage by raising awareness of your brand and cause among teachers, parents and young people.

Think about the fifth P of the marketing mix – place – (see Chapter 5) and ask yourself where your desired target audience is most likely to be found.

## Exercise: Marketing through public services

Think about the following public services. How relevant are their clients to your cause? What opportunities might they offer?

- Hospitals
- Health clinics
- GP surgeries
- Social services
- Residential care homes
- Schools
- Colleges
- Universities
- County, district and local councils
- Public libraries
- Quangos such as government benefit agencies, job centres, etc

Now consider the various ways that you might use these channels:

- Public exhibitions
- Leaflet dispensers
- Wall posters
- Special events – for example a talk in a local library
- Professional referrals – such as a social service recommending your service to clients
- Educational packs
- Presentations at training days
- Competitions

All of these openings and ideas can be made to work on either a national, regional or local level. The key principles for achieving success are to:

1. **Understand the decision-taking structure:** Who do you need to persuade in order for the public service to cooperate? If you are hoping to put up a poster or hold a talk in a local library, then the local library manager will most likely to have the authority to grant your request. On the other hand, a plan to insert your leaflet into a government agency mailout will require senior management consent at a national level, and that may take several months or more than a year to achieve.

2. **Work within public service constraints:** All public service workers are bound by operational procedures, confidentiality issues and codes of conduct. Find out what these are and construct your proposal to fit within them. No GP practice will welcome you with open arms if you begin by crassly asking for their patient list. However, a well-reasoned case for displaying your leaflet or poster in their waiting room may be granted.

3. **Nurture the gatekeepers:** You may have a pressing target to achieve, but that is unlikely to motivate a quango or care home – they have enough worries of their own to empathise much with yours. See the potential deal through their eyes and explain how your proposal will help them in their own work or meet their targets. Then they may be curious to learn more. For example, a care home's clients may include people with

a hearing loss and they may not know how to help them. Your training course or information pack will educate the staff to help the residents get NHS hearing aids and make use of teletext TV subtitles. The result: happier residents plus a care manager who is more amenable to distributing your leaflets.

4. **Be altruistic and don't oversell:** Even if your primary objective is to recruit new members don't be overly aggressive about it. Hard sell doesn't work here. Public sector workers will quickly smell a commercial rat. So be honest and say that you are offering membership but be public service minded about it. Your primary message is that you can support them to support their clients.

5. **Create a win–win situation:** Working in partnership requires a real effort from both parties to make it work. There is always a greater chance of success when you can define a win–win situation of mutual benefit to both the public sector body and your organisation. For example:

| How the public service benefits | How you benefit |
| --- | --- |
| • Public body is able to meet certain client needs not covered by their own service<br>• Motivating for professionals to be able to refer clients to you<br>• Public service outcomes are improved by added value from the third sector<br>• Save costs and time as the client makes fewer repeat visits | • Reach new audiences outside of your own contacts base<br>• Boost recruitment (so more of your target audience is helped)<br>• Generates funding/income<br>• Image of altruistic partnership with public services<br>• Share information and knowledge |

The following case study (reproduced from the *Guardian* 19 December 2003) is a good example of the kind of strategic thinking that can be applied to membership recruitment via public services:

## Weight Watchers

Overweight people may soon get slimming club membership on the NHS. Weight Watchers, one of the country's biggest slimming organisations, is drawing up plans with GPs and NHS trusts for patients to be referred to its weekly meetings.

Doctors and dieticians are backing the scheme, after hearing that the cost of a month's slimming club was far cheaper than the price of obesity drugs or surgery.

The House of Commons' health select committee, which is due to report on Britain's obesity epidemic next year, is considering whether to recommend that slimming clubs could be paid for by the NHS.

Paula Hunt, a nutritionist and dietician for Weight Watchers, told the select committee yesterday that the company was talking to "several" primary care trusts and GPs about such a scheme.

She said: "A lot of it is a question of time and motivation. There are huge time constraints within the NHS; doctors have 10 minutes to talk to their patients about everything, not just their weight.

"We can offer lifelong support and the motivation for people to lose the weight. We are very keen to get involved in partnerships with the NHS."

The Health Development Agency has also suggested that the NHS uses the experience of the multimillion pound commercial slimming sector to help tackle rising rates of obesity.

Weight Watchers is also one of the few programmes which has been subject to scientific studies. Research has shown that the slimming club regime, which involves allowing people "food points" rather than making them count calories, is effective and works better than counselling from doctors and self-help diets. Half of all people in Britain are now considered overweight and one in five are obese. The proportion of people who are considered too fat has doubled in the past decade.

Amanda Avery, a community dietician with the Greater Derby Primary Care Trust, said that a 12-week course at Slimming World cost £55, while a similar course of an anti-obesity drug would have cost £126 on the NHS. She told the committee: "One of the problems with the NHS is that obese people can be offered help or a referral to a clinic, but then that help is withdrawn because of a lack of money and resources. The slimming clubs don't have that problem because they have the money and the infrastructure."

**Partnership with companies**

As with the public sector, collaborating with the private sector can also open doors to new audiences for your scheme. The biggest companies have access to customer bases of hundreds of thousands or even millions of people. Local companies have the value of links with customers in your local community. Negotiating access to these is, of course, another matter. But with the onset of cause-related marketing (CRM), companies are often motivated to work with good causes too. Business in the Community defines CRM as a commercial activity by which businesses and charities, or causes, form a partnership with each other to market an image, product or service for mutual benefit.

CRM now forms a major part of membership recruitment at Diabetes UK. As previously mentioned, through its fundraising department, the charity struck a deal with the national chain of chemists, Lloyds. In the Lloyds retail outlets, staff position display banners and leaflets offering "free diabetes testing". If the test result is positive the customer is alerted and advised to contact their GP. The process also involves customers being told about Diabetes UK and many people have been recruited who would otherwise not have contacted the charity. There are many instances of local membership groups working with local companies, chambers of commerce or local rotary groups to similarly good effect.

It is important to be realistic; companies don't work with charities just for their own sake. In 2002, the UK business sector as a whole gave on average less than 1 per cent to charity (during a time of economic prosperity). The majority of companies view charities or voluntary partnerships in just the same way as they do for any commercial relationship. Any deal must include a convincing benefit for the company. I was once told by a senior executive of one leading high street brand: "I've had a bellyful of these disabled organisations approaching me. Who do they think we are – a social services department? The first thing I want to see when talking to a charity is a clearly thought-out business plan."

**The majority of companies view charities or voluntary partnerships in just the same way as they do for any commercial relationship.**

The table summarises the mutual benefits that businesses will expect to see:

| How the company benefits | How you benefit |
|---|---|
| • More business<br>• Enhanced public relations<br>• Increased awareness<br>• Perceived as a socially enlightened company<br>• Tool for motivating staff<br>• Boosts customer retention<br>• Introduces new customers<br>• Cross-marketing of their product via your own networks | • Increases public awareness of your organisation or cause<br>• Opens doors to new audiences outside your contact base<br>• Generates income<br>• Image of a dynamic partner who makes things happen<br>• Cross-fertilisation of information and knowledge |

Five key principles to keep in mind when researching a potential company to work with are:

1. **A common target audience.** In a successful tie-up, your organisation and the company will have similar or at least complementary target audiences. The respective audiences must need and want the other's service or product.

2. **Get the right fit.** Make sure that the buying public clearly sees a natural fit between you and the company. An ecological charity and a recycling company make perfect sense. A war games manufacturer and a peace campaign will be counterproductive and alienate many of your prospects.

3. **A win–win situation.** The partnership must be seen to be mutually beneficial to both sides in more or less equal proportion. If the company gains a lot more from the deal than the charity, then customers invariably find out. When certain charity Christmas card projects are exposed for giving only a tiny percentage to the charity, the deal is seen as exploitative and leaves the charity at risk of being perceived as shallow or conniving with cynical profiteering.

4. **Relationship management.** A successful business will not deal with time wasters. It must have complete trust and confidence in those who represent your membership scheme. Adopt an account management approach and assign a person to be the key contact person with the

company at all times. Don't allow sundry personnel to pester them with ad hoc communications and demands. If you can make the relationship work they will see it as a convenient arrangement and keep it alive.

5. **Be patient.** Often the bigger the company, the slower the decision-making process. A request to place your membership leaflets on the counter of local newsagent may be granted by the shop manager the same day, but the glittering prize of an endorsement by a national organisation will almost certainly mean the company's community relations manager first having to seek approval from the company board which might meet only quarterly.

## Media

Media stories can provide a dramatic window of opportunity to raise awareness of your organisation and so recruit new members.

### Case study – The Women's Institute (WI)

In September 2003, the film premiere of *Calendar Girls* achieved national media coverage for the Women's Institute. Initially, the coverage was for the wrong reasons. The *Daily Mail* placed a negative spin on the story when only six of the 11 real-life calendar girls, from the Rylstone WI group in north Yorkshire, were present at the Leicester Square premiere. The story focused on the absence of the other five women after quarrels about how the stunt to raise £1,000 was turned into a blockbuster film starring Helen Mirren and Julie Walters.

Side-stepping the *Daily Mail*'s loaded questions about the quarrels, WI's PR office chose instead to emphasise that the charity's 230,000 members were in fact very excited by film. The national office had received 50 membership enquiries on the night. Its 70 local federations were also boosting recruitment by organising local screenings of the film.

In a website message to all their local groups, WI chair Barbara Gill rallied her members with these words:

*None of us could have envisaged that producing a calendar would generate so much publicity for the WI. As an organisation we must now build on this publicity, because we know that there are potential new members waiting to join this organisation. Many will want to join a WI in their local area, whilst there may be a group of friends who would like to start a WI of their own, just like the group who have formed the Fulham WI. If you are having a special showing of the film in your area, do ask the cinema if you can have an eye-catching display of all the diverse things that the WI offers at local, federation and national level. We must not miss this golden opportunity, it may never come again and we all must embrace those prospective new members and give them a warm welcome.*

**Think creatively and enlist the support of a local celebrity or tie in with one of the newspaper's own running stories.**

Even if media coverage like this is rare for your cause, there is much you can do to try to make it happen. And media work isn't just for big organisations. If you are a local group, the local media is always seeking a local angle to their stories. You may have just the story they are looking for in a quiet period. You may have a fundraising drive or local campaign that gives them an easy story to run. You can think creatively and enlist the support of a local celebrity or tie in with one of the newspaper's own running stories.

The Further Reading section lists additional material about how to run a media or public relations campaign. We'll just mention here some tips for those seeking to raise awareness about their membership scheme.

1. **Don't start the story with your membership scheme:** No journalist is going to be very interested in running a story that begins with 'join this organisation'. Journalists want *news* and *human interest*. It is more effective to get the membership message across implicitly by embedding it within a story that is of genuine interest to their readers. It may be a piece of research, a technological breakthrough or a campaign. Use the news story as a peg to introduce membership rather than the other way around.

2. **Target your media work:** It is all to easy too bandy about terms like 'raising public awareness' or 'educating the general public'. Your target audience of prospective members is unlikely to be the entire 60 million plus population of the UK. Study the media closely. Consider which

newspapers, magazines, websites, radio or TV programmes are relevant to your membership prospects. This doesn't just mean the national newspapers. Your prospects are just as likely to read regional and local newspapers or listen to local radio stations (which according to polling research tend to be more trusted and believed than the nationals), or the trade press or special interest magazines. A one-size-fits-all approach to drafting your press releases won't work either. Make sure you target them. A Scottish story should use a spokesperson from that country. A story for the Oldham press can feature statistics about the local area, and so on.

3. **Quote your members:** Try to offer member case studies. Journalists love these as they afford human interest to flesh out the bare facts: " Local Ramblers' Association member, Angela Baverstock, who has been campaigning for footpaths in Wiltshire to be better waymarked, says ..." An opinion like this will be more powerful coming from someone actually affected by issues rather than a corporate press officer. You will also subtly draw your prospects' attention to the fact that you are a membership body.

4. **Compile a database of spokespeople and quotes:** When I worked at RNID we ran an initiative called Tell Us Your Story which invited members to write in with their experiences on a preset range of topical issues such as getting a hearing aid or using television subtitles. We asked each member to tick a box giving consent to their testimony being used in media work and whether or not they were happy to be interviewed by a journalist. This ensured that we had a readymade database of contacts for both long-term proactive media work and for same day reactive activity.

5. **Use your membership survey:** Another good way to lift a story is to position some membership survey results within your press release – whether statistical or anecdotal – for example, that 82 per cent of your members believe that supermarkets should stock more organic produce.

6. **Be proactive but reactive too:** Do plan your media campaigns but be ready to react quickly to breaking stories. Scan the media on a regular (even daily) basis and be sure that you are not missing out on opportunities in the outside

world simply because you are too engrossed with preparing next year's campaign. The WI example cited above is a classic example of good reactive work.

7. **Be prepared to fulfil enquiries:** Any proactive media campaign should bear in mind the possibility of a sudden increase in enquiries to your organisation once the story has broken. Ensure that you have enough people to handle the telephones or to fulfil postal enquiries (and that they are properly briefed to answer questions provoked by the media coverage and are tasked to sell membership). Third-sector bodies that do a great deal of media work, such as Greenpeace and Friends of the Earth, can be exceptionally good at turning media interest into newly recruited members and they prepare accordingly.

8. **Follow through:** Once a story has broken, it can act as a springboard for other media work. For example, you can appeal, as the WI did, for members to consolidate public interest by generating local initiatives or by writing letters to the local press. This has the doubly beneficial effect of making your members feel involved.

9. **Assess the risks and the opportunities:** Media work can be a double-edged sword. Always remember that journalists are not obliged to angle the story from your own perspective. There is a degree of risk because you are using a third party to relate your story in their own words. Negative publicity that isn't effectively countered can actually deter prospects from joining your organisation. On a positive note, while you don't have total control of the message, when you do get coverage you can access new audiences.

## Advertising

In contrast to press work, you have much more control over advertising. You choose the headlines, write the content and decide where and when it appears. On the other hand, you have to pay fees and it doesn't come cheap.

There are essentially two kinds of advertising:

- **Public awareness advertising:** which is generally aimed at increasing public awareness of your brand, your cause or your services.

- **Response advertising:** which is specifically geared to soliciting a response, usually via a postal coupon or a telephone hotline or website, and which may solicit donations, membership applications or campaign support.

At the top end of the market, mass membership bodies such as the Consumers' Association (with its subscription magazine *Which?*), the National Trust and the RSPB have a successful track record of national press and magazine advertising. At the lower end, it can still be affordable so long as you choose carefully focus on your local or specialist media, negotiate good rates and do small-scale tests before you splash the cash. The following principles apply:

1. Copywriting an advertisement is not the same as for a direct mail pack or leaflet. When readers flick through a newspaper or magazine you have just a few seconds to grab their attention and hold it. Good adverts stand out from the copy around them. Use an arresting headline and image and keep copy to the barest essentials. Think about the unique reason to join and key benefits (see Chapter 5). Make sure the advert is easy to respond to, via a coupon, website address or telephone hotline number.

2. Target your advertising. Any reputable newspaper or magazine will have a media pack detailing its readership profile – age, gender, income, special interests, etc. Match this profile against your desired target audience and select your media accordingly.

3. You could ask the editor for a list of forthcoming features and see if you can place your advert near it. Send the editor a list of feature ideas of your own and offer to supply information and pictures. At RNID we often targeted magazines that were primarily read by the over-50s – the group containing the greatest concentration of people with hearing loss. Many editors genuinely didn't know how many of their readers would be affected by the condition and were pleased to be alerted to the opportunity of a good story. Sometimes an article would be backed up with a paid-for membership advertisement or leaflet inserted into the same issue to reinforce the article with a call to join.

4. If you are new to advertising or unsure if a particular publication will work for you, then test on a small scale. Find out whether your target newspaper or magazine can do a split

run. Place your ad or insert into a segment of the print run, eg 10 per cent or a quarter or a half of its circulation. This has the advantage of allowing you to test on a low-cost basis. If the test results warrant it, you can follow up on a wider scale in the next issue. At RNID we once did this with the BBC's *Radio Times* magazine by inserting into half of the London area distribution. We did sign up some members but simply not enough to justify losing money by rolling out the insert nationally. By testing first, we avoided a very costly mistake.

5. Some newspapers and magazines sell distress space – that is, space still left unsold just prior to going to press. Not all will do so, but if you research their usual rates, the deadlines and time your approach to the last few days before they print there can be some good deals around.

6. Wherever possible, place an origin code on your response coupon. This enables you to trace the membership order back to the publication it was placed in, so you can evaluate the results and plan future advertising accordingly.

7. Whatever publishers, or their agents, say, there are discounts available to those who push hard enough for them. Remember they need your business too. First-time buyers can often haggle for lower rates on the basis that they don't yet know if the magazine will work for them and want to see the results first. A sequence of ads spread over several issues nearly always justifies a series rate – discounted against the standard one-off rate.

## Events and exhibitions

Whether it is a high-powered business-to-business trade fair, a specialist event or a popular gardening show, visitors usually attend with just one thing in mind – gathering information and advice. With an attractive stall, you can meet and greet people, explain yourself directly, answer questions, find out more about your prospects and how they perceive your work.

Exhibiting at large events isn't always cheap once you've paid the fee, produced the display materials and subsidised the travel costs. When making your case for a budget, it helps to be able to demonstrate a return on your investment. The following tips may aid you to make the case.

1. Don't fall into the trap of buying space at an exhibition simply because the word 'charity' is in the name. Define your target audience and research the events that they attend. The obvious events to attend might not always be the most productive ones for you – they may simply be visited by people who are already members anyway (which is fine for keeping in touch with them). You may find a much less obvious choice of event will have thousands of prospects who don't know much about you but who have needs and wants that you can satisfy.

2. Set yourself measurable targets so that you can evaluate the return on your investment; for example, the number of names and addresses captured, people signed up as members etc. For those people who sign up on the day, make sure you code the leaflets that they take away so you can trace the subsequent orders back to the event.

3. Publicise your stand at the exhibition in any mailshots you despatch in the weeks leading up to the event.

4. Organise a speaker or workshop at the event, which can then be used to direct people towards your stand. Hand out leaflets outside the main entrance or in the foyer.

5. Be selective about what you put on the stand. Some exhibitors will put everything but the kitchen sink on display, just to show how much they do. But a rainforest of leaflets, publications and brochures all screaming for attention makes it difficult for the visitor to navigate your stall. If you are aiming to recruit people on the day, organise your stand so that your membership offer stands out.

6. Attract children to your stand and the parents will soon follow – you can make fun items or balloons part of your display.

7. A single large powerful image that's easy to spot from a distance will carry more impact than a thousand words.

8. Think of something creative that will engage passers-by. For example, I once supervised a stand with a 'Spot the hearing aid' competition using a large poster of a crowd of people in the room. Not many people did but it was a fantastic device to stop people in their tracks and linger at the stall.

9. Organise a rota, plan sensible breaks with your colleagues and look around the exhibition to survey what others are doing. You'll be sure to come away with stimulating ideas and publications.

10. It takes less than three seconds for someone to walk past a stand. No matter how impressive it may be, it's often the way in which staff or volunteers behave behind the stand that first catches the eye. If they look passive, bored or are larking about, this can put people off. So don't invest money in a stand and then put people behind it who have no flair or enthusiasm for face-to-face work.

11. Handing someone a leaflet and promptly turning away gives your prospects an excuse not to talk to you. If you can, get their contact details because a high percentage of these leads can be converted at a later date when you follow up their visit with an inspirational reminder about your organisation.

12. Make it as easy as possible to join on the day. Attract attention to your membership offer by using banner stands – a roller blind-type display which works like a projector screen attached to a pole – or similar attention-grabbers that advertise your membership benefits.

13. Make your visitor feel special – for example, keep a supply of your most recent back issues of the membership magazine and then make an offer to "join today and take away a free issue of our magazine".

14. Talk with your visitors. What is it that makes them tick? What particular piece of information are they looking for? If someone is looking for ideas for organic recipes you can tailor your explanation about the membership scheme by pointing out that the magazine carries regular recipes for organic dishes.

## Action points

✓ Before you start your membership recruitment drive, make sure you have got the marketing mix right (see Chapter 5).

✓ Get your trustees and key staff to see marketing as an investment, not an expense.

✓ Start with your warmest audience – your enquirers and service users.

✓ Avoid relying on word of mouth alone and experiment with a range of different marketing channels.

✓ Systematically plan and evaluate all your recruitment activities so that you can make like-for-like comparisons using ROI, LVA or CBA analyses – and then focus your investment wherever you get the best return.

✓ Use your members' own contacts and networks to recruit other members.

✓ If you have no previous experience of direct marketing, first test on a small scale to see if you can get an acceptable return on your investment.

✓ Whatever type or size of membership scheme you run, the media (national, local or specialist) needs stories. Target the channels that reach your desired audience and then create the stories that will interest them.

✓ Ensure that your website functions as a recruitment vehicle.

✓ Think about how public-sector organisations and companies might open doors to new audiences for your membership scheme, but see the deal from their perspective as well as yours.

✓ Don't always rely on the same marketing channel for recruiting members. Keep experimenting.

# 7 Loyalty and retention

## This chapter covers:

This chapter looks at:

- The relationship between recruitment and retention
- Tailoring your own communications mix
- Welcoming your new members
- Building active relationships with your members
- Handling contacts from your members
- Using databases to build up a complete picture of each individual
- How to design a renewal programme
- Getting your lapsed members back
- The importance of making technology and data serve a human need

As discussed in Chapter 1, a key tenet of relationship marketing holds that you can't grow an enthusiastic long-term supporter base for your valuable cause without having a *loyalty and retention programme* that's just as effective as your initial recruitment campaign. Consider the following basic sums and you'll soon see how true that statement is.

**Anyshire Citizen's Alliance**
2003 membership = 5,000
2004 new members recruited = 1,250
2004 existing members renewed = 3,750 (75%)
2004 existing members lapsed = 1,250 (25%)
Year-on-year growth = 0%

In this scenario, a membership scheme has 5,000 existing members and then impressively recruits 25 per cent more members. But even with a solid 75 per cent of the existing 5,000 members renewing there is no overall growth for the scheme. This is because gain from the incoming 1,250 new members is cancelled out by the outgoing 1,250 lapsed members.

If this 25 per cent lapsed member rate is repeated each year, then the equivalent of an entire membership base must be replaced every four years.

For any organisation with a long-term mission to achieve a better world, that is a lot of wastage to contend with. For the more existing members who lapse, the more time and money has to be spent recruiting new people to replace them.

**Recruitment is just the beginning of the relationship marketing process, not the end of it.**

Clearly then, recruitment is just the beginning of the relationship marketing process, not the end of it. Yet all too often membership organisations fall into the trap of seeing marketing as just recruitment. The loyalty and retention aspects receive less attention or care than anything else. Cue an all too familiar scenario: some organisations lavish money, time and care on the glossy recruitment leaflet, while the renewal effort might comprise little more than a letter which gives the impression of having been dashed off as an afterthought, taking it for granted that a cheque will soon follow.

### More than just recruitment

Relationship marketing abhors the narrow stress on recruitment and focuses on a continuous process of:

1. Recruitment
2. Building loyalty
3. Retention

**Recruitment** is telling your prospects about your scheme, the value it offers and persuading them to sign up.

**Building loyalty** is the ongoing process of keeping your members continuously informed about what your organisation is doing for them and for the cause. The marketing objective is to stimulate your members to be active members. This is because the more active your members are, the stronger their appreciation of the benefits of your scheme and/or the stronger their commitment to your cause. In the long run, the more active your members are, the more likely they are to renew for another year.

The **retention** process is about transferring the member's loyalty from one year to the next, so that your cause has a long-term source of committed supporters and advocates.

### Activity versus inactivity

As you read through the following two pen-portraits, ask yourself which person is most likely to renew their loyalty to the scheme.

**The active member:** Sunita is a member of the Anyshire Nature Trust. During the year she receives four Trust newsletters. Each issue markets the scheme's benefits; so Sunita is reminded to take regular advantage of the free access to the Trust's nature reserves. She makes the most of the members' discounts on walking boots and outdoor clothes. Sunita is also moved by an appeal letter asking for people to write to their local MP to oppose industrial development on one of the Trust sites. She is especially pleased to read an update in the subsequent Trust newsletter, thanking the members for their support and explaining how this had persuaded the local council to refuse planning permission. At the end of the year, Sunita receives a personal letter inviting her to renew her support. The letter also acknowledges the value to the Trust of her recent purchases and advocacy support.

**The inactive member:** Gary is a member of the Friends of Anytown Museum. He joined to give something back to the cause. As a young boy he had fallen in love with the museum's dinosaur exhibits – an experience which sowed the seeds of his vocation as a palaeontologist. Shortly after joining he made a donation to a fundraising appeal. He heard nothing more that year from the museum until the membership renewal letter arrived. This was a greyish photocopied letter addressed to 'Dear Friend'. He hadn't got around to visiting the museum that year (he couldn't recall getting any publicity about the major shows). Accompanying the letter was a bald summary of the annual accounts with no explanation other than a short statement of thanks from the Friends chairman to a major bank that had made a big gift of a multimedia display for the museum foyer.

It doesn't take rocket science to work out which of the two is most likely to renew their support.

Prompted by quarterly reminders, Sunita has remained active throughout the year while Gary, after his donation early in the year, has been inactive.

Sunita's activity has been nurtured by the Trust's regular communications – reminding her of the benefits of the scheme and appealing for her support. Gary has heard nothing all year and so didn't take advantage of the benefits, even though these were spelled out to him in the membership leaflet he filled out when he joined. He'd simply forgotten what the benefits were.

A promising start to the relationship between Gary and the Friends had petered out when the Friends omitted to thank him for his donation. By the time he received his renewal letter, Gary had simply forgotten what the point of the scheme was. The note from the chairman thanking the bank for its big donation gave Gary the impression that the museum's future didn't really depend on his loyalty.

### Exercise: Are you an acquirer, retainer or relationship marketer?

Estimate the ratio of time, money and effort that your organisation spends on the three areas of recruitment, loyalty building and retention. Where does it stand in relation to the following typology?

- **Acquirers** – who concentrate most of their resources on membership recruitment at the expense of loyalty and retention activities.
- **Retainers** – who do little recruitment and focus most of their effort on serving and keeping the existing members.
- **Relationship marketers** – who see their members as long-term friends and continuously balance the time, money and effort spent on recruitment, loyalty and retention activities.

## The ten key ingredients for maximising loyalty and retention

As the above case studies suggest, the task of building long-term relationships can't be left to chance. It needs a relationship marketing strategy with the following key ingredients.

1. A relationship marketing model
2. An annual communications mix

3. A warm welcome
4. A commitment to building member-focused relationships
5. An integrated contact strategy
6. Database profiling and analysis
7. A systemic renewal programme
8. A lapsed reactivation programme
9. Systemic renewal data
10. A commitment to making technology and data serve human needs

## Ingredient 1: A relationship marketing model

When a new member joins, you should already have a clear membership journey mapped out with appropriate marketing activities in place – such as a newsletter or direct mailshots – for building the individual's loyalty and commitment.

The *membership trapezoid* (see Chapter 1) outlines the six stages of the membership journey. This offers a path for nurturing the member along the journey to higher levels of *behavioural* activity (using services, getting involved, making a donation, etc) or *attitudinal* commitment (identifying with the cause, a feeling of pride at being a member, etc).

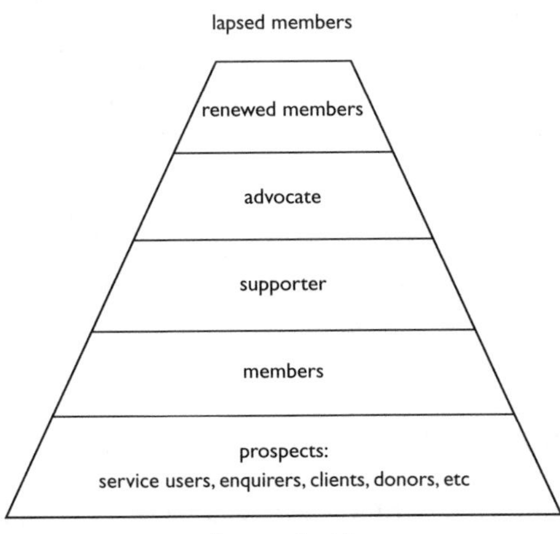


Your **members** will have already signed up to a certain package of benefits. Some benefits will be tangible (a magazine, access to privileges), some may be intangible (a feeling of enhanced self-esteem from supporting a cause). However, with ongoing marketing from your organisation (for example, a membership newsletter), a percentage of these can be upgraded into

**supporters**, ie members who give further support to your cause over and above their actual membership (for example, by purchasing other goods and services, making a donation or by getting involved in volunteering activities).

Ongoing marketing directed at your members can also convert a percentage of members and supporters into **advocates** – people who provide word-of-mouth endorsement for your cause (for example, they may actively support your campaign by lobbying an MP or writing to the local press, or they may do some of your marketing for you by attending events and introducing other people to your scheme).

The strategic objective of up-selling the member from one level of behavioural or attitudinal commitment to the next is to make it more likely they will reach the next stage of the membership journey; the decision to renew their commitment for another year.

Not every member will be a supporter or advocate. Some will be content to just passively consume the core member benefit (such as the newsletter) and not engage in any other way. Some may go from members to renewed members without any intervening stage. But think of the trapezoid as being like a ladder – if your people are on the bottom rung (members) it takes a lot more effort to get their feet on the top rung (renewed) than it would if you had helped them onto the middle rungs (as a supporter or advocate).

The following exercise encourages you to adapt this model to your own situation by defining the desired actions that you believe will identify those of your members who will also be your supporters and advocates.

## Exercise: Defining your supporters and advocates

What behaviours and attitudes will enable you to define who your **supporters** are?

What behaviours and attitudes will enable you to define who your **advocates** are?

## Ingredient 2: An annual communications mix

Relationship marketing seeks to nurture your members away from being passive consumers of your membership benefits to becoming active supporters and advocates for your cause. To achieve this, you need to invest time and resources in building active relationships between the members and the cause you represent. And any good relationship – at home, at work, at leisure – needs regular two-way communication. Without it, people – be they marriage or cohabiting partners, work colleagues, club members – slowly pull in different directions and eventually drift apart. So it is with membership schemes. With relationship marketing we can use the *communications mix* not only to retain the allegiance of our members but also to motivate them to higher levels of activity and support.

### The communications mix

Calling it a communications mix reminds you to try to get the balance right between the various ingredients. Your mix will most likely include some of the following communication channels:

- welcome pack
- membership card
- annual yearbook
- magazine/newsletter/journal/supplements
- website/microsite
- email
- mobile text
- face-to-face meetings
- direct mailshots
- market research/membership surveys

To choose the right mix, the organisation needs to consider:

- the frequency of contact required to achieve desired levels of member support and advocacy
- the available resources (editorial, production, distribution)
- the costs to the organisation

The organisation also needs to consider the members' needs:

- the frequency of contact desired/tolerated
- perceptions of the relevance of each communication
- convenience (eg do they prefer post or email?)

A good way to get the mix right is to develop an annual plan for all your membership communications showing a month-by-month breakdown of the various contacts you will make with the members (and with each segment) during the year.

**Annual member communications plan**

**April**
Quarterly magazine

**May**
Donation ask

**July**
Quarterly magazine with donation thank you letter inserted into it

**September**
Christmas catalogue

**October**
Quarterly magazine with notice of AGM inserted into it

**January**
Quarterly magazine

**March**
Campaign postcard

The virtue of the above sample plan is that the communications mix:

- is sequential, eg a donation ask is followed by a magazine containing a donation thank you (to avoid duplication and wastage);
- is spaced evenly throughout the year;
- includes response mailings – eg donation ask, Christmas catalogue plus the campaign postcard – that are each scheduled at least two months apart from the other, so that the response to one mailing doesn't cancel out the others.

An annual communications mix is especially important if the member is likely to be contacted by different departments or people. For example, in a medium to large-sized organisation there may be separate membership, fundraising, campaigns and service teams. Each team has its own target to meet – membership renewal, donations, campaign support, service usage, product purchases. The danger of all this is overkill; the member gets overwhelmed by too many messages and requests appearing in quick succession at certain times of the year and leaving the member with a feeling of being harassed.

With an annual communications plan we can avoid these haphazard patterns of communication and create a feeling of a true relationship. For example, if a member is sent a donation appeal and responds to it, the next communication that follows should naturally be a thank you letter for the donation.

**With an annual communications plan we can avoid these haphazard patterns of communication and create a feeling of a true relationship.**

### Magazine/newsletter

Regular communication with your members is the foundation stone of relationship marketing, and this is where newsletters and magazines really come into their own.

With the advent of desktop publishing it has never been easier for even the smallest groups to produce their own newsletter. The steady fall in full-colour printing costs has seen some third-sector organisations produce magazines on a par with the best newsstand titles. However, you shouldn't invest in a glossy magazine for its own sake. Match the design and production values to the members' expectations. For example, someone who joins expecting their fee to contribute to alleviating poverty may feel that a thick glossy magazine is inappropriate and that a modest newsletter is sufficient to keep up to date. On the other hand, if the magazine is the primary attraction for joining, the member will see full colour, professional design, good paper stock and excellent photography as value for money.

The typical content of a magazine or newsletter might include:

- news of your organisation's work and recent successes
- features about your goods, services and offers
- human-interest features about home, work or life issues affecting your members
- details of your campaigns
- details of your fundraising activities
- snippets of press coverage about your organisation's work
- letters and opinion pages
- forthcoming events
- entertainment (crosswords, puzzles, cartoons)
- profiles of your members
- display advertisements/small ads

**The vocabulary, style and tone of writing used by a membership scheme's newsletter or magazine speak volumes about its culture.**

A key challenge is to find the right voice. The vocabulary, style and tone of writing used by a membership scheme's newsletter or magazine speak volumes about its culture. The degree of formality shapes people's impressions about the friendliness of your host organisation; frequent use of academic jargon suggests a professional audience while using informal language conveys an organisation that serves a younger or teenage market. Develop a written identity that enables you to connect, practically and emotionally, with your members.

Rather than just dryly listing your activities, relate interesting stories about the impact your organisation makes on people's lives. When your members understand that their money funds an organisation that makes a real difference, it leads to improved loyalty and retention.

Use imaginative pictures. A picture of two 'suits' shaking hands in front of a giant cheque is so clichéd your reader's eyes will simply glaze over it. A good picture is worth a thousand words, so invest time and money in a handful of memorable ones rather than padding your publication out with dozens of eminently forgettable ones.

Your publication should not be a mere status symbol for your organisation – it should be a practical tool for your members. Don't fill your publication with self-indulgent or meaningless copy of interest only to the person that wrote it (what the chairman did on his holidays, etc). Make every single item count. If your members have a particular medical condition, or pursue a sport, then devote your features to bringing them right up to date with practical tips that they can use in their daily lives.

Don't ignore your members. Featuring only the staff's names, pictures, stories and quotes will paint an insular picture of your work and give the (albeit unintentional) impression that the members don't really matter. Harness your members' experiences, ideas, tips and feedback. Present your supporters and advocates as role models for other members.

Link your editorial features to your relationship marketing plan. If your strategy is to convert a percentage of your members into supporters and advocates, then the magazine can be used to cross-sell opportunities to purchase other goods and services. If you don't ask, you don't get. Human interest features (such as the real-life story of one of your members) are a powerful tool for appealing to your members to get involved.

Don't be worthy but dull. We live in an 'infotainment' age, where people expect to be both informed and entertained. Above all, make it the kind of magazine or newsletter that you'd like to read if you were a member yourself. Make this your litmus test when editing and designing your publication. If you feel informed, excited and inspired when producing your publication, then the chances are so will your members.

### Yearbook

You don't actually have to produce a magazine or newsletter at all if there is another medium that works better for you and your members. A yearbook is often more appropriate for membership schemes centred around information rather than continuous news; for example, a membership scheme for a profession or trade might focus on a yearbook containing detailed legal and best practice information, a directory of services and contacts which can be combined with a continually updated website for keeping members informed, plus regular email updates.

### Direct mail

Special messages that appeal to the members for support or advocacy can sometimes get lost within a magazine or newsletter. A direct mailshot has the advantage of focusing the member's attention on one message only without the distraction of other news and features. Some forms of relationship marketing, eg fundraising appeals, are more effective by using direct marketing to the individual at home. Further guidance on good practice in copywriting, producing and evaluating direct marketing packs is given in Chapter 6.

### Email

The advantage of emails is that they are cheap to send, have an immediate impact and the message can easily be tailored for different members. You can send one email to people who have a track record of supporting your fundraising appeals and a different one to those who would rather volunteer, and so on. Emails can be used to communicate newsflashes, send reminders or to draw attention to special offers. Email messages are best kept short and to the point with members given the option to refer to the newsletter or to click on a hyperlink to a website to obtain further details. Some professional schemes send newsletters only via email to save on costs. However, bear in mind that many of your members will not have a computer or mobile, especially older people, so for the time being at least email is generally best used to supplement existing communication channels and not replace them.

**Websites**

In the past decade, a website has become the worldwide window on the membership schemes of many non-profit organisations, marketing the schemes to prospects from Ipswich to Islamabad to Illinois. A good website can also offer a new outlet for member-only privileges via password-protected zones. While print media is static, your website offers interactivity and animation such as the chance to watch a video image of your organisation's leader making a public appeal for support or the opportunity to use a bulletin board enabling people to exchange opinions or practical tips. Information through print-based communication channels may quickly go out of date, but websites can be continuously updated. Websites allow members to view goods, publications and merchandise and then by clicking onto a secure server they can purchase them there and then. Most excitingly, new developments mean that websites and membership databases can interface dynamically with each other to create a personal home page for the individual member.

**Membership surveys**

These can be another powerful form of communication and loyalty-building: it shows you are listening and want to hear from your members. Be sure to accompany any survey with a covering letter explaining its purpose and how the results will be used. Take care to feedback the subsequent results too. Further information on survey techniques is given in Chapter 4.

## Ingredient 3: A warm welcome

The first ingredient in the communications mix, at least for new members, is a warm welcome. The member's initial commitment of signing up should be rewarded promptly and appropriately. A personalised and signed covering letter goes much further than an anonymous photocopied one.

Many new members will have joined by completing a simple leaflet or via a face-to-face encounter, so they may not yet be fully informed about your organisation's work, its services and the opportunities to get involved. Some form of welcome pack can be a highly effective tool for converting the new member's initial rush of enthusiasm into long-term support and/or advocacy for your cause.

**The welcome pack**

The pack does not have to be glossy or expensive, but neither should it be cursory or slapdash.

- Include a copy of the current (or most recent) issue of your newsletter.
- Assume no prior knowledge of your work but reaffirm who you are, your mission and values, your products and services.
- Start at the beginning. Explain what it means to be a member; how the cause, organisation and the members all benefit (the win–win outcomes).
- Tell them about your recent successes.
- Be brief, snappy, visual and alive, but don't overburden your new members with more information than they can absorb.
- Make it a practical resource that the new member will wish to keep handy (for example, with a directory of your organisation's services, useful contacts, website address, etc).
- Tell the reader how they can support or advocate for the cause.

Above all, make it the kind of welcome pack that you would have liked to have received had you joined yourself.

Some membership schemes also enclose a mini-questionnaire to enable them to begin building up a more complete picture of individual members. How would they like to be communicated with? What are their special interests? Provide tick boxes to allow people to state their interests and preferences and then data capture the responses onto your database for future action (see Ingredient 6: Database profiling and analysis).

### The membership card

Another way of extending a welcome is to enclose a membership card with your thank you letter to reinforce the new member's sense of belonging and/or pride at being a member.

The card may also have a practical and/or marketing application. For some schemes, a card is a practical necessity, eg to enable members to access a heritage site or to obtain a shop discount. Those schemes which have no practical use for a card may still issue them as part of their branding or marketing strategy, for example, by printing the organisation's contact details or their website address on it. The member is encouraged to retain the card in their purse/wallet as an ever-present reminder of your organisation's readiness to help.

Card production is usually outsourced to companies that can mass-produce them cheaply, either as simple paper-based cards or plastic/magnetic swipe cards.

## Ingredient 4: A commitment to building member-focused relationships

You've got the relationship marketing model (Ingredient 1), the annual communications mix (Ingredient 2) and you've extended a warm welcome to the new member (Ingredient 3). The next task is to convert all this planning and preparation into an actual relationship with your members. It doesn't matter whether you have 34, 340, 3400, 34,000 or 340,000 members – the same relationship marketing principles hold true. Start from where the members are and then strengthen their loyalty to your cause.

### Exercise: Getting started with relationship marketing

Imagine that you are secretary of a local park conservation group with 340 members. The initial motivation for members to join, is to financially support the upkeep of a park that they and their families have enjoyed, sometimes for generations. In return, each member gets a twice-yearly update from the senior park ranger but otherwise there is no expectation of practical involvement with the group's conservation work. The members generally assume this to be the work of park staff.

Yet like most local authority park services, your local one is cash-strapped and the staff cannot keep up with all the work that needs to be done. From the outset, your relationship marketing model is geared to converting a certain percentage of your members into supporters by persuading them to give of their time to help keep the park in good shape. How do you go about this?

Brainstorm a list of the kind of things you might need to do. The list might include some of the following steps:

- Write a personal note to each member individually.
- Invite them to your project office to discover more about your work.
- Make them feel at home with coffee and biscuits.
- Find out which aspects of the project excites most interest.
- Talk to each individual about their personal skills and

interests and make a note of them.
- Keep a copy of the notes on your file or computer.
- Offer to put them on a volunteer mailing list.
- Segment your mailing list, eg into three groups: one that can volunteer two Saturdays a month, another that will volunteer once a month, and another that will come to an annual park clear-up and barbeque.
- Offer a choice to each individual volunteer as to how they would like to be communicated with – by letter, telephone or email.
- Help the members to visualise what success looks like. How their local community will benefit if the volunteer project achieves its goals.
- When the project is completed give the members feedback and a share in the credit for its success.
- Write a personal thank you note to each one individually.
- Build on the project's success by thinking about how you can convert your new supporters into advocates – for example, by asking them to encourage friends and relatives to become new members and volunteers for the project.

From these simple first steps you will have established some of the building blocks of relationship marketing: a personal touch; the ability to listen; responsiveness to people's individual preferences; two-way communication; flexibility and choice. Does all of that sound a bit too labour-intensive? Wouldn't it have been quicker to have just mailed out a standard photocopied circular? It certainly would have been quicker but would it have generated the same level of support? Almost certainly not – this is the part of the challenge of relationship marketing. Being member-focused demands a lot more effort from your organisation, but in return you get a much higher level of member support.

**Being member-focused demands a lot more effort from your organisation, but in return you get a much higher level of member support.**

Segmenting your communications is important because not all of your members will be inclined to higher levels of support or advocacy – indeed some members will be apathetic or may even feel threatened by the idea of getting involved. Remember the so-called Pareto principle discussed in Chapter 3: around 80 per cent of your sales (or advocacy) will come from around 20 per cent of your customers. By taking the kind of relationship marketing approach described above, you will be able to discern which of your members are most likely to form the 20 per cent and tailor your approach accordingly.

## Ingredient 5: An integrated contact strategy

For small local groups, the relationship marketing approach described in the local park case study works well if you have an active membership secretary who has local knowledge, the contacts and the initiative to tailor different levels of contact with different subgroups of members. On a larger scale, you need a relational membership database to replicate the creative skills of the local membership secretary. In the right hands, a relational database will not only store names and addresses, it will also act as a kind of superhuman membership secretary and perform the following functions on a scale of hundreds or thousands of members:

- assure that people in the various membership categories each receive their chosen benefits and communications;
- store special instructions from individual members (for example, the number of appeal mailings they wish to receive);
- keep a contact history of each and every member's contact with your organisation, when and how they joined, which category, what other transactions they have made – from donating to purchasing merchandise;
- keep a copy of all correspondence between you and each individual member, tagged to the member's record for easy retrieval;
- store demographic data about your members' (age, gender, region, etc).

For such a model to build up a complete picture of each individual, those who administrate the membership scheme must have an *integrated contact handling* strategy that databases every single transaction between the scheme and the members.

Some host organisations have the resources and skills to do this internally, while others prefer to outsource their database, fulfilment and enquiry handling to an external company. The following case study illustrates an example of how an integrated contact strategy can bring benefits.

## The Macular Disease Society

The Macular Disease Society represents people with a condition that affects central vision. The charity provides information and support to enable members to make the most of their remaining sight.

Like many third-sector bodies, the society lacks the infrastructure to link all its contact points to a central database. So it has outsourced its contacts handling to an external company. The Society's strategic aim is not only to keep good records but also to reduce wastage, boost income and improve the service to its members.

When it began the search for an outsourcing partner, the most important criteria for the society was trust. It would have to trust the partner with its most valuable assets – its members, both existing and potential. The partner would need to become an extension of the organisation, not just a supplier. As well as administrating the membership records, it would have to be empathetic to the Society's 13,000 members, many of whom are elderly and tend to worry about membership matters. The customer care offered by the partner would directly impact on how the members regarded the charity and whether or not they continued to support it.

The tender of the outsourcing contract involved the Society drawing up a detailed specification of its own requirements and a thorough check on the background of the potential partner – checking industry accreditations to see whether it demonstrated best practice, looking at the potential partner's record with other clients, and its ability to provide ongoing advice and feedback on how to use its data to better manage the charity's relationships with its members and supporters.

After outsourcing to Associa, the Macular Disease Society was able to reduce wastage via a general clean-up of the Society's database records which still held 'gone aways' and people who had died. By cleaning the data it was also able to identify those members who not yet registered for Gift Aid contributions (see Appendix). Within six months, it had boosted member income from Gift Aid by 93 per cent.

For the first time, the Society was able to truly integrate all its contact points – from post, telephone, fax, email or the internet. For example, in the past, new members joining via the website had to fill in their details on the website enquiry form and then await a reply from the Society. The reply letter unhelpfully asked them to fill in the details again and send the information back in the post before they were accepted as a member. With outsourcing, this duplication is a thing of the past. All the website details entered by the member are now automatically linked into a letter from the Society which is sent to the member with their unique reference number already allocated to make the member feel part of the Society.

With an integrated contact history of each member, Associa lends a more personal touch to the Society's direct mailings. For example, every member giving £1 more than their annual subscription now receives a thank you letter for their support. Members donating over £200 receive a thank you letter from the chairman.

Outsourcing has empowered the Society to prepare the ground for future campaigns to widen public support for its cause. For example, it found that non-members had sought to financially support the cause by requesting Christmas cards through the members themselves. Information about these non-members was now captured on the database for use in future public awareness and fundraising campaigns. These new contacts, often relatives of people affected by the condition, will now receive an annual publication aimed at further building their support for the work of the society.

As can be seen from this case study, an integrated contacts strategy is much more than just about keeping your records up to date – it goes right to the core of relationship marketing's aim to create friends for life.

## Ingredient 6: Database profiling and analysis

With a relational database (see Chapter 8) all data yielded by an integrated contact handling strategy (see Ingredient 5 above) is stored in a series of two-dimensional tables. The following case study offers a flavour of how database profiling and analysis can be used to build stronger relationships with your members.

## NFU Countryside

NFU Countryside is the National Farmers Union's membership organisation for people with an interest in rural affairs. It offers a 100-page monthly Countryside magazine, access to exclusive members' events, a fully searchable database of nearly 5,000 farm shops plus a wide range of affinity services and brand discounts – from a legal helpline to money off at selected independent garden centres.

Working in collaboration with the outsourcing company Associa, NFU piloted a database linked to an integrated contacts system. According to their individual contact history, the database allocates each member to one of four distinct groups, each with a different set of behavioural or attitudinal characteristics:

**Advocates**
high behavioural and
high attitudinal commitment

**Spuriously committed members**
high behavioural but low
attitudinal commitment

**Latently committed members**
low behavioural but high
attitudinal commitment

**Non-committed members**
showing low behavioural
and low attitudinal commitment

The Associa model is similar to the membership trapezoid (at the beginning of this chapter and used throughout this guide), but focuses on the middle three layers – the members, supporters and advocates.

In the Associa model, the most committed NFU Countryside members, or the **advocates** show *high behavioural commitment* (they use the scheme's services and benefits, such as helplines or discounts, on a regular basis) and also display a *high attitudinal commitment* (such as a feeling of pride at belonging and a readiness to recommend the scheme to others).

**Spuriously committed members** are those who are active or use the membership benefits but no longer show empathy or loyalty to the organisation. They are less likely to recommend the scheme to others and yet place a disproportionately large demand on resources. In other words, they exhibit *high behavioural commitment but low attitudinal commitment*.

Opposite to the spurious group are the NFU Countryside's **latently committed members** who show *low behavioural commitment with high attitudinal commitment*. These members are less likely to be active or to use member services, but they feel a strong allegiance with the organisation and its value. This group was felt to be ripe for encouragement to become more committed once the behavioural barriers are understood (ie why they are not using the services).

The final group are the **non-committed members**. This group shows *low behavioural and low attitudinal commitment*. They are not involved in activities, nor do they use the NFU Countryside's membership services. This group is also likely to be dissatisfied with their membership and is the most likely to lapse.

The value of such a model is that when individuals are identified as belonging to one group or the other, NFU Countryside can cost-effectively target communications to the right places. For example, it introduced Countryside Friends for the advocates – members who visit their local events (fairs, fêtes, etc) and promote and raise awareness of NFU Countryside. These people already have a great interest in the countryside and are able to talk knowledgeably about rural life. Although there is no formal contract between NFU Countryside and the Countryside Friends, they receive out-of-pocket expenses and commission for

> each membership sold. They are also encouraged to enter people into a prize draw which enables NFU Countryside to collect names and addresses of potential members who can then be targeted in later direct mail campaigns. The Countryside Friends are provided with all the training, information and marketing materials needed and while NFU Countryside is able to recommend places for the Country Friends to visit, they are also given scope to build a programme of activities throughout the spring and summer months to suit their own personal circumstances.
>
> For the majority group of members – the 68 per cent who made up the latently committed members group – NFU Countryside is now able to tailor marketing messages aimed at activating this cohort of members who feel a strong attitudinal commitment to the cause but who have hitherto displayed little behavioural activity – for example, purchasing goods or making a donation.
>
> By separating out its non-committed members, NFU Countryside is able to focus special incentives for remaining a member to people who need a quite different approach than for the more committed members.

## Ingredient 7: A systematic renewal programme

**The renewal letter is a key event in your loyalty-building programme.**

The renewal letter is a key event in your loyalty-building programme. It is the chance to make the member feel special for having supported your cause in the past year, and to build the case for renewing that support for another year.

Yet no matter how strong your membership product is, without a multi-stage renewal programme a fair percentage of members will lapse out of sheer inertia. Think about it, our usual reaction to seeing the utility or phone bills hit the doormat is invariably the same – 'I'll put that in the drawer and deal with it later.' Most people only get around to filling in a form when it becomes imperative. Local membership groups have always known that simply sending out renewal forms does not on its own guarantee that people will actually complete them. Cue the membership secretary mingling at the branch meeting and collecting the dues. Most national organisations have no such face-to-face opportunities and must rely on direct mail. One renewal mailing almost certainly won't be enough. A typical multi-stage programme includes:

Initial membership renewal letter
⇩
Reminder letter
⇩
Final reminder
⇩
Lapsed reactivation letter

The number of stages isn't fixed. As a general rule, you can keep sending renewal letters to your members until the response rate drops so low that the income earned does not recover the costs of sending them out. The business sector did its homework quite some time ago. After much testing, subscription-based magazines worked out that an initial invitation to renew followed by two reminder letters is generally the optimum number. That plus an additional letter sent to lapsed subscribers. This would indicate that most found that a fifth letter cost more than the income it generated. In the US, it is not unknown for some leading magazines to send up to nine letters – starting halfway through the current subscription. But in relationship marketing terms you are left wondering what impression this makes on the recipient.

For each stage of the renewal programme, you can do an ROI analysis (see Chapter 6) to work out the optimum number of stages for your renewal programme. Whatever approach you take, one stage will almost certainly not be enough. As a Christmas gift, I once received a subscription to the impressively well-written *Prospect* magazine. A year later I did get an invitation to renew. Thanks to my own inertia, I just didn't get around to filling it in. Then I lost my form or it was inadvertently thrown out; I didn't get another reminder. It was my loss but it was theirs too. You probably have a similar story to tell about a magazine or newsletter you once read. There are two different types of renewal programmes:

**Fixed date:** these renew the entire membership base at a certain fixed date during the calendar year. This works best for schemes such as a sports club, where the benefits are seasonal. People joining late may be offered a reduced rate. Other organisations choose a fixed-date system because it is easier to administrate; rolling systems are more complex and require intricate database management. For larger schemes, the downside of fixed-date systems is that all the renewals have to be processed at once causing sudden pressure on those who administrate it.

**Rolling date:** these renew each member individually when their membership becomes due 12 months from the day (or month) that they originally joined. So a member who joined in May 2003 will renew in May 2004, but one who joins in July 2003 will renew in July 2004, and so on. These have the advantage of spreading the administrative workload across the calendar year and of allowing every member to enjoy a full year's worth of benefits. That said, they do require continuous all-year-round database administration.

### The renewal letter

There is no one-size-fits-all template for the perfect renewal letter but the sample below illustrates several aspects of good practice:

Anyshire
Nature
Trust

Anyshire Nature Trust (ANT)
Grange Park
Anyshire AY1 2XE

Ms A Sample
1 Sample Road
Anytown
Anyshire AY1 6LP

November 2003

**Your membership helps us to help the environment – and you!**

Dear Ms Sample

Your annual membership of Anyshire Nature Trust (ANT) expires on 7 January 2004 and so I would like to invite you to renew your membership for another year.

Renewing your membership of ANT will ensure that you continue to benefit from:

- All the latest news and stories via *Busy Bee* – our quarterly magazine.
- Our comprehensive annual yearbook with an up-to-date listing of all the local sites of interest, nature reserves and guided walks.
- NEW! In response to popular demand, we are introducing discounts on well-known brands of nature-watching equipment and leisure wear.

When you renew your membership, would you consider using direct debit as your method of payment? This would mean less paperwork for you in the future and it would reduce our administration costs so that an additional £2 of your fee could go straight into our Anyshire Marshes fighting fund – to protect it from industrial development.

With Gift Aid your membership contribution to ANT is worth 28% more to us, at no extra cost to you. If you are a UK taxpayer and have not already completed a Gift Aid form, simply read and complete the attached coupon.

As well as being of direct benefit to you, your membership of ANT brings hope to everyone living in Anyshire.

In the past year, ANT persuaded Anyshire Council to reject the proposed planning development of the Freeman's Meadows. Not only is this a breeding area for a number of uncommon bird species, but a favourite family walking habitat has been preserved for future generations.

We cannot be complacent; our countryside is under threat as never before and there are more battles to be fought. **The more people like you support our work, the more our voice will be heard.**

Quite simply, we couldn't do it without you.

Yours sincerely

Julia Millais
Director, Anyshire Nature Trust

PS Please ignore this reminder if you have already renewed your membership. Thank you. (Your payment may have crossed our letter in the post!)

This sample letter demonstrates sound relationship marketing principles:

- It personalises the letter by mail merging the member's name into it.
- The letter text has added impact with the use of the

pronouns 'you' and 'your'.

- It appeals to self-interest – with a prominent statement of the benefits.
- It stresses the organisation's *ongoing* need for campaign support (the fight isn't over yet).
- It appeals to altruism – your loyalty will benefit the environment.
- It introduces a NEW benefit (it isn't merely a 'more of the same' offer).
- It acknowledges the member's contribution to a recent campaign success.
- Direct debit and Gift Aid are promoted in terms that stress the benefit to both the member and the cause.

**Minimising gone aways**

Two ever-present reasons for lapsing are deceased members and gone aways (people who move home without a forwarding address). No one has yet come up with an answer to the former issue but the latter can be minimised if not totally eliminated.

If you have a high proportion of gone aways, try to make it easier for members to inform you of their new address. For example, you can overprint your magazine mailings with 'Tell us your new address' coupons.

Sometimes the fault may lie with incorrectly inputted addresses or postcodes on your mailing list. With a good database, these mistakes can be minimised via the use of a database checking facility, such as the Royal Mail's PAF file which holds 27 million addresses and automatically highlights any inappropriately inputted address or postcode.

**Effect of payment methods**

It is now widely recognised that the methods of payment offered can have a significant, even dramatic, impact on membership retention rates.

The introduction of **direct debit** will almost always create a significant uplift. The Consumers' Association magazine *Which?* is only available by direct debit while many voluntary organisations such as the RSPB have systematic programmes for persuading existing members to move away from cheque or cash payments in favour of direct debit. There is no great mystery about this: once the member signs a mandate allowing your organisation to automatically deduct the membership fee from their personal bank account – each year, quarter or month – there is no need for you to send a renewal letter at all. While you must still notify members of any proposed price increase you do not need their consent to deduct it. This method takes advantage of the inertia principle. In other words, the member doesn't have to make an effort to renew, but has to make an effort to cancel the mandate.

A **standing order** payment is less common to membership schemes than they once were. While they do allow fees to be deducted automatically, the membership fee cannot be changed without the member's consent.

**Credit and debit cards** are now a fairly widespread method of payment for membership renewals. The renewal is processed electronically using a telephone between your organisation (or external outsourcing company) and the merchant bank. With a secure server your website can also process credit card payments with the minimum of hassle to both parties.

### Is the future electronic?

It is easy to see the exciting future potential of email to save on traditional paper-based renewal costs – the unit cost of sending an email is a fraction of the usual letter, envelope and stamp.

But first your organisation's data collection strategy must accommodate the systematic collection of email as well as postal addresses. If the majority of your members joined in the past, their existing records may not include an email address. So consider inserting a new email address field into all new membership application and renewal forms. There are also technological considerations such as: Can your computer or database output bulk email mailings? Will your fulfilment team cope with mass email returns? (Email addresses change with greater frequency than postal addresses; 'unknown to sender' returns may be high and there is no readily obtainable background cleaning file for email addresses to come to the rescue).

Nonetheless, the long-term cost efficiency will surely make it worth the effort to overcome these issues. Establish a long-term data collection strategy for incrementally building the number of email addresses on your membership database. Explain to those of your members who have email facilities that if they consent to receive future communications by email then it will reduce your organisation's costs. Do small-scale test mailings to evaluate the cost/benefits of email and compare them with postal methods.

Greenpeace was among the first to facilitate renewals through the internet. By way of typing a unique individual pin number into a field within the membership section of the website, it gives the individual access to his/her own secure, personal page – allowing them to change contact details, upgrade or renew. All this, without impacting on the workload of Greenpeace staff!

## Ingredient 8: A lapsed reactivation programme

Any renewal programme needs to do more than just collect fees from committed members. It must also diagnose the underlying reasons why less committed members lapse. As with Diabetes UK (see case study below), you might consider doing a lapsed subscriber survey using a mailed questionnaire, telephone interviews or focus groups, to probe into the reasons why they no longer wish to be a member (see Chapter 4 for further discussion of these and other research methods).

Consider every possible reason – big or small – why any member might not wish to renew and then see if you can reduce or eliminate these factors.

### Exercise: Why do your members lapse?

- Indecision
- Lack of time to complete the form
- Lost the form
- Financial circumstances have changed for the worse
- Unmet expectations of the service
- Not getting the information initially hoped for
- Getting the information sought and then losing interest
- Cold recruitment brings in uncommitted members who quickly leave
- Inadequate customer service from other departments
- Aggravated by your junk mail/repeat demands for money
- Perception of ineffective campaigning
- Perception of wastage by your organisation
- Found another organisation that delivers a more relevant service
- Unresolved complaint handling
- Gone aways
- Deceased

This exercise can make a good team-building event for the key people involved with delivering your scheme. Make sure you involve your front-line staff or volunteers too. As they deal directly with both satisfied and dissatisfied members, they will be sensitive to the more qualitative factors. Other key sources of lapsed data might include:

1. Annual membership survey.
2. Database analysis of demographic, behavioural and attitudinal characteristics of lapsed members.
3. Letters of complaint.
4. Telephone conversations.
5. Face-to-face conversations at events.
6. Benchmarking the experiences of other third-sector bodies.

**Analysing the reasons why people lapse means being committed to acting on the results.**

Analysing the reasons why people lapse means being committed to acting on the results. Avoid the filing cabinet syndrome of just skim-reading and filing the results away when the findings are inconvenient or problematic to address (see Chapter 4). Even when feedback is negative, it can often be turned to advantage. For example:

- If some members did not get the information they hoped to find in your magazine then integrate those topics into your future editorial plans.
- If some members say that they are getting too much mail or the wrong kind of mail from your organisation, then consider how you might in future offer members the flexibility of choosing what they want to receive.
- A relatively high percentage of dissatisfied members citing unresolved complaints might indicate a need to tighten up your complaints procedure. Do you have a systemic report for analysing the number and type of complaints? Is each complaint logged, tracked and resolved?

Taking action on the reasons behind people lapsing has the wider benefit of improving the service for satisfied members too.

Take every action you can, no matter how great or small, to improve member satisfaction. It is not always the case that one single factor can explain why most of your members lapse. There may be a host of factors involved. Even if each factor accounts for only one per cent of your lapsed members leaving, then tackling five of them could incrementally improve your renewal rate by a valuable five per cent.

## Diabetes UK

In 2003, Diabetes UK had 175,000 individual members – people with diabetes, their families and friends – plus 6,000 professional members, mainly GPs and practice nurses.

The news that every person with diabetes wants to hear is that a cure has been found. It's not an impossible dream but it won't happen overnight. In the meantime, Diabetes UK champions the cause of medical research and offers up-to-date information and advice to enable people to manage their condition on a day-to-day basis.

Once acquired, diabetes is a chronic condition that requires people to manage their daily nutrition and lifestyle. This creates a natural incentive for members to stay in touch with the charity and in 2003, an average 82 per cent of people renewed their membership. To discover ways of reducing the 18 per cent churn rate, Diabetes UK commissioned independent research into why some people lapse.

For any scheme that recruits heavily via direct mail, around five per cent of the churn rate can often be attributed to people who have moved address without notification (the so-called gone aways) and deceased members. But the Diabetes UK research identified another factor: people lead increasingly busy lives, put off taking action and often just forget to renew – even after three letters. As a result, Diabetes UK undertook trials of a fourth lapsed mailing. These reintroduced five per cent of lapsed members. For this mailing, the outer envelope was redesigned to make it more self-evident that this was a renewal pack. The previous outer envelopes were sometimes perceived by the recipient as containing a request for a donation or a general mailing and so were often left unopened or thrown away.

Another research-driven tactic used by Diabetes UK for reducing the attrition rate was to incentivise people to take out direct debit by offering members a £1 discount. All its letters now include a carefully worded statement that this is cheaper for the charity to administrate and so allows more of the membership fee to be devoted to vital research.

Another loyalty device is the membership card which is mail merged onto the first renewal letter and peeled off by the recipient. This credit card-sized membership card not only carries the member's name and number and the key Diabetes UK helpline numbers, it also allows space for the GP and hospital clinic phone numbers to be written on it. The card isn't an unnecessary piece of frippery. It is designed to be practical and reinforce brand loyalty to the charity.

Diabetes UK is now in the process of collecting email addresses from its members. By mid-2003, just 10 per cent of members had submitted an email address but with the exponential growth of PC usage among even older groups, the charity expects the percentage will increase year on year. In future, emailed renewals are potentially both convenient for the member and cost effective for the charity. Increasing the percentage of life members from the current 13 per cent is another long-term goal. Plans are in hand to test both email and the internet. Renewing by mobile phones is not a short-term prospect, but the charity is open to considering any channel that will "make it as easy as possible to renew". The principle is not just to maximise the renewal rate – although that is the outcome – but the desire to offer convenience and "provide old-fashioned customer service".

### Lapsed reactivation programmes

When running a lapsed member reactivation programme, avoid references in your letter to 'your previous membership' or 'our lapsed members'. A large number of won't have taken a conscious decision to lapse at all – they just haven't got around to renewing yet. Phrase your approach along the lines of "you may have missed your most recent magazine" or "we just wanted to get in touch with you to check that ..."

To quote the old Joni Mitchell song Big Yellow Taxi – "Don't it always seem to go / You don't know what you've got until it's gone". Many people defer taking action until it has been made clear that the benefit is lost – such as access being denied to the members' only area of the website. Therefore, a lapsed reactivation programme tends to work best when timed not too soon after the membership has lapsed, but not too long afterwards either. Depending upon the frequency of your magazine mailings, for example, that could be two to four months after lapsing or when one or two issues of your magazine have been missed.

## Ingredient 9: Systematic renewal data

Some third sector bodies have no idea how much each renewal stage costs them, or whether they have an optimum number of renewal stages. Consider how much wastage that implies.

Statistics alone do not provide the full picture, but they are an essential ingredient to maximising your retention rates.

With a database you can systematically document the results of your renewal programme. The exact data collected will vary for one organisation to another, but will include the costs and income, the renewal rate (numbers of people who rejoin) and the attrition rate (numbers of people who lapse).

The data table overleaf shows a six month report of the four stage renewal programme of the Anyshire Nature Trust. Like any detailed spreadsheet, at first glance it looks intimidating. But with a little practice and routine use it is quite easy to interpret.

**Statistics alone do not provide the full picture, but they are an essential ingredient to maximising your retention rates.**

The first renewal letter is sent in month eight of the member's current one year subscription. The second in month ten, with a final reminder just before the subscription is due to expire. If a person's membership expires, a 'reactivation' letter is sent two months later to try and revive their interest.

Over the period, a total of 3,440 members were due for renewal (row 1). At the end of the period 80 per cent rejoined (row 32). The cumulative cost of the programme was £2,310 (row 34). Annual income was £34,313 (row 35) with a £32,003 profit/surplus (row 36).

But the report also highlights some underlying issues that could be tackled:

- Of the 80 per cent of members who renewed, 27 per cent did so automatically by direct debit (row 3). Once this has been taken into account, the Trust retained just 53 per cent of those who paid by cheque or cash.
- With a very modest 15 per cent response (row 8), the first renewal letter is wasteful. Many members complain that it is arriving "too early".
- The response to the reactivation mailing shows large seasonal fluctuations (row 26) – ranging from 19 per cent in May to zero in August.

Possible courses of action might be to:

- implement a programme to upgrade more members to direct debit
- move the first letter back to month 10 to increase response rate and reduce complaints from members receiving their renewal letter early
- boost the response rate of lapsed reactivation mailings by posting them quarterly, rather than monthly, to avoid the dry summer when people are less responsive.

| | | APR | MAY | JUN | JUL | AUG | SEP | TOT |
|---|---|---|---|---|---|---|---|---|
| 1 | Numbers due to renew | 1000 | 800 | 750 | 400 | 90 | 400 | 3440 |
| 2 | Numbers renewing/direct debit | 270 | 216 | 203 | 108 | 24 | 112 | 933 |
| 3 | Response rate (%) | 29 | 28 | 27 | 26 | 26 | 28 | 27% |
| 4 | Costs @ 40p per transaction | 108 | 86 | 81 | 43 | 10 | 45 | £373 |
| 5 | Income @ £12 average | 3420 | 2592 | 2436 | 1296 | 288 | 1344 | £11376 |
| 6 | Surplus / (deficit) | 3312 | 2506 | 2355 | 1253 | 278 | 1299 | £11003 |
| | | | | | | | | |
| 7 | Numbers still to renew | 730 | 584 | 547 | 292 | 66 | 288 | 2507 |
| 8 | Actual response rate (%) | 18 | 16 | 15 | 14 | 14 | 13 | 15% |
| 9 | Cumulative response rate (%) | 40 | 39 | 38 | 37 | 36 | 37 | 38% |
| 10 | Costs @ 30p per pack | 219 | 175 | 164 | 87 | 20 | 86 | £751 |
| 11 | Income @ £12 average | 1560 | 1152 | 984 | 480 | 108 | 449 | £4733 |
| 12 | Surplus / (deficit) | 1341 | 977 | 820 | 393 | 88 | 363 | £3982 |
| | | | | | | | | |
| 13 | Numbers still to renew | 600 | 488 | 465 | 252 | 57 | 250 | 2112 |
| 14 | Actual response rate (%) | 50 | 52 | 48 | 46 | 43 | 46 | 48% |
| 15 | Cumulative response rate (%) | 70 | 68 | 68 | 66 | 65 | 66 | 67% |
| 16 | Costs @ 30p per pack | 180 | 146 | 140 | 76 | 17 | 75 | £634 |
| 17 | Income @ £12 average | 3600 | 2784 | 2700 | 1392 | 313 | 1392 | £12181 |
| 18 | Surplus / (deficit) | 3420 | 2638 | 2560 | 1316 | 196 | 1317 | £11447 |
| | | | | | | | | |
| 19 | Numbers still to renew | 300 | 256 | 240 | 136 | 32 | 136 | 1100 |
| 20 | Actual response rate (%) | 37 | 34 | 31 | 32 | 31 | 32 | 33% |
| 21 | Cumulative response rate (%) | 81 | 79 | 78 | 77 | 76 | 77 | 78% |
| 22 | Costs @ 30p per pack | 90 | 79 | 72 | 41 | 10 | 41 | £333 |
| 23 | Income @ £12 average | 1320 | 1056 | 900 | 528 | 119 | 528 | £4451 |
| 24 | Surplus / (deficit) | 1230 | 977 | 828 | 487 | 109 | 487 | £4118 |
| | | | | | | | | |
| 25 | Numbers still to renew | 190 | 168 | 165 | 92 | 22 | 92 | 729 |
| 26 | Actual response rate (%) | 16 | 19 | 9 | 0 | 0 | 4 | 8% |
| 27 | Cumulative response rate (%) | 84 | 83 | 80 | 79 | 75 | 78 | 80% |
| 29 | Costs @ 30p per pack | 57 | 50 | 50 | 28 | 7 | 27 | £219 |
| 30 | Income @ £12 average | 360 | 384 | 180 | 0 | 0 | 48 | £972 |
| 31 | Surplus / (deficit) | 303 | 334 | 130 | (28) | (7) | 21 | £21 |
| 32 | TOTAL RENEWALS (%) | 84 | 83 | 80 | 79 | 75 | 78 | 80% |
| 33 | TOTAL ATTRITION RATE (%) | 16 | 17 | 20 | 23 | 25 | 22 | 20% |
| 34 | TOTAL COSTS (£) | 654 | 536 | 507 | 275 | 64 | 274 | £2310 |
| 35 | TOTAL INCOME (£) | 10260 | 7968 | 7200 | 3696 | 1428 | 3761 | £34313 |
| 36 | TOTAL SURPLUS (LOSS) (£) | 9606 | 7432 | 6693 | 3421 | 1364 | 3487 | £32003 |

## Ingredient 10: A commitment to making technology and data serve human needs

Does a member join your scheme in order to have a relationship with a database or a membership number? Obviously not, yet that's exactly how many allegedly service-based industries relate to us. From credit card companies to banks to insurance brokers, all too frequently their correspondence and call centres reduce you to a number first and a person second. As do many third-sector organisations if we're frank about it.

It is all too easy to become seduced by technology and data and to lose sight of our members as living breathing individuals that we are meant to serve. Technological and data-driven relationship marketing is a means to an end, never an end in itself. It is not the object of your relationship but a channel for managing the relationship between your cause and the members. Good relationship marketing isn't just about the hard skills of marketing strategy, there's a softer set of skills involved too: honesty, sincerity and commitment. There's the art of making members feel valued, wanted, listened to, involved, and so on. *Technology and Data In Relationship Fundraising,* Ken Burnett[1] lists nine of these softer keys to securing the loyalty of hundreds or thousands of donors. With just a little adaptation, the same keys apply to members too.

- **Be honest:** While public trust in institutions is at an all-time low (see Chapter 5 on the first P, philosophy), non-profit groups are an exception to this rule. This trust is one of your most priceless assets. So be open and transparent in all your actions and don't allow your members to feel that you are being anything less than honest in all your dealings with them.
- **Be sincere and let your commitment show:** Members join because they care. Allow them to see that you really care about both their welfare and the cause. Reinforce this in all your communications – from the incoming telephone call to the newsletter to the renewal letter. When they can see this, members will be all the more prepared to come out and respond to your appeals for support.
- **Be prompt:** Set yourself clear and appropriate targets to reply to each member request or complaint within seven working days. Promptness shows that you really value hearing from your members.
- **Be regular:** Develop an annual communications mix (see above) with a regular and logical sequence of contact with your members – via email, newsletters, appeals, and so forth. Communicate at least quarterly, if not more. Regular

contact keeps your relationship alive. Long periods of silence followed by a sudden out-of-the-blue contact may leave the member feeling treated like an afterthought.

- **Be interesting and memorable:** Don't fall into the trap of being worthy but dull. The very fact your members have joined your cause means that they should find your communications exciting and memorable. You have the news, the information, the stories and the ideas they want. Exploit these riches to the full and be interesting and memorable.
- **Be involving:** Research shows clearly that the more your members are involved, the higher the eventual renewal rates. So positively promote regular opportunities for your members to input or feedback into your work; from membership surveys to the magazine letters page, from the annual conference to head office open days.
- **Be cheerful and helpful:** Advertise your willingness to help and never let members feel unsure about asking for it. Assure that all your colleagues know the importance of good customer care so that your members feel that the whole organisation is there for them, not just the membership department.
- **Be faithful:** Keep your promises. Honour your membership offer, be faithful to the mission and values that your members signed up to.
- **Be cost effective:** Avoid conspicuous waste and regularly feedback to your members on how their membership fees are invested back into the cause.

## Action points

✓ Recognise that relationship marketing isn't about sales. Relationship marketing = recruitment, loyalty building and retention.

✓ Plot the six key stages of the membership journey in advance of your new members joining.

✓ Always extend a warm welcome. The quickest way to dampen the rush of enthusiasm felt by the new member is to make an impersonal welcome, or none at all.

✓ Tailor the right annual communications mix for your members (and segments).

✓ Some members quickly forget why they joined. Use your newsletter, emails and other communications to continuously reiterate the benefits, the services and the opportunities to get involved.

✓ Periodically reiterate your organisation's purpose. Tell great stories about the impact your organisation makes on people's lives.

✓ Be involving and keep your members active. The more involved and active they are, the more they'll recall the benefits when later asked to renew.

✓ Database your members' contact histories and use it to build a complete picture of each individual.

✓ Harness the power of databases to target your benefits, offers and communications to different subgroups within your membership base.

✓ Put as much of your time and resources into creating an inspirational renewal letter as you do for the initial effort.

✓ Beware the inertia factor: one renewal letter won't be enough. You will need to send two, three or four.

✓ Analyse the cost, income and response rates for each renewal stage. Don't stop sending letters until the response becomes unprofitable.

✓ Don't neglect the views of your lapsed members. Find out what lessons you can learn from them and then implement a lapsed reactivation programme.

✓ Invest in a direct debit programme and give your existing cash- or cheque-paying members every chance to upgrade.

✓ Prepare to convert as many of your members as you can to internet and email-based renewal systems. Electronic renewals will cost a fraction of traditional paper-based systems.

✓ Make data and technology serve a human need.

✓ Play the nine keys of relationship marketing: be honest; be sincere; be prompt; be regular; be interesting and memorable; be involving; be cheerful; be faithful; and be cost effective.

---

1. Burnett, K (2002) *Relationship Fundraising: A Donor-based Approach to the Business of Raising Money*, Jossey Bass Wiley

---

# 8 Membership databases

The membership database is much more than just a humble list of names of who is and who is not a member. As discussed in Chapter 1, it is a key part in the relationship marketing toolkit.

If the ultimate objective of any membership scheme is to manage one-to-one relationships, no matter how many hundreds or thousands of members it has, then the database can help it to replicate the personal touch used by the old corner shopkeepers to inspire loyalty from their customers: "Hello Mr Jones – as it's Saturday evening I assume you've popped in for your weekly *Sporting Life* and packet of Polo mints. By the way, we have now introduced a stock of pipe-cleaners after you enquired about them last week."

Obviously, we cannot keep this sort of personal knowledge inside our heads for hundreds and thousands of members all at once. But a well-managed database can become the modern equivalent of the old shopkeepers (see Chapter 7, Ingredient 5: an integrated contact strategy).

With a *relational database* all the subsets of membership data are stored in a series of two-dimensional tables. These are inter-connected so that a table with the individual member's name and identifying number is linked to an address table, to a membership category table, to a contact history table and so forth. Over time, you can add as many new tables as are required to serve the evolving needs of your scheme.

Obviously, membership databases can't quite recreate the one-to-one relationships found in the old corner shops, but what they do instead is to segment the overall membership base into subgroups of people who share common characteristics, such as a group of new members due to receive their welcome pack, or people who supported a recent campaign appeal and who are due a thank you letter, or those who are about to renew, and so on.

As discussed in Chapter 5, segmentation is a powerful tool that can offer your members a reasonable choice of how they wish to engage with your organisation. Some people may consent to receive appeal mailings, other people may loathe seeing them land on their doormat. The database is the engine that stores and manages these choices and assures that we honour and deliver them. Segmentation enables you to build a set of relationships with different groups of people. Quite simply, tailoring your service in this way can make the difference to whether or not the individual renews their membership.

A well-chosen software package can also save you a huge amount of time and money by integrating your membership records with your host organisation's accounts, word processing and spreadsheet packages. Without this, the process of managing subscriptions and renewals soon becomes unfeasible.

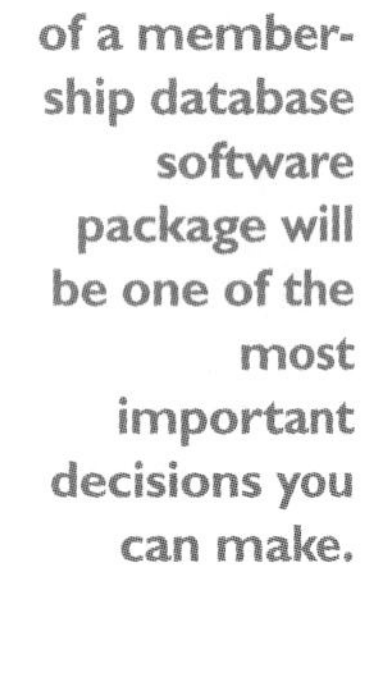
Your choice of a membership database software package will be one of the most important decisions you can make.

In summary, your choice of a membership database software package will be one of the most important decisions you can make. You may have the right product, price, promotion and people, but all of that will count for little if the membership records are inefficiently stored and your computer can't segment the lists or effectively automate your communications. A good database can not only significantly reduce your costs and boost income, but it can also help assure that your organisation is legally compliant with data protection legisation. This chapter covers:

- Selecting a database solution
- In-house or outsourced?
- Creating a database specification
- The cost of databases
- Keeping accurate records
- Data collection
- Managing your data
- Conforming to data protection legislation

## Selecting a database solution

At its most basic, a database is a list of people. Very small or local groups may hold the data on a card index file or some other informal storage and retrieval system. But with the exponential growth of home computers, even those with minimal resources are now most likely to have computerised the data, if only by using a popular word processing or spreadsheet package.

To the novice or home computer user, the more sophisticated database software packages can at first sight seem awesomely difficult, intricate and fiddly. In practice they are not, providing you bear in mind some basic features that will be inherent to any system you choose. At the bare minimum, the membership record will always include the name and address linked to the date and type of membership, the renewal date and a history of the communications that have taken place in between joining and lapsing. The system will offer data views in a user-friendly format that empowers you to look at the same set of records and data in different ways – allowing managers, marketers and volunteers alike the opportunity of calling up screens specifically tailored to their own day-to-day needs.

The type of data collected may include, but need not be limited to:

- Salutation (Mr, Mrs, Ms, Miss, Dr, Sir, Lady, options for non-conventional titles)
- Forename or initials
- Surname
- Suffixes (OBE, MBE, etc which may be important to some members)
- Spouse, other family members
- Full address (street number/name, village/district, town/city, county, postcode)
- Delivery address (if different from billing address)
- Telephone, fax/mobile, SMS numbers
- Email address
- Origin source (how the member was originally recruited, for example, at the AGM, by direct mail or website)
- Membership start date
- Duration of membership
- Category of membership
- Fee paid
- Optional donations paid
- Other status (eg one-off donor, committed giver, legacy pledger, volunteer, campaign advocate)
- Contact flags (to show which correspondence or packs have been received by the member, and which appeals have been responded to)
- Renewals (first reminder, second and final renewal letters, which one was responded to, reasons for lapsing if known)
- Opt outs (eg from appeal mailings)
- Special instructions (eg does not wish to receive annual report and voting papers, or other ad hoc requests)

The greater the range of data that you handle, the more likely it is you will need specialist database software (especially if you have a membership scheme with tiered categories), as opposed to the simpler off-the-shelf database solutions that suffice for more basic schemes. But choosing the right software package is a challenging task. You can take your pick from more than 100 fundraising or membership packages on the market. Whether it is free shareware or a customised database costing thousands of pounds, the choice is perplexing but can be broken down into three broad options:

- **Off-the-shelf package.** These are sold as standard packages. While their one-size-fits-all approach is unlikely to cover all of your requirements, they offer entry-level solutions at a reasonable cost.
- **A bespoke database.** These databases are tailored by the supplier to the very specific needs of your non-profit organisation. They cost more and to be successful, you will first need a very clear long-term strategy and a detailed plan as to how your database marketing will fit into this.
- **Hybrid solutions.** As an alternative to the two options above, you can specify a hybrid that utilises an off-the-shelf package and combines these with features adapted to meet your own needs.

### In-house or outsourced?

Will the database run in-house at your office or will it be outsourced to an external company? Doing it in-house may give you greater ultimate control over your data, but your organisation will also have to budget for capital expenditure on hardware, software, cables, plus the variable costs of software development and maintenance. Outsourcing the membership database to an external database and fulfilment bureau was once the preserve of very large organisations who now increasingly buy in-house facilities. However, the advent of the internet has now opened up the outsourcing route to smaller organisations.

Whether you choose to keep it in-house or go outside, you should go to a competitive tender. Some organisations feel confident that they are the best judges of what they need, but most will at the very least get the wise advice of a database expert who can help them match what is available out there to their specific needs. A consultant can help you to prepare a full specification of your requirements and check your potential supplier exhaustively against it. Get your system users or fulfilment team involved too – ask them to give you their own assessment of the basic features, screen layout and ease of navigation around the system. Ask them to test load some of your current data onto their system (if that doesn't work, it might signal potential future problems). Don't base your decisions on a single sales pitch. Ask for references or preferably a full client list, and conduct some benchmarking visits. Ask impertinent questions – is the computer platform stable? Have the bugs been ironed out of the system? Is the telephone helpline really as accessible as it says in the brochure?

One pitfall with some database suppliers is the overuse of technological jargon when talking to lay users. Some will seek to impress their clients by wrapping technology in mystique. But you should treat with caution any company that fails to communicate clearly how the technology works and how it applies to your situation. In relationship marketing terms, databases are there for managing long-term relationships. So your supplier must convince you that it will make a suitable long-term partner who will always communicate clearly with your end users, not just at the sales presentation. Purchasing the kit is just the beginning. You might be working with that company for a decade or more. Be wary too of systems that run on obscure programming languages. Whenever problems occur, you will become over-dependent on an elite cadre of technical experts.

Whether you are starting a membership database from scratch or looking to upgrade your existing systems, make sure you compile a checklist of items to feature in your audit of needs. The following exercise offers a template for your own checklist, though it is by no means exhaustive and you will most likely add a few more items of your own.

## Exercise: Creating a database specification

Whether you are looking for a new database package, upgrading your existing package, or just want to assess how you are doing with your current set-up, use the template below to audit your requirements and to stimulate further thinking on your specific needs:

**Checklist of key requirements for a membership database**

**General**

- Was it designed with UK non-profit organisations in mind?
- Will it enable your membership administrators to talk to other teams – such as fundraisers, event coordinators, sales staff, marketing, finance?

- Will it integrate with popular accounting, word processing and spreadsheet packages?

**Contact management**

- Does it provide for a full contact history for each individual?
- Will it save your word processed documents on the database?
- Is a full mailing history automatically generated for each record – inclusive of initial membership application, renewals, donations, gifts, enquiries, purchases and all other transactions?
- Can it customise a variety of pages and fields for your specific data needs?
- To comply with the Data Protection Act, are mailing flags available to prevent specific mailings going to people who don't want them?

**Security**

- Check that user identity and password access features are included and that it allows for someone to be assigned as the System Administrator who has access to the records, who can only view records and who can amend them.

**Data entry**

- Does the system feel user-friendly for data input staff? (It should most likely be a Windows-type or at least have a Windows-type look and feel to it)
- Has it got a rapid address and bank account entry?
- Will it allow data import into, and export from and to, other databases?
- Can it automatically check duplicate records and merge them together?

**Membership administration**

- Does it support tiered membership schemes?
- Will it handle membership renewal and lapsing processes?
- Has it got the flexibility to schedule either fixed or rolling renewal dates?
- Can it generate membership cards?

**Finance**

- Is a full financial transaction history maintained?

- Does it record full range types (what the money was for) and source (why it was given)?
- Will it import bank files for automated standing order reconciliation?
- Has it got a BACS facility for paperless direct debit?
- Can it handle Gift Aid processing?

**Internet**

- Given the unlimited future potential of the internet can the database interface with it, or is it capable of being upgraded to do so?

**Recruitment campaigns and appeals**

- Does it produce automated campaign reports enabling you to see, at a glance, overall campaign performance against target, response rates and return on investment?
- Will it allow users to write their own reports and queries and then store them in an internal library for future use?
- Can you take advantage of instant visual campaign and appeal status – graphs, pie charts, statistical tables?

**Technical and system requirements**

- Will it sit on your organisation's computer server, or can the supplier deliver a server for you?
- What version of Windows, or other operating software, does it require?
- How many users (your staff) will the licence allow for?

**Technical support and upgrades**

- Does the supplier offer unlimited access during office hours to telephone support?
- Are free upgrades included or are they paid for?
- Is there a user group to enable both supplier and customers to exchange ideas and feedback?
- Does it take an account management approach to guiding your organisation on its strategic and problem-solving needs?

You may not be able to afford, or even need, every feature that is on offer from the supplier. You may find the so-called Moscow rules handy (must have; should have; could have; and will live without). Moscow rules encourage you to prioritise the features that you really need over those which might be nice to have but aren't strictly essential. For example, would you really prefer a 24-hour support contract to a user-friendly interface?

## The cost of databases

In recent years, the exponential growth in fundraising has seeded a lucrative market in building and supplying donor databases. Often membership databases are spin-offs from a company's initial investment in fundraising support systems. So be wary of compromise solutions. Look out for the companies who have gone the extra mile in tailoring their products specifically for membership managers.

Whatever the price quoted, fundraising and membership databases aren't cheap. There is a valid reason for this – they demand a lot of research and software development on the part of the supplier (sometimes even more so than customer databases used in the commercial sector). From this complexity springs the need for sound training and support systems including ongoing consultancy to enable membership organisations to make the best strategic use of the system and human resources for staffing the telephone helpline.

As stated earlier, an alternative to buying your own software package is to rent it. Outsourcing bureaux can offer the economies of scale that come with communal working arrangements. They connect with remote membership departments via dial-up access to communal software facilities over a digital telephone line. Remember that a database isn't a one-off investment; there needs to be ongoing investment in staff training and consultancy, and support from the supplier (often a monthly fee).

Whichever route you choose, do a cost-benefit analysis of your prospective new or upgraded system. This involves weighing up the increased loyalty and income that is forecast to be achieved from a well-managed relationship marketing strategy and relational database, and demonstrating to your trustees or chief executive how the new or upgraded system will more than repay for itself with long-term membership success. Don't underestimate the time that needs to be invested in choosing and implementing a new database. Allocate sufficient time to allow for a detailed specification to be drawn up, tendering and staff training. If it doesn't all go to plan it's all too easy for organisations to blame the supplier and not look at their own project management.

**Keeping accurate records**

Good databasing isn't just about technology – the human element is vital too. To coin an old phrase that's long been a mantra in the computer industry – Garbage In, Garbage Out (or GIGO to cite the acronym). The task of inputting data is critical. Even the perfect all-singing-all-dancing membership database will be severely compromised if your record keeping is inaccurate. If good data gives you good answers, then nobody has yet invented the database that stops poor data giving you very stupid answers.

Good quality data rests on two irreducibly human tasks: one is producing a strategy for *data collection* – looking at all the information that is sloshing around your organisation before deciding what and how to collect it. The second is defining a clear plan for data management – how to look after and take care of your data once it is on the system.

**Data collection**

Over and above the membership application or renewal, consider what is happening in your organisation on a day-to-day basis that is currently generating useful information. For example, information enquiries, complaints, purchases, completing a membership survey, Gift Aid, donations, committed giving and legacy pledges. But also bear in mind that the more data you collect, the greater the time demands will be for the people inputting it. So whether you are starting from scratch or working with an existing system, prioritise your data needs against what your organisation is trying to achieve. For example, a local conservation society might keep details of its individual members' contact details and the skills and knowledge that each is prepared to volunteer to local projects.

**The more data you collect, the greater the time demands will be.**

As a rule of thumb, if you cannot think of a reason for having the data, don't collect it. Collecting too much information is as expensive and wasteful as having too little. The key principle is to select information not collect it for its own sake. For a corporate membership scheme, it might merely be interesting to know the number of employees working at each of its corporate members, but such data might be superfluous. On the other hand, if it is to be used to tailor services and promotional offers to large and small companies, it would be justifiable to collect it.

Ensure that the response coupon on any form, leaflet, brochure or advertisement allows sufficient room for clear and legible names and addresses. If the address field in the coupon is too small, or you have left insufficient space for the lengthy email addresses that abound, then you increase the probability of collecting poor data.

A word about the people who do the data inputting – whether in your organisation or at the fulfilment house. Typically, these people might be among the lowest paid staff or they may be volunteers. So the task of ongoing data collection is a real management issue. If staff feel disinterested at the prospect of repetitive inputting or collecting ad hoc data (enquiries, complaints, etc), then data quality is inevitably going to be patchy. They may understandably think: 'What's in it for me?' You will have to work at communicating the value of the organisation to the members and indeed to the staff or volunteers themselves. Some managers seek to avoid boredom and fatigue through task rotation and involving team members in strategic discussion and team issues, so that small matters such as accurate inputting assume the strategic importance that they deserve.

**Managing your data**

Databases have to be scrupulously managed if they are to be the springboard for effective membership growth. The following elements of good practice will go a long way to ensuring this:

- Appoint a data supervisor to monitor quality control, whether in your own organisation or at the fulfilment house. The data supervisor acts as the gatekeeper to the database and he/she is pivotal to assuring that your organisation abides by a set of pre-agreed rules as to which types of data can be stored on the database and which are irrelevant and will not be entered.

- Make use of quality control functions within your database to validate the (hopefully already careful) work of the data inputters. Validation tables are powerful instruments – they ensure that only valid entries of personal salutations or campaign origin codes will be accepted by the database and that any human errors will be flashed up or corrected automatically. The tables also pick up duplicate names and addresses and if instructed, will merge them too.

- Most databases now offer background cleaning of addresses. If you're inputting several dozen or a hundred records a day, it is perfectly human to input the odd postcode slightly wrong, but a piece of software supplied by the Post Office will automatically correct this by cross-checking via a background file of addresses and postcodes.

Where the human element becomes crucial once more is in picking up ad hoc instructions, comments or complaints from your members and adding these to the database record. These might include a change of address or special preferences ('Please send me just the one donor appeal a year' – 'I don't want a copy of your annual report, keep it and save the money'). Feeding such requests into the database means you can rest assured that it will remember the instruction when the appeal or annual report mailings come around. The result: another satisfied member who will be more likely to renew.

If your organisation has more than one database, it is worth trying to centralise them where possible. The ever-present risk with holding a member's details on more than one database is the prospect of duplicated or uncoordinated mailings and the annoyance that it causes. If you can't centralise your records, an alternative is to de-dupe your lists by running a programme which spots and removes duplicate names and addresses before your mailing goes out.

Finally, you must keep up to date on the changing requirements of the data protection legislation at all times and ensure that they are enshrined into your daily practice.

**Keep up to date on the changing requirements of the data protection legislation at all times and ensure that they are enshrined into your daily practice.**

## Conforming to data protection legislation

Almost any commercial, public or third-sector organisation operating a membership scheme will have to comply with legislation that enshrines the rights of individuals whose personal details are stored, processed and supplied. There are several laws pertaining to this including:

- *Data Protection Act (1998)*
- *Freedom of Information Act (2000)*
- *Privacy and Electronic Communications Regulations (2003)*

Even if you hold only such basic information as a name and address, you must notify the office of the Information Commissioner to clarify what data you hold and exactly how you intend to use it. This applies whether your records are stored manually or electronically.

As a data controller, you will have to anticipate all the various ways that you might put your data to use, and declare them to the Information Commissioner. In the first instance, you will be holding the data for the purpose of delivering the membership benefits that your members have paid a fee to get. It must also include other intended purposes, such as:

- using telephone numbers to cross-sell other services offered by your host organisation; or
- sending reciprocal fundraising appeals from other charities.

The Information Commissioner keeps a public register of data controllers. Each entry details the name and address of the data controller and outlines their use of personal data. Individuals (such as your members) can view the register to learn what types of personal data are held by your organisation and how it is used.

Notification has to be renewed annually for a small fee. Some non-profit bodies are exempt from notification. Further information about notification is given on the Information Commissioner's website at www.information-commissioner.gov.uk.

## Action points

✓ See databases as integral to the whole process of relationship marketing, not merely as a piece of kit for keeping name and address lists.

✓ Recognise the complexity of databases and seek advice when purchasing or upgrading systems.

✓ Don't under-invest in membership database hardware and software, but equally don't purchase what you don't essentially need. Use the Moscow rules (must have; should have; could have; and will live without).

✓ View your supplier or external bureau as a potential long-term partner. Look beyond the sales pitch to check out their ongoing training and customer support services.

✓ Have a data collection strategy and prioritise your data needs. Don't collect too much or too little data.

✓ Use databases as a tool for personalisation not just automation.

✓ Use databases creatively, interrogate your data and see what it tells you about your members, their needs and values.

✓ Prize your data as one of your most valuable assets. Keep it clean and up to date.

✓ Appoint a data supervisor to monitor access and quality control.

✓ Remember the human element of data inputting.

✓ Stay up to date with data protection legislation and respect it.

# 9 Governance and representation

The overriding theme of this guide is relationship marketing – a marketing ethos which focuses on the vital bond between the host organisation and the members. The key goal is to create and nurture that bond and to avoid anything that might weaken or threaten it. Every action you take must ensure that the members feel valued and listened to, which has the benefit of securing long-term support for your cause. But where does the business of governance fit into all this?

Governance is about the leadership, monitoring and control of an organisation at the highest levels. Good governance inspires trust and confidence from the organisation's investors and supporters.

**Good governance inspires trust and confidence from the organisation's investors and supporters.**

Well-publicised scandals in the business sector indicate that sometimes the boards that were assumed to be controlling the business were not doing so in reality (or else they were running them to a hidden agenda). Such scandals have brought into focus the vital importance of shareholder trust and confidence in a company's board. Without trust, shareholders will lack confidence in the company's integrity or ability, which puts its future at risk.

In order to halt the decline of investor confidence, regulators have issued a steady stream of best practice guidelines. At the heart of best practice is the presence of open and transparent protocols and an active board that is publicly accountable to the company's shareholders. Fewer shareholders are willing to place blind faith in a company's board merely on the grounds of its past track record. Now and in the future, businesses must strive harder to retain trust and confidence.

Through the Charity Commission and the National Council for Voluntary Organisations (NCVO), the third sector has also been busily producing best practice guidelines on governance. Non-profit organisations are accountable to trustees rather than shareholders, but their members, supporters and funders have the same need to know that the organisation they have invested in is wisely stewarded. In order for members to develop loyalty towards an organisation they need to know that their membership subscriptions are well invested in the purpose for which the organisation was established. Members must be able to see that their trustees are acting in the best interests of the organisation and are exercising real control over its affairs. Likewise, the trustees must be clear that ultimately it is they who are accountable when things backfire.

The Charity Commission reports that over 70,000 organisations – 44 per cent of the UK's charities – have voting members who control or influence the charity's governance.[1] For some schemes, being involved with governance is central to why people become a member – for others it ranks low on the list of reasons that motivate people to join. As discussed in Chapters 1 and 2, the most popular reasons for joining are to support the cause and/or to take benefits. Be it attending trustee meetings or debating policy motions at a conference, governance is often typecast by most people as being worthy but dull – strictly reserved for committee junkies and the activists. Of course, this perception belies the vital role of good charity governance in fostering the trust and confidence of members. The irony is that when governance proceeds smoothly, few members pay much heed to it. It is only when things go wrong – a serious board dispute or a constitutional crisis with a knock-on effect on the funding and delivery of membership services – that its true importance becomes painfully clear to all. Without good governance, a charity cannot properly manage its affairs and the interests of the members will suffer too.

**Without good governance, a charity cannot properly manage its affairs and the interests of the members will suffer too.**

But if few members cite getting involved in *governance* as a reason for joining, many more people will seek *representation*. The difference is subtle but crucial:

- **governance** is the *control* by the trustees of strategy and policies
- **representation** is the *influence* that members exert on strategy and policies and the way that the trustees take account of it

If good governance is ultimately about control, good representation is about relationships. Whether through membership surveys, policy forums, participative campaigns – good representation means having a range of interactive channels to enable members to influence the key decisions of the trustees. It means embodying the influence of the members in the organisation's projects, services and campaigns. Ultimately, it strengthens the bond between trustees, staff and members, so that the whole organisation adds up to more than the sum of its parts and can punch above its natural weight.

Conversely, with poor representation, the members may feel undervalued by the organisation, or ignored by it, with negative results. What should have been a potentially united cause may be soured by the wider perception of a charity more focused on internecine disputes than fulfilling the mission to deliver a better world. The effect may have insidious long-term implications; fewer people join or more people lapse than would have otherwise.

Balance is crucial – and tricky – when it comes to the question of governance and representation. As many of the case studies in this chapter testify, it is not easy to arrive at a perfect equilibrium that allows strong, effective governance while satisfying members that their interests are being served. Poor or inappropriate governance structures can often lead to a breakdown of continuity between the wishes of the majority of members and the leadership, resulting in frustration and conflict. By conducting governance reviews and adopting more suitable governance practices – better trustee selection, accountable voting, systematic handling of strategic issues – organisations can respond to member concerns more effectively. Yet any change, even for the better, can be controversial. To be successful, restructuring needs to have the support of the membership. This implies a process of consultation and communication that will help members understand why change is necessary and ensure that they understand both the issues facing the organisation and that the current governing body is acting for the common good.

In short, governance is much more than a minority sport; it matters to everyone and it sits at the heart of any relationship marketing approach to growing your support. In this context, this guide is less concerned with the legal minutiae of governance (already admirably covered by *The Good Trustee Guide*[2]) than with integrating governance with representation, hooking it up into the wider process of managing good relationships between your organisation and its members. This chapter aims to help you understand how the following factors impact on your scheme:

- your governing documents
- your institutional structure
- your trustees and their role
- the electoral methods for appointing trustees
- the composition of your trustee board
- your business meetings
- your criteria for defining who is and who is not a member
- the balance between governance and representation

## Your governing documents

All membership bodies that are registered charities must have a governing instrument or a set of rules under which they operate in a form acceptable to the Charity Commission. Broadly speaking, there are two basic forms of legal structure, each with its own type of constitution (there are also other less common legal forms):

**1. Unincorporated association:** which involves a group of people who come together to pursue a shared aim. It is particularly suitable for membership bodies where the members desire a close involvement with the running of the organisation. This legal structure is commonly found in:

- Self-help groups
- Local societies
- Local campaigning organisations

The governing document of an unincorporated association will usually be a *constitution* which sets out the name in which the association will be administered, the charitable objectives, trustees' powers, financial matters and the procedure for amendment or dissolution. It will normally specify:

- who is eligible to be a member of the charity
- procedures for election of trustees and voting rights
- rules and procedures for calling an AGM, including quorums and voting
- how a person's membership can be suspended or terminated
- how constitutional amendments or the dissolution of the charity is agreed

The advantage of the unincorporated association is that it is simple and flexible to set up and inexpensive to administrate. The constitution can be tailored to suit the unique needs of each organisation and its members. The disadvantage is that the trustees – and in exceptional circumstances, the wider membership – have unlimited liability if the association has insufficient assets to pay its debts (see *The Good Trustee Guide* for further guidance).

The Charity Commission publishes a *Model Constitution for a Charitable Unincorporated Association* (see Further reading). This offers a template for creating your own governing document and setting out the clauses which define how the membership is to be managed.

**2. Company limited by guarantee:** which involves a charity set up as a limited company to carry out charitable activities. In this case, the company has a membership instead of shareholders (which means that the members accept a degree of limited liability, usually a nominal sum of between £1 and £5).

This legal structure is ideal for the more complex legal responsibilities of larger or national charitable membership bodies which:

- enter into contracts with third parties in the name of the charity
- own their own property
- can raise investment without having to pay dividends to shareholders
- employ large numbers of staff

The governing document is usually in two parts: the *memorandum of association* and the *articles of association.*

The memorandum states the charity's name and its objectives or aims. It will detail the powers of the trustees to achieve the objectives as well as explaining what will happen to the assets if the company is wound up. It will also spell out:

- the fact that members' liability is limited
- the size of the members' guarantee

The members may need reassurance that signing the guarantee is a standard feature for this type of organisation. The articles of association give the rules and regulations which govern the internal proceedings of the company. These usually include:

- who can become a member of the company, and the types of membership available
- how members (and other stakeholders) elect the trustees
- procedures for holding meetings – including annual general meetings (AGMs), extraordinary general meetings (EGMs), and for voting
- procedures for becoming a member and for expelling a member

A register of members must be kept. The Charity Commission has published a *Model Memorandum and Articles of Association for a Charitable Company* (see Further reading). This includes clauses that the commission recommends charities adopt when setting out how the membership is to be managed.

In addition to these two common legal structures, other forms may include:

- a trust
- an industrial and provident society
- a body created by royal charter or by an act of parliament

At the time of writing, the government's draft Charities Bill includes a provision for a charitable incorporated organisation. This provision will mean that in the future, an organisation that registers as a charity will also be able to become incorporated (take on a legal identity as an organisation) without having to register as a company, if the trustees choose to do so. Also at the time of going to press, the government's Companies (Audit, Investigations and Community Enterprise) Bill includes proposals to create community interest companies (CICs).

### Exercise: How well do you know your governing documents?

It is not unusual for the people who administrate or market membership schemes to be unfamiliar with their governing documents. Often this is because matters such as admitting or renewing members, organising the AGM or sending out voting papers become part of the 'way that we do things'. But over time, and with staff turnover, sometimes unconstitutional habits – such as not giving adequate notice of the AGM – can innocently slip in, or go unnoticed by trustees or staff until a stickler-for-detail or disgruntled member rightly points it out.

So be sure to know your governing document and the key requirements that it makes on your membership work. Some governing documents may make for turgid reading and be impossible to learn by heart; if so, make it your business to know the key requirements and integrate them seamlessly into your relationship marketing, while keeping a copy to hand to be consulted whenever more unusual situations crop up.

**Be sure to know your governing document and the key requirements that it makes on your membership work.**

The institutional structure of your host organisation will have a strong bearing on the kind of governance input or influence that your members have.

According to Mike Hudson, the wide variety of institutional structures adopted by third-sector organisations can be placed on a continuum with, at one end, a linear structure and, at the other end, a federal structure.[3]

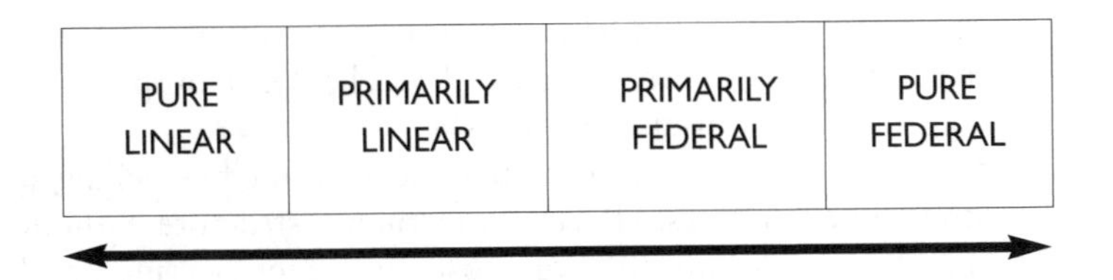


Linear organisations have a straight-line structure. The members appoint a board of trustees to oversee their organisation's governance. In turn, the board appoints a chief executive who leads the staff management team responsible for the day-to-day business of the organisation. Well-known linear examples include the RSPB, the RNID and the Consumers' Association.

**Federal organisations** are characterised by a circular form of ownership and control. The board governs the organisation but is accountable to the branches and is appointed by them. Classic examples of membership bodies with a federal structure include The Ramblers' Association, Arthritis Care and the Citizens Advice Bureaux.

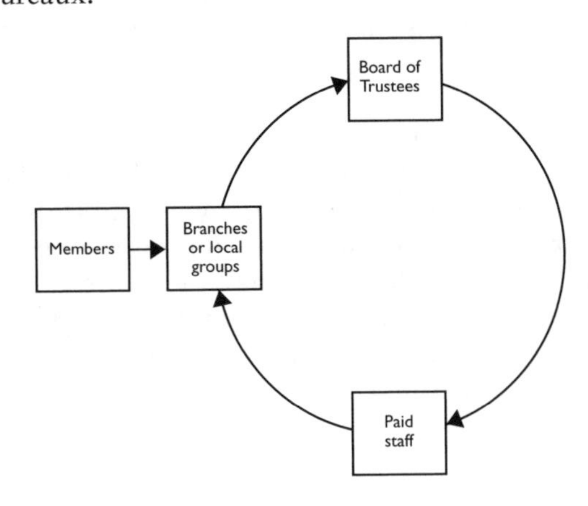

## The pros and cons of linear and federal structures

Linear structures work well for membership organisations that:

- have only (or mostly) individual members who belong to the centre;
- achieve their mission through centralised services and campaigns;
- raise most of their funds/subscriptions at a national level (so the centre has a greater need than the local outposts to control the organisation's affairs);
- focus expenditure on achieving the mission by seeking a streamlined and cost-effective governance structure without the higher administrative costs of empowering and consulting all the local outposts;
- are able to respond quickly to external opportunities (for example, media debates or government consultation documents) without the time-consuming factor of having to consult all their local outposts.

Federal structures may be more appropriate for membership bodies whose:

- individual members belong to the local branches, not to the centre;
- mission is achieved primarily through voluntary branches;
- and where most of the funding/subscriptions is raised locally (so the local outposts have a need or desire to influence the organisation's national management).

Both federal and linear structures have inbuilt strengths and weaknesses, and organisations should choose the structure that has the most advantages and the least disadvantages for their own situation.

### Your trustees and their role

Whether the charity's structure is linear or federal, the trustees ultimately control the organisation by law. The trustees are people who are entrusted to look after money (or other resources such as land or property) given to the organisation. Once appointed, the trustees are legally obliged to ensure that this money is used effectively to achieve the particular purpose for which it was given. For example, the trustees of the MS Society assure that subscriptions paid by their members are spent on multiple sclerosis-related activities. The trustees must act collectively in the best interests of their beneficiaries and avoid conflicts of interest.

### Who are the trustees?

Depending on your organisation's terminology, the trustees may be known as:

- Trustees
- Council members
- Executive committee members
- Governors
- Other terms

The proliferation of terms is unfortunate and confusing. Whatever title they are given, if they are a member of the governing body of a charitable membership organisation, entitled to take part in the decision-taking process and vote at meetings, then they are a charity trustee. To avoid further confusion, NCVO recommends that all charity people with legal responsibility for trusteeship are referred to as *trustees*. The committee or council on which they sit should be referred to as the *board of trustees*. These titles are therefore used throughout this guide.

In a charitable organisation which is limited by guarantee, the trustees and the company directors are one and the same.

### Duties of the trustees

Under charity and company law, the duties of the trustees are:

- The duty to comply with the governing document.
- The duty of care in all financial, legal and managerial matters.
- The duty to comply with charity and company law requirements, as appropriate.
- The duty to protect the organisation's property.
- The duty to act in the best interests of beneficiaries and avoid conflicts of interest.
- The duty to act collectively – no trustee can act alone unless specifically authorised to do so.
- The duty not to benefit financially and so avoid any conflict of interest.

Trustees must act in the interests of the organisation at all times and failure to exercise due care may make them personally liable, for example, for a breach of trust such as distributing assets on a cause that falls outside the objectives of an organisation. Further details on trustees' duties and liability are given in *The Good Trustee Guide*.

Boards must be alert to particular issues that may arise when a member joins a board of trustees, for example:

- When a member has joined the board and has a particular issue to pursue: is it in the best interests of the organisation to pursue it?
- Is a member who has become a trustee acting objectively as a trustee or do they have outside interests in the matter, such as championing the needs of their local branch (over and above other branches)?

**Relationship between trustees, staff and members**

The relationship between trustees, staff and members varies from one organisation to another but is usually as follows:

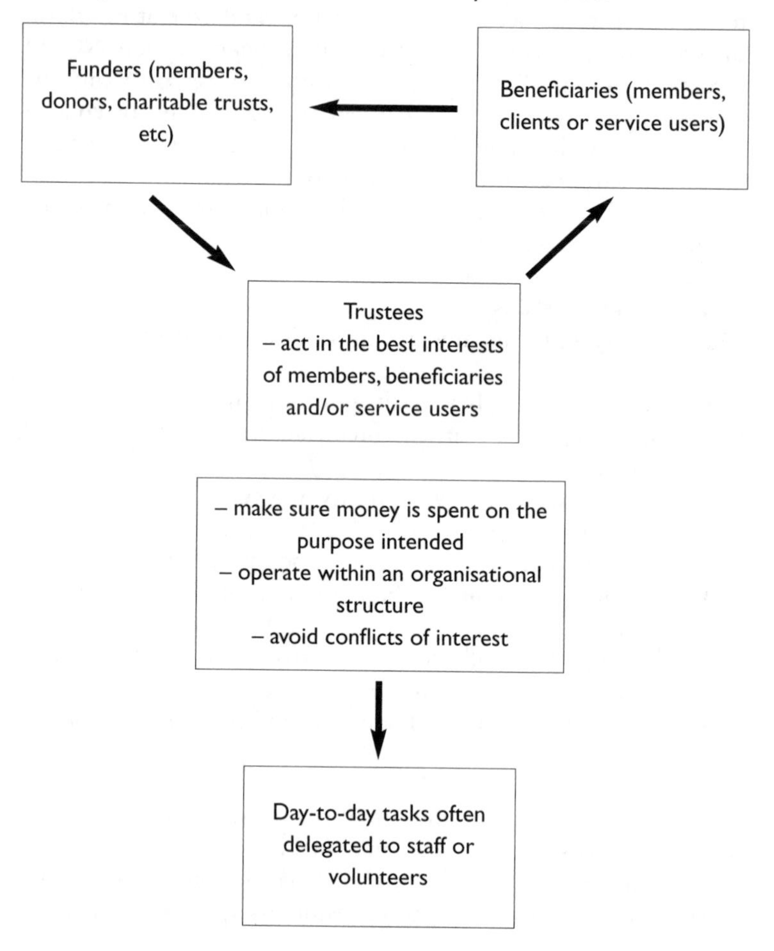

## The electoral methods for appointing trustees

The following are the most common methods for appointing trustees:

| | |
|---|---|
| Membership only elections | Individuals may be elected at an annual general meeting (AGM) and/or by postal ballot. Candidates may be drawn only from the membership, or may include non-members who have been nominated and seconded by a member. |
| Collegiate elections | Sometimes members share power with an electoral college where the right to appoint a trustee is shared between a pre-defined combination of stakeholders – eg a specific group of members or other interest groups or by geographical areas. |
| Co-option | A number of trustees may be appointed by the trustees themselves, often to fill a particular skills gap. |
| Appointed from outside | One or more trustees may be appointed by an external body, such as a significant funder. |
| Ex-officio | One or more trustees may be appointed by virtue of the office they hold, eg a mayor or vicar. |

Check your governing document to see what it says about your own procedures for electing/appointing trustees. The Charity Commission has useful guidance in this area, in *Trustee Recruitment, Selection and Induction* (see Further Reading).

**What are the board of trustees' strategic responsibilities?**
The following list is adapted from *The Good Trustee Guide* to take into account the specific needs of membership organisations:

1. Determine the organisation's mission
2. Engage in strategic planning
3. Formulate needed policies
4. Approve and monitor the organisation's programmes and services
5. Ensure adequate financial resources
6. Provide effective fiscal oversight and ensure sound risk management

7. Enhance the organisation's public image
8. Carry out board business efficiently
9. Oversee the election (or selection) and induction of new board members

Where staff are employed:

10. Select and support the chief executive and review his or her performance
11. Act as a responsible employer
12. Understand and respect the relationship between the board and staff

Where members are concerned, the board must determine their needs and wants and then match its resources to delivering a cost-effective membership scheme. The board should also match its governance structure to the degree and nature of the members' engagement with the organisation. The board should facilitate appropriate mechanisms for taking into account members' views on strategy, policy, services and campaigns. With other stake-holder groups in mind, the board should balance the expressed wishes of the members with its wider duty to fulfil the organisa-tion's mission.

**The board should balance the expressed wishes of the members with its wider duty to fulfil the organisa-tion's mission.**

**Getting the most from your members**

Good boards need good quality member-elected trustees. Yet in many organisations, most members aren't really aware of what being a trustee is about. Some hints and tips:

- Circulate information to the members highlighting the skills and experiences required by the board, the responsibilities of the trustees, and how to nominate and elect candidates.
- Open up communication channels between the board and members – via the newsletter, conferences, open forums, etc.
- Create an advisory board or similar forum where members can gain experience that enables them to become more confident about standing for election to the board.
- Create a mentoring programme to enable members elected to the board to make the transition.
- Review board performance to highlight off-putting gover-nance procedures – such as long, boring meetings. Are your board meetings welcoming and inclusive to new partici-pants?

## Your business meetings

The business meetings that must take place to enable your organisation to be accountable to your members will be determined to some extent by your legal structure and governing document.

### Annual general meeting (AGM)

For incorporated organisations, company law mandates that an annual general meeting (AGM) will be held and that specific rules are observed viz. members' meetings and trustees' meetings. The governing document for unincorporated organisations must specify similar arrangements.

Invariably, an AGM will cover:

- a report to the members on the activities of your organisation over the past year;
- discussion of the issues arising from the report;
- endorsement of the annual report and accounts, with the confirmation by independent auditors that the accounts are a true reflection of the organisation's financial affairs;
- reporting to members the results of the election of the board of trustees (or part of it);
- the appointment of the auditors for the following year;
- approval of the previous year's minutes of the AGM.

The procedural obligations for giving advance notice of AGMs and for conducting them will be set out in the governing document and, where applicable, company law. In *Charities and Meetings*, the Charity Commission gives further advice on good practice in organising an annual general meeting and related issues (see Further Reading).

### Extraordinary general meeting (EGM)

Occasionally, the AGM may also raise more fundamental issues such as amending the governing document to adapt the charity's name or objectives, a merger with another body or the question of whether to wind up the organisation. However, a fuller debate and a decision on these crucial matters will often be the subject of an extraordinary general meeting (EGM). If your governing document allows it, members may call an EGM to debate exceptional circumstances and to participate in critical decision making.

## The criteria for determining who is and who is not a member

Who is and who is not a voting member is another issue that should be clearly spelled out in your governing document. Confusion can arise if care is not taken when using the term 'member' to differentiate between those who are in a strict legal sense a member (who is entitled to control or influence governance), and when the term is used more colloquially to mean someone who pays an annual subscription or is receiving services from the charity, who may in law only be an affiliate or associate member.

### Eligibility for membership

In membership charities, eligibility will usually fall into one of the following categories:

- **Open membership:** anyone can join irrespective of their beliefs, circumstances, qualifications or other criteria. Applications to join are not scrutinised by the board although it retains the power to refuse an individual's membership or to terminate it.
- **Restricted membership:** prospects may join providing they fulfil specific criteria laid down in the charity's governing document. For example, being a resident of a specified geographic area or by practising a named creed or faith. Under the law, these restrictions are allowable providing that the *test of public benefit* is met).

In some cases, an application to join a restricted membership scheme will need to be proposed and seconded or may be subject to the approval of the trustees and/or members. In these cases, care must be taken to avoid indirect discrimination which may be subject to legal action, for example, on grounds of race or gender.

## Do the members control or influence?

The handle that members have on governance will fall into one of the following four areas:

**Absolute control:** where the members directly elect or appoint all the trustees who govern the charity.

**Partial control:** where the election or appointment of members to the board of trustees is balanced by the inclusion of people from other pre-defined stakeholder groups.

These other trustees may be appointed from outside by external organisations, ex-officio people appointed by virtue of the office they hold or co-opted people appointed to fill skills gaps.

**Direct influence:** where members do not elect or appoint members to the board of trustees, but are able to use other formal mechanisms to directly influence the trustees. This may happen via a member-elected assembly which advises a trustee body but which cannot control it. In some cases, the member-elected body may itself appoint people to the board of trustees.

**Indirect influence:** where members neither elect nor appoint members to the board of trustees nor have any formal mechanism for influencing the organisation's governance.

There is no standard template. The issue of whether or not members of a given organisation should have absolute or partial control, or a direct or indirect influence, will be affected by many variables – from the organisation's history and culture to the member's latent expectations about the degree of participation they feel they should exercise. Inevitably it can be a source of strong debate, as evidenced by the next case study.

**The issue of whether or not members of a given organisation should have absolute or partial control, or a direct or indirect influence, will be affected by many variables.**

## The Ramblers' Association

With 143,000 members (in 2004), the Ramblers' Association is Britain's biggest organisation for walkers.

The roots of the ramblers' movement lie in the 1920s when walking in the countryside became popular with people of all ages and incomes. The year 1932 saw the Kinder Scout Mass Trespass – a defiant act of civil disobedience by young walkers marching onto private land to call for open access to all countryside. In 1935, the Ramblers' Association was founded to unite the disparate local groups and get the law changed. With little money and no paid staff, the association secured the 1949 *National Parks and Access to the Countryside Act*, the first of many campaign victories. Today, the Association has a modern administrative structure with paid staff, but much of the work is still carried out by member volunteers – the walk programmes, the clearing of blocked paths and local campaigning.

With this proud history, the modern Ramblers' Association has a strong culture of grass-roots involvement. Members of the 450 local groups elect their representatives onto 54 area councils who in turn elect delegates to the general council (GC) which elects and advises the charity's trustees on the executive committee (EC).

In 2003, an internal dispute was sparked over which group – the GC or EC – ultimately controls the association.

Following a visit by the voluntary sector regulator, the Charity Commission, the Ramblers' Association was advised to clarify its governing documents which did not make it sufficiently clear that, under charity law, the trustees (ie the EC) must ultimately be responsible for the charity's policies and actions. This rankled with some GC members who perceived the grass-roots input of the Association would be compromised if they were not able to both advise and control the trustees.

The confusion was understandable. As is generally the case when members join a medium to large-sized charity, members of the Ramblers' Association belong to a *mission-driven* organisation not a purely *membership-driven* one. To qualify for the tax privileges of charity status, the charity must fulfil a mission to deliver public benefit, including, but not exclusively meeting, the needs and wishes of the members. And under charity law, the trustees are made legally responsible for the use of charitable funds.

As a charity, the Association delivers many public benefits, for example, looking after Britain's footpaths which often become illegally blocked, obstructed and overgrown. This means recognising that many other stakeholders have a vested interest in the charity. Without amending the governing documents, the Association would be in danger of 'mission hijack' by unrepresentative groups that do not have this public interest at heart. On 25 February 2004, chief executive Nick Barrett, told *Third Sector* magazine: "While your membership is important and influential, it cannot be the only voice that you listen to."

"We want our members to continue to have an influence over policy and to call trustees to account," Barrett continued, "We need to have a single identifiable body in charge of the organisation. We want the trustees to be advised by the members and not mandated by them. We want members to have a voice, but they are not the only stakeholders."

With feelings running high, a Charity Commission representative sat in on the April 2004 GC meeting and made a presentation on the legal issues. To allow time for proper debate and consensus, the trustees scheduled the proposed amendments to the governing document be put to the vote of the GC the following year in 2005.

## Balancing member input with other stakeholders

Other stakeholder groups served by charities may have quite different needs from those of the members. For example, in the case of disability charities, the service users may include highly vulnerable people who are dependent on its care services. Some charitable activities may involve contractual obligations to public services with significant legal and financial implications. So there are pros and cons involved with absolute or partial member control. On the plus side, the host organisation will, at least in theory, be well clued up to the needs and desires of its target audience – assuming that members and non-members have broadly similar needs and interests. On the down side, if most members are apathetic about governance (eg do not attend conferences or cast their vote) there is a risk that small, well-organised cliques will seek to gain power – as happens when animal rights groups seek to infiltrate animal or heritage charities in order to pursue singular and controversial goals.

In order to create both a balanced range of inputs into charity trusteeship and avoid entryism, many organisations with membership schemes take steps to apportion the degree to which members control or influence their affairs. There are several ways in which this can be achieved:

**Many organisations with membership schemes take steps to apportion the degree to which members control or influence their affairs.**

- **Apportioning the number of member-elected seats on the board of trustees:** members nominate, stand for and elect other members to the board but the number of seats that they take up is limited to a pre-defined ratio (eg the governing document of a board with 25 members may determine that five, 10, 15 or some other number of seats are elected by the members).

- **Creating an advisory body:** members stand for, propose and directly elect other members or nominees. They don't stand for the board of trustees itself, but for an advisory body (sometimes called an assembly or consultative group). The advisory group has no mandatory power but acts as a strong influence on the governing body (and sometimes elects its own members onto the board of trustees).

- **Creating a trust:** members join the trust rather than the organisation itself. Members are given the opportunity to vote on trust-related issues, but not on the host organisation's policy and strategies.

Whichever mechanism is adopted, the organisation must take into account a range of variables:

- the demand (or the latent expectation) of the members for participation in governance;
- the range of other stakeholders (service users, allies, funders) whose needs must be taken into account;
- the optimum balance between user (member) input and specialist (usually professional) input;
- the skills and experiences required by the board to play an effective role;
- the historical baggage acquired by the organisation, which may either facilitate or obstruct attempts to tamper with governance structures;
- the appropriate balance between governance (control) and representation (influence) by the members (which will be discussed later in this chapter).

There is a widespread trend for large unwieldy boards of trustees to be streamlined into smaller, more diverse boards with large representative advisory bodies. That said, there is no single answer to the question of balancing the needs of multiple stakeholders. As the next case study illustrates, each organisation must consider all the above factors when devising its own unique solution.

## Royal National Institute of the Blind (RNIB)

Traditionally, RNIB governance was dominated by the charity's historical roots as a federation of local organisations for blind people. These were mostly led by professionals who were not themselves blind or partially sighted – leading activists to accuse the RNIB of benevolent paternalism towards blind people.

The RNIB introduced a radically new and streamlined system of governance in April 2002. Key features included:

- The replacement of a large and unwieldy 100-member executive council with a 24-strong board of trustees.

- The creation of a 90-strong member-elected assembly to advise the board and to elect most of the trustees.

- A legally binding requirement by its governing document that a majority of the board of trustees, the assembly and the wider membership are themselves blind or partially sighted.

- While 18 of the 24 trustees are member-elected, six are co-opted by the rest of the trustees to ensure the board has (as far as possible) the right balance of people in terms of age, ethnicity, gender, skills, experiences and background.

The following process for framing recommendations on the six co-opted members of the board was agreed in February 2002:

- A skills audit would be conducted of existing trustees to identify gaps in respect of skills, experience and background.
- Advertisements would be placed in the national and voluntary sector press inviting applications, particularly from those meeting gaps identified in the skills audit.
- Formal and informal networks and cost-free brokerage services would be used to attract candidates.

The skills audit found a gap among existing board members in respect of:

- Women
- Minority ethnic groups
- Younger people

- Experience of working with business (particularly large corporations)
- Working with and for central government
- Working with and for the health service

In Spring 2002, advertisements were placed in the national and specialist press, trustees and senior staff passed details to their contacts, details were circulated to a range of networks and agencies including the City Women's Network, Business in the Community, Black Londoner's Forum and the Work Foundation – 60 applications were received, 15 candidates were interviewed by a panel and the six recommended people were presented to the trustee board and duly appointed.

The RNIB's governance restructure reflects current thinking on best practice. Many charities are now shrinking a preciously large (and unwieldy) governing body into a streamlined board of trustees. The new slim-line RNIB board empowers trustees to meet more often, take real responsibility, reach quicker agreement and act decisively – all vital for survival in a global economy driven by rapid social and economic change.

Meanwhile, the larger 90-strong RNIB assembly has the virtue of allowing members to participate in a broad church of voices in a way that the new slimmer board of trustees can't accommodate.

## Balancing governance and representation

As the Ramblers' Association and RNIB case studies affirm, voluntary organisations need both good governance and representational structures and processes.

To clarify, *governance* is the control by the trustees of strategy and policies while *representation* is the influence that members exert on strategy and policies and the way that the trustees take account of it.

There are four key elements to **representation:**

- listening
- taking action
- participation
- feedback (into governance, strategy, policy, and action)

These four acts may take place at a macro level where inputs are fed into governance – eg through a membership survey that is reported to the board of trustees – or they may take place at a micro level – eg complaints handling, where inputs are not directly fed to the board of trustees but may influence the way services are delivered.

**Listening**

In a healthy organisation, even one where few members are interested in formal governance, listening to the members can still take place through many other representational channels with varying degrees of formality:

- non-governing assembly bodies
- open forums
- open days/meet the management
- market research
- membership surveys
- website forums
- telephone helpline
- the postbag
- the complaints log

**Taking action**

Whether on a macro or micro scale, taking action converts the act of listening to members into action by the organisation:

- strategy
- policy
- research
- development
- service delivery
- campaigns
- public awareness
- media and public relations activity
- replies to correspondence
- response to complaints

**Participation**

Participation means channelling the energy of the members and enabling them to get involved in the above activities to the extent they wish and as far as is practicable and desirable for the organisation to allow them to do so. Member participation in taking action may take place through activities such as actively advocating the organisation's campaigns to local politicians or being quoted as a case study in a media case. Not all members will participate, but if they can see that others do, it enhances the perception of an involving and representative scheme.

**Feedback**

**It is not enough just to listen and take action – you have to be seen to be doing so. Reporting back on the outcomes is critical to keeping your members' trust and goodwill.**

It is not enough just to listen and take action – you have to be seen to be doing so. Reporting back on the outcomes is critical to keeping your members' trust and goodwill. For example, using your member newsletter to report back on:

- key market research outcomes and what action will be taken as a result
- AGM decisions and trustee elections;
- membership survey results and how they will be followed up;
- how member inputs helped your campaigns, fundraising appeals, service developments, etc.

When there are adequate forms of representation, the members feel that they are valued and listened to, and that their concerns, wishes and ideas are taken into account when the organisation makes decisions on strategy and policy. Not all input will be fed into governance, and you might not always be able to give the members the answers they seek, or take the actions that they want. But this does not detract from the benefits you will gain if your members can see that yours is a *listening organisation* (see Chapter 3).

How would members feel with inadequate representation? Undervalued? Neglected? Dissatisfied? More likely to lapse?

## Reviewing your governance and representation

As the next case study illustrates, even thriving membership bodies must periodically review their governance and representation structures:

### The National Trust

With 3.4 million members, the National Trust is the largest membership body in the UK's voluntary sector, the custodian of several hundred of Britain's most loved houses, gardens and natural landscapes. In its own words, the

Trust is "completely independent of government, therefore relying heavily on the generosity of our subscribing members and other supporters."

Just how dependent the Trust is on its members is made clear by the fact that four in every five of its historic houses runs at a loss. Yet in the eyes of some of the Trust's members, the charity's governance lacked openness and transparency. In response, the Trust set up a year-long independently chaired governance review.

The review's report noted that members "without existing contacts within the Trust often feel that there is a circle into which they cannot break." It called for the Trust to put "clear and transparent procedures in place for elections and appointments. Any criteria would be published and, as a general rule, posts should be advertised." In future, the report said, the members would be informed when vacancies on the council arose.

On proxy voting, the report stated: "There is deep suspicion on the part of a significant number of the Trust's members about the proxy voting system, particularly in relation to elections to the council." Many charities operate a proxy voting system which by the very nature of the operation can be confusing to the members. In short, a proxy voting system is designed to enable any member who is unable or does not wish to attend the AGM to assign another member to cast their vote on their behalf. In practice, this may lead to someone, for example the chairman, casting several hundred or even thousands of votes for particular candidates. While this is perfectly legal, the way in which such proxy votes are cast often becomes a subject of debate and suspicion. The Trust report recommended replacing proxy voting with a postal or electronic ballot before the AGM.

On AGMs, the report recommended: "It should be made more obvious that the AGM is an opportunity to hear from members of the Trust as well as an opportunity to provide them with information. There should be sufficient flexibility in the timing to allow ample scope for questions on the day. Questions and answers should be published on the Trust's website, including answers to any questions which there was not time to cover at the meeting. The Trust should be less defensive in dealing with concerns or views of members, or suggestions from them. The National Trust Acts give members the important right to propose and debate resolutions but they also make clear that resolutions are not binding on the trustees, who are obliged to act as they think right in the interests of the nation."

On transparency and communication: "As well as the AGM there are many other ways in which the Trust and its members can exchange information, views and ideas. The Trust should undertake further work to explore how it can better communicate effectively... The Trust should make information on its decision-making processes and its decisions, more readily accessible, making full use of its website and its magazine."

The Trust's council accepted the recommendations of the report which were then put to vote at the Trust's 2003 AGM and endorsed by the members.

Even in the best-run membership organisations, governance doesn't always run smoothly. If this happens, openness and transparency is the best policy. After all, your members are your organisation's friends. With friends you can share both the good and bad news. Your members benefit from the work that you do, and share in your successes and failures. They will tell you when what you are doing is right and when they feel it to be wrong. Be honest, and your members will respect you for it – just as the National Trust's members saluted their organisation's honesty by overwhelmingly mandating the conclusion of its governance review.

## Exercise: A governance and representation health check

Fill in the following questionnaire to assess how you and your colleagues see your organisation in relation to the following issues. (Where 1 is very poor and 5 is very good indeed.) Also, if you are ready to take a risk, ask some key trustees and members to fill this in too.

| | | | | | |
|---|---|---|---|---|---|
| **Governance and representation** | | | | | |
| Our organisation knows the difference between governance and representation | 1 | 2 | 3 | 4 | 5 |
| We have clearly differentiated structures and processes for governance and representation | 1 | 2 | 3 | 4 | 5 |
| **Governing document** | | | | | |
| We are familiar with the key obligations as set out by our governing document | 1 | 2 | 3 | 4 | 5 |
| We adhere to the letter and spirit of the rules as set out in our governing document | 1 | 2 | 3 | 4 | 5 |
| We periodically review our governing document to ensure that it is up to date | 1 | 2 | 3 | 4 | 5 |
| **Institutional structure (linear or federal)** | | | | | |
| Our institutional structure is up to date and it has more advantages than disadvantages | 1 | 2 | 3 | 4 | 5 |
| **Your trustees** | | | | | |
| We have the right balance of members and other stakeholders on our board of trustees | 1 | 2 | 3 | 4 | 5 |
| Our trustees are committed to determining the needs and wants of the members | 1 | 2 | 3 | 4 | 5 |
| Our members have appropriate input into electing trustees | 1 | 2 | 3 | 4 | 5 |
| Our members are informed who the trustees are, how they operate and their key decisions | 1 | 2 | 3 | 4 | 5 |
| **Definition of voting membership** | | | | | |
| We have clear and appropriate criteria for who is and who is not a voting member | 1 | 2 | 3 | 4 | 5 |
| **Representation** | | | | | |
| We have a range of listening channels through which our members can communicate with us | 1 | 2 | 3 | 4 | 5 |
| After listening to our members we take action | 1 | 2 | 3 | 4 | 5 |
| We offer our members opportunities to participate in our work | 1 | 2 | 3 | 4 | 5 |
| We regularly feedback to our members on how their input is taken into account in our actions | 1 | 2 | 3 | 4 | 5 |
| **Openness and transparency** | | | | | |
| We are open and transparent in all aspects of our governance and representation | 1 | 2 | 3 | 4 | 5 |

As a membership organisation, what are your strengths and weaknesses according to this assessment? What areas do you either need or want to develop? If there are a number of areas requiring work, can you prioritise three aspects to improve in the short term, then three more in the medium term, and so on?

*The Good Trustee Guide* contains further guidance on governance review strategies.

## Action points

✓ Practise good governance and representation as an integral part of your relationship marketing strategy.

✓ Get the right balance between member input into governance (control) and representation (influence).

✓ Make your governance processes open and transparent by reporting key outcomes to the members.

✓ Combine your AGM with an interesting event to attract and involve your members.

✓ Lay down structures and processes for collecting data and input from your members – from advisory groups to membership surveys to complaint logs – and assure your trustees are well briefed about the results.

✓ Know the four key steps to representation: listen, take action, involve and feed back.

✓ Remember that listening without action and feedback invites cynicism.

✓ Provide opportunities for those of your members who wish to participate in your work to do so.

✓ Periodically review your governance and representation. Be honest about your strengths and weaknesses, take action and your members will respect you for it.

✓ Be honest about your mistakes. Any attempt to do otherwise merely invites suspicion and ridicule.

✓ Be proactive. Discuss and have a dialogue on the overlap between governance and representation, and agree a strategy to enhance the effectiveness of the organisation.

1. Charity Commission (2004) *Membership Charities*
2. Dyer, P (ed.)(2003) *The Good Trustee Guide*, NCVO
3. Hudson, M (2002) *Managing without Profit*, Directory of Social Change

# Conclusion

In 2001, the American sociologist Robert Putnam spawned a national debate with *Bowling Alone*. His groundbreaking book argued that the community-orientated values of the older community, shaped by the experience of world war two, were being diluted by their more individualistic beliefs of their children and grandchildren. Generational change, the emergence of two-career families, the rise of electronic entertainment – TV, video and the internet – was causing increasing numbers of people to withdraw from civic life. Putnam's driving metaphor was bowling; from 1980 to 1993, the total number of bowlers increased by over 10 per cent, yet league bowling fell by more then 40 per cent. People, said Putnam, are bowling alone rather than with their neighbours. He argued that the very fabric of community life was weakened by these changes. *Bowling Alone* puts forward a seven-step programme of civic renewal. At the top of this list was an appeal for a renewal of social relationships and group membership.

**The common goal of membership schemes**

The UK has a different history of civic participation, but the central idea of this book is that all third sector membership schemes, of any kind, share the same goal. That goal is bringing people together and managing relationships. You might be the secretary of a social club or the marketing manager at a large charity. Your members may be individuals, or organisations, or other membership bodies who have joined an umbrella scheme. Whatever your scheme is, it is a channel for managing relationships between your cause and like-minded people. The glue that binds these relationships is the two-way flow of value, that is, the member gains real value from the relationship which converts into value for the organisation.

**Why people join**

To attract people to join, your scheme must offer real value to the members. The most common benefits include:

- Personal development
- Social and networking opportunities
- Preferential access to goods and services
- Financial benefit
- Representation
- Self fulfilment through altruism to others

Not all of these will have equal appeal to all members. However, through market research or dialogue with your members, it is possible to establish which benefits your members perceive as being the most important.

### Getting value from the members

By delivering member value, your organisation in turn will gain value from some combination of one or more of the following benefits:

- Revenue from membership fees
- A warmer audience for trading activities
- Increased fundraising
- More volunteers
- Greater lobbying strength
- Stronger governance and representation
- Improved branding

### Finding 'win-win' situations

Getting the right two-way flow of value is crucial. The challenge for any person or team responsible for membership affairs is to balance these demands that organisations and members make on each other and to find 'win-win' situations for both parties. For example, if an organisation's scheme is set up to fundraise for it, and it is losing money, and the trustees and staff do not see any other value in it – for example, as a source of volunteers – then the organisation's investment in the scheme will most likely atrophy, even if its members appreciate the benefits. The reverse is also true; if the same scheme has fundraising value for the organisation but the members do not perceive any tangible value (such as privileged access to benefits) or intangible value (a feeling of gratitude from the organisation) then the scheme will decline from a lack of public support.

The ultimate challenge of membership strategy is to get the right balance. As case studies in this book testify, the most effective schemes achieve win-win outcomes of mutual benefit. With members feeling satisfied and cared-for, the organisation gains 'friends for life', a group of loyal supporters and advocates in both good times and bad.

### Satisfaction, activity and growth

For any charity or voluntary organisation, the ability to recruit 'friends for life' is crucial because:

- people who renew their membership are satisfied with your work and the benefits you offer
- satisfied members are more likely to support you in other ways, from donating to campaigning, from volunteering to buying merchandise
- satisfied members are more likely to be good ambassadors for your cause and refer other prospective members to it
- satisfied members fuel growth
- growth inspires the organisation's trustees and management to invest further in your scheme, and the confidence in your prospects to join it

**Surviving in a global economy**

Yet building loyalty is a challenging task. In the 21st century the global economy has changed for ever the rules of engagement between brands and their customers. With increasing choice and competition people are more easily able to transfer their brand loyalties if unimpressed with the goods or service offered by their existing supermarket or department store, car dealer or travel firm. With customers more aware of their power to 'shop around' even the leading brands – such as BT and Marks & Spencer – have to work much harder to keep traditionally loyal customers. Likewise, the third sector is no longer immune from competition. For example, children's and youth groups must work harder and smarter to keep themselves relevant in an age when boys and girls are immersed in a wider environment of aggressively marketed children's television, internet, electronic games, fads and fashions.

**Why marketing matters to nonprofits**

The key to membership survival in this global economy is marketing. Robert Putnam's vision for civic renewal is tempered by the acknowledgement that civic groups must borrow and adapt some of the tools of the new marketing-driven society. We are immersed by smart media campaigns aimed at capturing our imagination – and money. Yet traditionally, marketing has been seen by many in the voluntary sector to be just another term for 'selling', linked to profit-making and irrelevant to their needs. In recent years, this perception is changing. Marketing, as we have seen, enables charities and voluntary groups to build lasting relationships – internally (with trustees and staff) and externally (with enquirers, members, donors, etc). A good marketing plan will:

- link membership recruitment to your organisation's vision and mission; the reasons why you exist in the first place!

- outline research on your prospective and existing members' needs and wants
- explain how your membership service will meet those needs
- make a business case for delivering the service profitably (or with a subsidy your organisation agrees it can afford)
- set down specific, measurable, agreed and time-related targets, costs and income
- identify the 'win-win' situation; how your plan's success mutually benefits both the cause and your beneficiaries' lives

Looked at this way, marketing is the opposite of selling people something they don't want. It is responsive to member needs. It is inclusive and motivates your staff, trustees and volunteers. And if you make a profit it doesn't go to shareholders – it is re-invested in the cause.

**Managing the marketing mix**

Whether you work from a national head office or a local community centre, an understanding of the marketing mix can help you to grow your membership support. The mix includes the so-called eight Ps. It means assuring that your target audience knows and empathises with your *philosophy* (the vision, mission and your values). It means that you are offering the right *product* (the brand, the membership service and benefits), that it is in the right *place* at the right *price*. It means communicating the benefits clearly (*promotion*). It means providing *physical evidence* of the benefits. It means being confident that all your organisation's *people* are fully behind it and that you have a user-friendly *process* of joining up.

**Marketing as investment**

For most organisations, no single recruitment channel will reach all of its prospective members. The widest possible audience can be reached only by using a range of different channels. Yet most schemes are still promoted using little more than 'word of mouth' or leaflets given out at face-to-face situations. This guide looks at a wider range of options from direct marketing to partnerships with public services. Yet many voluntary organisations are risk averse and don't invest in marketing for fear of expensive failure. The key to getting around this block is to use marketing evaluation tools such those described in this guide – Return on Investment (ROI), Lifetime Value Analysis (LVI) and Cost Benefit Analysis (CBI). These enable new ideas to be tested for their cost effectiveness and marketing spend to be invested only where it brings the best return for your cause.

**Are you in it for the long run?**

But relationship marketing is not confined to recruiting members. The ultimate goal is to develop more lasting relationships. The analogy used earlier in this book was that membership is like a bath; you can turn on the taps and fill it up (recruitment) but if there is no bath plug (retention) your members drain out as quickly as they arrive (lapse). Rather, relationship marketing is a three-stage process:

1. Recruitment: Communicating the benefits of your scheme and persuading people to join.
2. Loyalty: Keeping your members informed of what your organisation is doing for them and the cause. Getting your members active as supporters and/or advocates. The more active your members are the stronger their appreciation of the benefits of your scheme and so the more likely they are to renew for another year.
3. Retention: The use of renewal programmes to carry the member's loyalty from one year over to the next, so your cause has a long-term source of committed support.

**The six stages of the membership journey**

Building loyalty and retention programmes means taking your members on a six-stage journey:

- **Prospects** – your users, enquirers, donors, etc, who have not yet joined but who are most likely 'warm' to your cause.
- Members – those prospects who have consolidated their transactional contact with your organisation by joining it.
- **Supporters** – members who give further transactional support by purchasing your goods and services (knowing that income supports the cause) by volunteering, making a donation, etc
- **Advocates** – members who go one step further and actively promote your cause to others, e.g. by supporting a campaign or recruiting new members
- **Renewed** – satisfied members, supporters, advocates who make the commitment to renew for another year
- **Lapsed** – those who have left your scheme but who may be re-activated at some point in the future

By using this relationship marketing 'ladder', large and small bodies alike can tailor their communications to nurture their members to higher levels of commitment.

**Getting the right balance between recruitment and retention**

Nurturing people along the six stages of the membership journey needs careful planning and the right balance of time, money and effort spent on the three areas of recruitment, loyalty building and retention. Where does your organisation stand in relation to the following typology?

- 'Acquirers' – who concentrate most of their resource on membership recruitment at the expense of loyalty and retention activities.
- 'Retainers' – who do little recruitment and focus the majority of their effort on serving and keeping the existing members.
- 'Relationship marketers' – who see their members as long-term friends, and continuously balance the time, money and effort spent on recruitment, loyalty and retention activities.

**Governance and representation**

A key task of relationship marketing is to create and nurture a bond between your organisation and the members, to avoid anything that might weaken or threaten it. Every action is geared to making the members feel valued and listened to, which has the benefit of securing your long term support. This means getting the right balance between governance and representation:

- governance is the control by the trustees of strategy and policies
- representation is the influence that members exert on strategy and policies and the way that the trustees take account of it

If good governance is ultimately about control, good representation is about relationships. Be it through membership surveys, policy forums, participative campaigns – good representation means having a range of interactive channels to enable members to influence the key decisions by the trustees. It means embodying the influence of the members in the organisation's projects, services and campaigns. Ultimately, it strengthens the bond between trustees, staff and members, so that the whole organisation adds up to more than the sum of its parts and can punch above its natural weight.

**Membership... a beacon, not a bolt on**

The status and position of membership within any third sector organisation is usually a clear indicator of the effectiveness of their scheme. Those with growing or active support see membership more as a 'beacon' and less as a 'bolt on'. As the many case studies in this book show, the more people in your organisation – trustees, staff, volunteers, members – who understand and promote two-way value between the organisation and members, the greater the recruitment, loyalty and retention.

Creating such a pan-organisation commitment is not easy, but the rewards are great. If there are key decision takers in your organisation who remain to be convinced, whose support and commitment is as yet untapped, involve them in some of the team-building exercises in this guide. Or present them with a copy of this book!

# Glossary

**Ansoff matrix** – useful aid exploring the strategic options for the different stages of the membership life cycle

**Break-even analysis** – method using the fixed and variable cost analysis whereby organisations can work out how many members their scheme will need to break even on income and expenditure

**Cause-related marketing** (**CRM**) – commercial activity by which businesses and charities, or causes, form a partnership with each other to market an image, product or service for mutual benefit

**Costs** (**fixed and variable**) – fixed costs do not alter in proportion to the number of members, variable costs change in proportion to the number of members in the scheme

**Cost benefit analysis** (**CBA**) – evaluation model which considers marketing costs against the wider benefits. Typically used in schemes where membership is subsidised or makes a loss

**Cross marketing** (also referred to as **cross selling**) – using your organisation's other products and services to promote your membership scheme

**Database** – see **relational database**

**Data Protection Act 1998** – law pertaining to the collection, storage and use of data on individuals and companies by organisations

**Demographics** – tangible factors that we can record or measure such as age, gender, address, occupation, building up a picture of basic population, or *target audience*, characteristics

**Direct marketing** – method of marketing based on individual customer or member records . Contact is made directly with the individual through, for example, email, post or telephone

**Doner pyramid** – encapsulates the life-cycle of a typical doner. General public, to inquirers, to responders, to doners, to committed doners, to big gifts, to bequests

**E-marketing** – electronic marketing activity utilising new technology such as email and websites to reach the *target audience*, often at a fraction of the cost of traditional methods

**Gift Aid** – government scheme whereby charities can claim up to 28 per cent of donations (and in some cases membership subscripptions) from taxpayers back from the Inland Revenue. See appendix

**Hierarchy of needs** – Maslow's famous model describing individual's behaviour and motivations. The five stages are physiological, safety, social, ego and self actualisation

**Integrated contact handling strategy** – a process of recording every single transaction between the scheme or organisation and the member in a database, and using the contact history to plan and monitor effective, targeted communication

**Lifetime value analysis (LVA)** – model which measures the organisation's costs and income against the lifetime of each member

**Market research** – the collection, analysis and interpretation of data on individuals or organisations, which allows organisation to diagnose and deliver effective marketing communications and strategies

**Marketing mix** – a set of controllable tactical marketing tools and the blend between them. Classically made up of the four Ps – product, price, place and promotion. Now with added elements philosophy, people, process and physical evidence

**Membership trapezoid** – represents the idealised journey which the organisation wants the members to take through different stages of membership. General public, to prospects, to members, to supporters, to advocates, to renewed, to lapsed

**Member get member (MGM)** – schemes whereby members recruit new members for the scheme, often with an incentive to do so

**Mission statement** – details the organisation's role in achieving the vision, a statement of organisational purpose

**Performance indicators** – a set of defined indicators by which an organisation can measure its performance. May be descriptive and qualitative or statistical and quantitative in nature

**PEST analysis** – a template offering a straightforward way to organise a 'scan' of the outside world. Considers political, economic, social and technological factors

**Prospects** – potential members who fit the characteristics of an organisation's *target audience*

**Public relations (PR)** – the planned and sustained effort to establish and maintain goodwill and mutual understanding between an organisation and its *target audiences*

**Psychographics** – the collective essence of an individual's attitudes, beliefs, opinions, prejudices, hopes, fears needs, desires and aspirations which taken together, govern how he or she behaves and that, as a whole expresses itself in a lifestyle

**Qualitative research** – is based on exploratory research methods such as open-ended interviews, and collects data which uncovers motivations, attitudes and behaviours

**Quantitative research** – is based on data collection from a sufficient number of respondents to allow statistical analysis. Usually records variables which can be measured numerically such as age, gender, earnings

**Recruitment** – the process of telling your *prospects* about your membership scheme, the value it offers and signing them up

**Relational database** – where subsets of membership data are stored in a series of tables, enabling the organisation to *segment* the membership and maximise the use of tailored communication

**Relationship marketing** – a member-focused approach to building relationships between the host organisation and its members

**Retention** – the process whereby member's loyalty is transferred from one year to the next, so that the cause has a long-term source of supporters and advocates

**Return on Investment (ROI)** – analysis which looks at the costs and income of individual promotion to evaluate its financial cost effectiveness

**Segmentation** – a defined group of the organisation's *target audience* who are, for example, expected to respond similarly to a particular type of communication

**SMART** – classic formula for setting objectives. States that objectives should be specific, measurable, achievable, realistic and time-related

**SWOT analysis** – classic assessment technique which draws attention to the critical organisational strengths, weaknesses, opportunities and threats. Can be used at both micro and macro levels, focusing on single issue or problem, or looking at the wider organisational *mission*, vision and values

**Target audience** – individuals or groups who are identified as having a direct or indirect interest in the organisation or a need for the services it provides, and which have common needs or characteristics. They are then selected to receive marketing communications

**Transactional marketing** – marketing activity which focuses on the initial sale

**URJ (unique reason to join)** – development of the classic term 'unique selling proposition'. Characteristics of the membership scheme or purpose (*mission, vision and values*) of the organisation which distinguish it from other organisations

**USP (unique selling proposition)** – see URJ

**VALS framework** – a system devised by American sociologist Arnold Mitchell, for categorising citizens by their social values and behaviour. The eight personality types are: innovators, thinkers, achievers, experiencers, believers, strivers, makers and survivors

**Values statement** – expresses the values an organisation holds and by which it will operate, for example, committing to staff development and equal opportunities

**Vision statement** – expresses the desired future for the organisation's users, members and the world at large

# Further reading

## The history of membership schemes

Dekker, P and van den Broek, A (1998) 'Civil society in comparative perspective', *Voluntas* (International Journal of Voluntary and Nonprofit Organizations), Vol. 9, No. 1, 11-38

Inglehart, R *World Values Study* data, as distributed in 1990, see www.worldvaluessurvey.org

Jochum, V (2003) *Social Capital: Beyond the Theory*, NCVO

Charity Commission (2004) *Membership Charities*

## Relationship marketing

Burnett, K (2002) *Relationship Fundraising: A Donor-based Approach to the Business of Raising Money*, Jossey Bass Wiley

Christopher M, Payne A and Ballantyne D (2002) *Relationship Marketing*, Butterworth-Heinemann

Keaveney, P and Kaufmann, M (2000) *Marketing for the Voluntary Sector: A Practical Guide for Charities and Non-government Organizations*, Kogan Page

Levitt, T (1968) *Innovations in Marketing*, Pan Books

Moss Kanter, R (1992) *When Giants Learn to Dance: Managing the Challenges of Strategy, Management and Careers in the 1990s*, International Thomson Business Press

NCVO Research Team (2003) *Voluntary Sector Strategic Analysis 2003/04*, NCVO

## Intrinsic motivations

Alderfer, CP (1972) *Existence, Relatedness and Growth: Human Needs in Organisational Settings*, Free Press

Maslow, AH (1970) *Motivation and Personality*, Harper and Row

Mitchell, A (1978) *VALS™*, inaugurated by SRI Consulting Business Intelligence, see www.sric-bi.com

## Mission and strategy

Buzan, T (1995) *The Mind Map Book*, BBC Books

Copeman, C and others (2004) *Tools for Tomorrow: a practical guide to strategic planning for voluntary organisations*, NCVO

De Bono, E (1990) *Lateral Thinking*, Penguin

Handy, C (1988) *Understanding Voluntary Organisations*, Pelican

Harris, J (2002) *The Good Management Guide*, NCVO

Hayes, D and Slater, A (2003) 'From "social club" to "integrated membership scheme": developing membership schemes strategically' in *International Journal of Nonprofit and Voluntary Sector Marketing*, Vol. 8, No.1 59-75

Palmer, P, Severn, J and Williams, S (2002) *The Good Financial Management Guide*, NCVO

Saxton, J (1996) *It's Competition, But Not As We Know It*, Third Sector Publications

Saxton, J (1998) *What Are Charities For?* Third Sector Publications

## Market research

Hannagan, T J (1992) *Marketing for the Non-Profit Sector*, Macmillan

## The marketing mix

Adkins, S (2000) *Cause Related Marketing*, Butterworth-Heinemann

Bruce, I (1998) *Successful Charity Marketing*, ICSA/Prentice Hall

Saxton, J (2003) *Polishing the Diamond: Values, Image and Brand as a Source of Strength for Charities*, nfp Synergy

## Recruitment

Gilchrist, A (1998) *Effective Media Relations*, Charities Aid Foundation

Theaker, A (2004) *Public Relations Handbook (media practice)*, Routledge

## Membership databases

Bremridge, T (2003) 'Outsourcing the servicing of supporters' in *Charities Management*, Autumn issue

Bremridge, T *Seeing a Clear Case for Outsourcing*, case study of the Macular Disease Society, at www.associa.co.uk

## Governance and representation

*Charities and Meetings* (2002) Charity Commission

Dyer, P (ed.) (2002) *The Good Trustee Guide*, NCVO

Hudson, M (2002) *Managing without Profit*, DSC

*Model Memorandum and Articles of Association for a Charitable Company* (GD1) (2003) Charity Commission

*Model Constitution for a Charitable Unincorporated Association* (GD3) (2003) Charity Commission

*Trustee Recruitment, Selection and Induction* (2002) Charity Commission

# Appendix: Gift Aid

**Gift Aid – what is it?**

Gift Aid is a remarkably easy-to-run scheme that enables charities to reclaim the basic rate of tax on donations received from UK taxpayers. When it was first introduced, Gift Aid could only apply to donations of £250 and above. But in the 2000 Budget, the government revoked this minimum level making it available to all taxpaying donors.

With certain constraints (listed below), membership fees are considered by the Inland Revenue as a donation to the charity and so qualify for Gift Aid.

**What are the benefits?**

Put simply, Gift Aid can boost the value of individual donations or membership subscriptions by 28 per cent. If your basic membership rate is £10 then your charity can claim back £2.80 in tax. If the rate is £20, then £5.60 can be reclaimed, and so on.

For the charity, claiming back the tax is straightforward. Many software packages will produce the claim for you, while some agencies offer support services. There is relatively little effort involved, but the financial gain can be enormous.

Another attractive feature of Gift Aid is that charities can back-date the tax claim on all the contributions received from donors/members from 6 April 2000 onwards.

There is an additional, more intangible, gain: the newly joined member, or renewed member, can feel the warm glow of inner satisfaction at performing an altruistic act of financial support to the cause.

**Does my membership scheme qualify for Gift Aid?**

As a general principle, Gift Aid applies whenever the donor or member does not gain in return any material benefit that has a financial value equivalent to 25 per cent or more of the donation or subscription itself. The Inland Revenue will not accept a Gift Aid application if the value of the benefit exceeds the limits shown below:

| Donation/Subscription (£) | Value of benefits |
|---|---|
| £0–£100 | 25% of the donation |
| £101–£1000 | £25 |
| £1001+ | 25% of the donation |

These amounts are annualised – the cost of the annual membership subscription is compared against the value of the benefits within that same year.

When estimating the value of membership benefits, it is important to note that the Inland Revenue will apply a financial value of nil to certain membership benefits. These include:

- Right of admission to view heritage property or wildlife.
- Provision of literature produced for the purpose of describing the work of the charity and relevant to furthering the objects of the charity. This includes newsletters, bulletins, annual reports, journals, members' handbooks and programmes of events.

If you are going to use Gift Aid for the first time, you need to contact the Inland Revenue so that it can recognise you for tax purposes and give you a reference number.

**Maximising your members' uptake of Gift Aid**

If you have persuaded someone to join as a member, then you are already two-thirds of the way to converting that person into a Gift Aider. Most membership charities now incorporate a Gift Aid tick box towards the bottom of the application form.

You may already have a substantial number of existing members on your database who have yet to sign a Gift Aid declaration. Consider targeting these members with a Gift Aid form either during:

- the renewal stage
- or, through forms distributed via your newsletter or website

While Gift Aid conversion is straightforward, it is vital to recognise that for most donors and members, Gift Aid only became an option from June 2000 onwards. Many charities were initially slow to take up the scheme and public awareness of it is far from universal.

A 2001 survey carried out for the Giving Campaign found that some people recognised the name, but could not explain what it meant. Some perceptions were confused – for example, people believing it to be a scheme which meant charities did not have to pay tax. A number of people had made a Gift Aid declaration without fully realising what they were agreeing to. Some people were looking for the catch. There was a clear dislike of describing the amount as a percentage – it was deemed to be confusing. There was greater support for stating clearly that the charity gets an extra 28p for every £1 given.

Undoubtedly, public awareness of Gift Aid will increase exponentially in the future but it is vital to explain it concisely and persuasively on your membership form.

Most people are positive about Gift Aid once they understand what it is about. All they want to know is that it is simple to do, costs them nothing and that the charity gains financially. People will use the scheme if it is prominent on the application form and accompanied by a brief explanation of how it works. Too much information deters people from completing the form but too little might mean it's overlooked.

Here is a sample description of the kind of concise text that gets the message across.

> *Use Gift Aid and you can make all your donations/membership subscriptions worth more. For every £1 you pay us, we get an extra 28p from the Inland Revenue. So, if you are a UK taxpayer, just tick here. There's no extra cost to you. It's that simple.*

Depending on your charity brand and activities, you might choose to further incentivise gift aiding by briefly illustrating how the additional money will be put to use, for example, for research and campaigning.

**Gift Aid – how does it work?**

Step 1: For tax purposes, register with the Inland Revenue and obtain a reference number.

Step 2: Obtain a Gift Aid declaration from your donor – this doesn't involve data-capturing a mass of information – just a full name, address (including postcode), details of the donations covered by the declaration and confirmation that they are a UK taxpayer. Declarations can apply to future donations and can be backdated to 6 April 2000, enabling you to reclaim tax on donations you have received since this date and in the future. Donations can also be made orally, by telephone or face to face – although research indicates that some people, particularly older people, may not be comfortable with this. You must keep details of the oral declaration and send a written record to the donor.

Step 3: Keep simple paper or computer records showing that your donors have agreed that you can reclaim their tax.

Step 4: Claim the tax back from the Inland Revenue – manually, using computer software packages, or using specialist organisations such as CAF.

**Gift Aid logo**

In 2002, the government launched the Giving Campaign to increase public awareness of Gift Aid. The campaign produced this logo

giftaid it

and encouraged charities to insert in their materials, leading to increased recognition and use of this tax-efficient giving method. According to the Giving Campaign: "The more the brand is used, the more the public will see a clear and consistent image of Gift Aid – an image that is positive, friendly and simple." This guide advises: Use it!

The Giving Campaign offers a free online toolkit which includes downloadable giftaid it logos and sample forms showing how the logo can be incorporated into your charity materials.

**Gift Aid – further information**

Further information on Gift Aid is available via the Giving Campaign website at www.givingcampaign.org.uk (the campaign itself has now closed but the website is maintained by the Inland Revenue.

# Feedback

We would very much appreciate your comments to help make future editions of this Good Membership Guide as relevant as possible.

1. How did you hear about this guide?

- ❑ My organisation
- ❑ Voluntary Sector magazine
- ❑ NCVO members' mailing
- ❑ Press coverage
- ❑ At an NCVO seminar/conference
- ❑ Advertisement
- ❑ Mailshot
- ❑ Recommendation
- ❑ Other, please state

2. How many people in your organisation will use this guide?

---

3. Which parts of the guide have you found most useful?

---

---

---

---

4. Why?

---

---

---

---

5. Which parts of the guide have you found least useful?

---

---

---

6. Why?

_______________________________________________

_______________________________________________

_______________________________________________

_______________________________________________

7. What additional information would be useful to include in future editions?

_______________________________________________

_______________________________________________

_______________________________________________

_______________________________________________

8. How would you rate the guide overall?

❑ Very useful
❑ Fairly useful
❑ Not very useful
❑ Not at all useful

9. We would appreciate your comments on the content, language and layout of the guide.

_______________________________________________

_______________________________________________

_______________________________________________

_______________________________________________

10. How will you use this guide?

❑ Inform myself
❑ Brief trustees
❑ Other, please specify

11. Which organisation do you represent (you do not have to give this information)

_______________________________________________

12. Are you a

- ❑ Trustee
- ❑ Staff member
- ❑ Professional advisor
- ❑ Other, please specify

13. Is your organisation a member of NCVO?

- ❑ Yes
- ❑ No

14. What size organisation do you represent?

- ❑ Small charity (less than £100,000 income)
- ❑ Medium-sized charity (£100,000 - £1m income)
- ❑ Large charity (over £1m income)

15. Would you like to be sent information about membership and other services available from NCVO?

If so please give details

Name ____________________

Position ____________________

Organisation ____________________

____________________

Address ____________________

____________________

____________________

Tel/fax ____________________

Email ____________________

**Data protection**
The information you provide will be held in accordance with the Data Protection Act 1998 and will be used by NCVO and its agents to supply the services which you have requested. We may wish to contact you from time to time with information on other products and services available from us, which we believe will be of interest to you.

❑ If you would like to be contacted please tick here.